The Ultimate Guide To Social Media For Business Owners, Professionals and Entrepreneurs

Jon Mitchell Jackson, Esq.

ISBN: 978-1-79-0591961

DEDICATION

A big thank you to Lisa, Alexandra, Garrett and Bleu,
for your love, support, and always reminding me to
make each day my masterpiece.

Social Media Marketing and Business Experts Share Thoughts About How Mitch Jackson Uses Social Media

"Being truly human and connecting in today's tech age isn't easy, but if anyone exemplifies how best to engage people in the new digital ecosystem it is Mitch Jackson. If you have the chance to learn or work with Mitch, consider yourself lucky. The ROI of the value provided is undoubtedly going to be worth it."

Shama Hyder– CEO of Zen Media and known as the "Zen Master of Marketing" by Entrepreneur Magazine and the "Millennial Master of the Universe" by Fast Company. Shama is an acclaimed international keynote speaker who has been invited to share the speaking stage with the world's top leaders, including President Obama and the Dalai Lama. https://zenmedia.com

"Mitch Jackson is the real deal. Rarely have I seen anyone combine high tech with high touch in such a powerful, effective and uplifting way. He's as authentic as they come and is absolutely focused on providing exceptional value to the lives of everyone he touches!"

Bob Burg is coauthor of the Go-Giver book series including "The Go-Giver" and "The Go-Giver Influencer", and author of "Endless Referrals" and "Adversaries into Allies." He is also a highly sought-after speaker for company and organizational conferences. Burg is host of the very popular weekly, The Go-Giver Podcast. https://burg.com

"Mitch Jackson leverages online channels like video and social networks to reach out and connect with people both on a personal level as well as a professional level. His efforts have taken him from being successful in his offline world to finding a whole new level of influence online, as well. In a very short time, Mitch has been able to reach out and connect with a lot of successful online influencers, and has been able to translate this into mutual value. Beyond all this, he's a great guy and doing yeoman work. I recommend him without hesitation."

Chris Brogan is president of Chris Brogan Media, offering business and marketing advisory help for mid to larger sized companies. In addition to being a keynote speaker, Chris is also a New York Times bestselling author of ten books. https://chrisbrogan.com

"I first met Mitch in Orange County at a LinkedOC event. Since then we've stayed connected on Twitter, Spreecasts and enjoyed a few podcasts together.

I've watched Mitch's use of social and he does a great job of connecting and engaging others at a very human level on the various digital platforms."

Gary Vaynerchuk is the co-founder and CEO of VaynerMedia, NY Times bestselling author and internationally acclaimed social media marketing expert and speaker https://vaynermedia.com

"Mitch is a master connector. He's humanized his law practice with online content and through social networking. In fact he does such a great job that I've written about him in my books and discuss his ideas in my many speaking engagements around the world."

David Meerman Scott, international bestselling author of "The New Rules of Sales and Service" and nine other books. David is an internationally acclaimed marketing and sales strategists who has spoken on all 7 continents and in 40 different countries. His book, "The New Rules of Marketing & PR is in its 6th edition and has been translated into 26 languages. It's used as a text book in hundreds of universities and business schools worldwide https://www.davidmeermanscott.com

"Mitch is a rare breed of early adopters who can bring what's next from the edge back to the center to help everyone understand what's coming and what to do about it."

Brian Solis, digital analyst, anthropologist, and futurist. In his work at Altimeter Group, Solis studies the effects of disruptive technology on business and society. He is an avid keynote speaker and award-winning best-selling author who is globally recognized as one of the most prominent thought leaders in digital transformation https://www.briansolis.com

"Many leaders know how to talk. Mitch shows us how to actually share a message. His insight, knowledge, and incomparable touch make him the consummate communicator."

Sally Hogshead– Hall of Fame speaker, best-selling author, and the world's leading expert on fascination https://www.sallyhogshead.com

"Mitch has done nothing but good for the social community and is someone who is trusted and highly regarded by myself and many others in this space. He provides incredibly valuable and consistently worthwhile content to many around the world and is a true educator and trailblazer. Most importantly, he's there for you. Mitch has personally provided with invaluable advice and guidance in the past, and I'm lucky enough not just to call him a great lawyer,

but my friend."

Alex Pettitt is a tech broadcaster, interactive live producer, consultant and speaker. http://alexpettitt.tv

"Mitch Jackson is one of the most unique Human Beings I know and the fact that he is a Lawyer makes him even more amazing. He lives every day to help the people around him become better, smarter, faster by inspiring and educating people about how they can grow. It's an honor to know him and I am proud to call him my friend."

Jon Ferrara is an American entrepreneur and the founder of Nimble. He is also best known as the co-founder of GoldMine Software Corp, one of the original contact management software companies https://Nimble.com

"Mitch Jackson is the epitome of someone who does social media right who is in the service based business. He is creative and approachable – always giving value to the audience he serves. Mitch is my go to example when I speak about how to use Instagram for those in service based industries."

Sue B. Zimmerman a speaker and expert on Instagram. She teaches entrepreneurs and marketing pros how to use Instagram to get tangible results https://suebzimmerman.com

"Mitch Jackson brings a rare combination of intelligence, clarity of communication, and strategy when it comes to helping people leverage technology and social media to further their business goals. I highly recommend that you pay attention to what he has to share."

Chris Lema is a product strategist, public speaker and blogger. He's a WordPress and WooCommerce evangelist and the creator of CaboPress. Chris is the VP of Product @liquidweb and you can connect with Chris at https://ChrisLema.com

"Mitch is living proof that you can be professional and personable at the same time in business. He is one of the best communicators I know and proves this in the way he teaches others how to be effective in communicating. Whether it be speaking, writing or using video, Mitch demonstrates what he teaches."

Tim McDonald– Previous Director of Community at The Huffing Post

"Mitch and his team are expert communicators who understand the fast-moving

targets of digital and social and weave in the very much needed human and relationship aspect of business. A lot of people can talk theory or great ideas, Mitch actually executes, usually with amazing results."

Bryan Elliott is Executive producer, writer & host of The GoodBrain Digital Studios http://www.behindthebrand.tv

"Mitch Jackson is most definitely a giver as he is extremely generous with his sound and insightful advice regarding all matters human interaction. To me, it is no surprise that Mitch is having a significant impact on people way beyond his courtrooms as he aptly translates the life lessons learned in such a high-pressure communications context to valuable communications tips to people from all walks of life including my grateful students. Mitch's interest in people is sincere and he is an extremely empathetic listener which allows him to find the perfect blend of professional and human elements of communication whether it be on or offline."

Niklas Myhr aka "The Social Media Professor" | Chapman University | https://NiklasMyhr.com

"Mitch is an amazing social networker and an all-around likable guy. I've watched his spreecasts and have been really impressed with his guests and the content. He's had so many notable people join him including Seth Godin, Leigh Steinberg and Chris Brogan. It's not at all surprising that influential people from many walks of life want to talk to Mitch because he asks great questions, he's extremely smart, and most of all, he's a super nice guy."

Jeff Fluhr, CEO and Co-Founder at Spreecast and former founder and CEO of StubHub https://www.linkedin.com/in/jefffluhr

"Mitch is a lawyer of tomorrow, today. He's the kind of lawyer and business man who can make rain shine. Totally client focused with an aptitude to make you feel like the most special and important person in the world. He reaches out and touches you where it matters most – in your mind and heart. He builds a relationship with you fast, to last; seemingly effortlessly – it's his human nature and star quality."

Chrissie Lightfoot | CEO EntrepreneurLawyer Limited | CEO Robot Lawyer LISA http://entrepreneurlawyer.co.uk

CONTENTS

PART THREE: SOCIAL MEDIA COMMUNICATION AND SUCCESS TIPS

FOREWORD

BY DAVID MEERMAN SCOTT

Today, buyers are in charge! The idea of mystery in the sales process is over. We research someone online before agreeing to a first date—is he a creep? We fire up LinkedIn an hour before an initial business meeting—does she have anyone I know in her network? We watch an on-demand movie trailer before deciding which film to see that night at the theater. We check out restaurant reviews and browse menus before booking a reservation.

But there's a huge disconnect between the way people research products and services they are interested in and the way companies and professionals market and sell.

We're fed up with unwanted phone calls interrupting us at home and work. We hate wading through hundreds of unsolicited emails. We've had it with intrusive social media messages. We're tired of poor service from companies that don't treat us with respect or that send us into a phone mail maze that wastes minutes of our time and never connects us with a living person.

We're especially annoyed with those who only focus on their own interests. Many people steeped in the tradition of product promotion naturally feel drawn to prattle on and on about their products and services. Yuk! But I have news for you. Nobody cares about your products and services (except you). Yes, you read that right.

What people do care about are themselves and how you can solve their problems. People also like to be entertained and to share in something remarkable. In order to have people talk about you and your ideas, you must resist the urge to hype your products and services. Instead, create something interesting that will be talked about online. When you get people talking on the Web, people will line up to learn more and to buy what you have to offer.

The good news is we can do something about this and Mitch Jackson is here to show us how in "The Ultimate Guide to Social Media for Business Owners, Professionals, and Entrepreneurs."

I connected with Mitch years ago. How? On social media of course! I was intrigued about how a lawyer was able to become so adept at creating content on the Web, reach his audiences via social media, and grow his business. I especially loved how Mitch took an idea I pioneered, Newsjacking—the art and science of injecting your ideas into a breaking news story to generate tons of media coverage, get sales leads, and grow business—and expanded on it to include such things as newsjacking through live video streaming on services like Facebook.

I love that Mitch has a thriving law practice and never needs to spend a penny on marketing. And I also love that he shares his knowledge through his social platforms including Streaming.Lawyer and LegalMinds.Lawyer. In fact, Mitch's ideas are so important that I've written about him in my books and have had him present with me to thousands of people at several Tony Robbins Business Mastery events.

That's exactly why Mitch is the perfect person to learn from. He takes the best of what's out there and makes it even better.

In this book, you'll learn from people I know and trust such as Jay Baer, Bob Burg, Mark Schaefer, and Chris Brogan. These folks share what they know best, and Mitch puts it all into context for professionals, and he adds a healthy dose of the formulas that have worked for him.

In the new world of human connections online, smart professionals have a tremendous opportunity to communicate directly with the public. They are transforming themselves and their businesses into content creators and enjoying tremendous success.

But there is another benefit you may not have thought of. Fun! It's incredibly enjoyable to engage with people online, to make friends, and to develop professional relationships. Just take a look at any of Mitch's feeds such as Twitter or Instagram—Mitch is always smiling, and you can be too.

I use the ideas in this book myself, and they work.

Here's to your success and your personal fulfillment!

———

David Meerman Scott
Marketing strategist, entrepreneur, and bestselling author of ten books including "The New Rules of Marketing & PR"
www.DavidMeermanScott.com
@dmscott

INTRODUCTION

We put up our first law firm website in 1996 and eight months later, pulled in a million dollar case through the site. Now I've never been accused of being the sharpest knife in the drawer, but at that moment I knew there was something special about this whole Internet thing.

Fast forward to today. Because of what we've experienced with social media, my enthusiasm is ten times what it was 23 years ago. The ability to build, market, and brand a business on social media is almost unlimited. In this book, I share not only what works so well for me, but also what has works for other professionals and experts from around the world. The approaches we share are broken down in three easy to digest, but important sections.

The Social Media Mindset

First, understanding the social media mindset is EVERYTHING. Making sure you're always adding value and showing your human side on social media is critically important to your success. Focus on helping others and building relationships in all that you say and do. Section I of my book shows you everything you need to know to develop the right mindset and build a unique brand on the digital platforms.

How To Use The Platforms

Second, each social media platform has its own personality. Sharing great content in the right context with each platform's personality in mind is key to marketing your business and building your brand. Add your personality into the content creating equation and your success is all but guaranteed. Section II of my book shows you how to do this the right way.

Communicating on Social Media

Third, I believe that sharing emotional stories on social media will get you the same explosive results as pouring gasoline on a digital fire. Adding pictures, videos, and the persuasive techniques shared in this section of my book will get you noticed and help you build a special community. You'll empower people to take action. Some of the best communication experts on the planet show you exactly how to do this in Section III of the book.

I always do my best to walk my talk on social media. I also know that protecting your time and attention is important to you. So, rather than telling you what you have in your hands, I invite you to turn the page and immediately get started on your social media success journey.

Enjoy, prosper, and make each day your masterpiece!

PART I

THE SOCIAL MEDIA MINDSET

CHAPTER 1

THE "SUCCESS MINDSET" OF SOCIAL MEDIA

BY MITCH JACKSON

Success on social media is about having the mindset of always listening, helping others, and adding value. You need to be yourself, selectively transparent, and show your human side. Being genuine and allowing your personality to shine for the world to see is a requirement and not an option.

This is precisely where I see most business owners, professionals, and entrepreneurs drop the ball. If you don't fully embrace the above mindset on social media, then you're wasting your time and setting yourself up for failure.

Another aspect of social media is appreciating and embracing the fact that building relationships and marketing your brand on the digital platforms isn't a sprint or marathon (like many experts say). In reality, there is no finish line. I believe that building your brand on social media is more like a good exercise routine or healthy diet. It's an ongoing and always changing process. If done right, it's also fun and personally and professionally rewarding.

My first website and online efforts began back in 1996. It took time to get things rolling and I wasn't even sure if having a website would help my practice. About eight months after putting up the website, our first seven figure case came in through the website. Now I've never been accused of being the brightest bulb in the lamp, but I knew right then that there was something special about this internet thing.

Motivated by this big case, I worked hard each day to learn the digital dance, create and publish content, engage with others and add as much value as I could to my online community. When social media rolled out, I saw the upside and raised the content and engagement bar even higher. The end result was more clients, opportunities and income.

You can do the same thing.

Be patient and don't be afraid of putting in the time and work. Using social media, give yourself time to change your business, practice and even your life.

Use these tools to expand your brand from local to global. Yes, good things can happen much faster and that's great. But what I've found to work well is simply focusing on using the methods, tools and approaches shared in this book. Sharing useful, helpful and engaging content, in a consistent fashion, while showing your human side, is the key to success on social media.

Before you share your first post, it's important to understand that sharing your unique personality while using good people skills will separate you from everyone else in town. I say this because while the social media platforms will come and go, relationships can last a lifetime. It's those relationships that I want you to start and build on the digital platforms.

The Content Mindset

What's the best content to post on social media?

My answer to this question might surprise you. For professionals, it's not all about you or your practice. When it comes to building a brand, relationships and referrals on social media, most people don't care about your professional products or services. What they care about is getting their needs taken care of. What they care about is fixing their problems and moving forward with their lives.

What I recommend you do is figure out your WHY. Take a moment and give deep thought and consideration to what really motivates you to get out of bed in the morning? What are your interests and passions? What gets you excited about life?

After you figure out the answers to these questions, start sharing your "why" on social media. Blend into your content examples or stories relating to what you do for a living.

I call this the online human "digital dance" and it's the most effective way I know to build relationships and bring in new customers, clients, and patients into your practice. It's also the best way I know to generate a constant stream of new clients and referrals from not only your city and state but also from around the world.

I also recommend that you get comfortable sharing your human side. What I'm talking about are your family experiences, hobbies and everything else in-between. I believe it's the sharing and engagement surrounding these interests that leads to your brand being noticed. Doing this is what will get new clients to contact your office, and new referrals sent your way.

Let's say you're a lawyer who enjoys riding horses, flying drones or standup paddle boarding. You may want to share posts about your latest ride, flight or experience out on the water along with pictures and videos of you enjoying these activities. Every once in a while, you can include a post about equine, drone, and admiralty laws, regulations and even discuss related legal cases your firm has handled. Doing this will allow you to connect with your audience on a deeper level.

At the same time, you might share pictures from your child's soccer sidelines or maybe a short video of your child's dance recital at school. Posting church, Rotary, and other community activities will also help people, over time, get to know, like, and trust you as a human being. The "professional" conversations will eventually happen. Just start with showing your human side first.

Pictures and videos increase visibility and engagement. Always try to add an image or video to each post you share on social media.

Make sure to share content in the form of interesting, engaging and entertaining stories. There's no better way to build rapport than in a short written, audio, and video story. I share chapters in Section III of this book that will show you how to tell a good, persuasive, emotional story.

If your personality allows you to do so, don't be afraid to take a controversial position on a matter that's important to you. Heck, that's why I became a trial lawyer, to take on the bad guys in the world. Social media now allows me to do this on a much larger scale than in years past. It also allows me to connect and build professional relationships with others who feel the same way that I do.

Now, having emphasized the human side of who you are, I still want you to use the tips, approaches and ideas in this book to show your professional side too. For maximum impact, blend all of this it into the human story you share.

Embrace Your Expertise on Social Media

Taking all the above into consideration, if you are a professional on social media, DO NOT shy away from who you are and what you do.

Go ahead and embrace your expertise. People will place a great deal of weight on what you say and do. This is a secret weapon that most professionals have but just don't use correctly.

Famed Psychologists, Robert Cialdini, calls this "directed deference." His findings show that people are conditioned to respect and follow the edicts of an authority figure.

Most of you are already experts and authority figures. For the above reasons, don't shy away from this on social media. But show your expertise in a human, kind, and giving way. Being an expert, or perceived as an expert, is a powerful brand building tool.

For those of you just getting started on your journey, work daily to establish yourself as an expert and reputable source on social media. Then, leverage this to build trust and influence.

Having this mindset, and then executing on it, is the best way I know to build your brand on social media. Now you know this too.

But there's one more "concept" about social media that you need to know.

Social Media is Constantly Changing. Unlearn Your Old and Outdated Habits.

The fact is, the world is changing at an exponentially fast pace. Consumer expectations are changing quickly too.

To have an impact on social media, you must take these changes into consideration. The consumer is holding all the cards. Attention spans are incredibly selective, and everything consumers want or need is a simple tap or swipe away on their smartphone.

Understand this new dynamic, and you'll be in good shape. Failing to change what you're doing and how you're doing it is going to expose you to an uncomfortable reality check down the road.

Another thing that's changing on social media is how consumers are interpreting the context of your content. They are more savvy than ever and are good at reading between the digital lines. Whether you know it or not, the complete message of who you are and what you do you is often times much more than what's in your last post or comment.

Your social media community is bigger than you think and growing at an exponentially fast pace. They are talking about you and sharing your content 24/7 on a global level. For this reason, you need to know how to create and share content, the right way and in the proper context, so that consumers will appreciate, understand, take action and share your message.

To be successful on social in today's world, you need to pay attention to, and understand the new customer journey. You have to embrace the consumer experience on social media. Build relationships and communicate on a global level. Focus on helping others, building your brand, top of mind awareness, and your business.

Another important thing to do is take time to unlearn your old outdated habits. Take a step back and give some thought to how you can start disrupting your industry, who you are, how you market, how you interact with your audience, and how you build your brand on social media. Give yourself permission to be unique, have an opinion, show your human side, and stand out.

In Summary

I want you to wrap your head around being strategically transparent and showing your human side on social media. Don't come across as "that professional" on social media with the personality of a wet dishrag sitting at the bottom of the kitchen sink. Instead, give yourself permission to share the dynamic human being that I know you are, and share the interests, passions, and desires you've been wanting to tell the world about. By how you create and share your content, let everyone know that you're interested in helping others and adding value to their lives.

Sharing your "why" and showing your human side on social media is how you can rise above all the noise. It's how you can stand out above your competition. Being genuine when doing so will allow you to expand your brand from local to global, amplify your voice, and become a top of mind resource for new customers, clients, and referrals.

Social media has changed my law firm practice and life. Follow the approaches, tips, and advice in this book, and social media will change your life too!

CHAPTER 2

THE GO-GIVER WAY TO ENRICHING YOUR PRACTICE VIA SOCIAL MEDIA

BY BOB BURG

The intuitive notion regarding how to succeed utilizing Social Media is to use it as a platform to demonstrate your expertise. In other words, if you can let your target market know how knowledgeable you are about your field—that you are the expert—then logically speaking it only makes sense that you will drive them to seek out you and your firm.

It is intuitive, but it's also incorrect. And more and more professionals "trying out" the world of social media as a way of creating business are just as quickly leaving social media because, "well, it doesn't work."

Actually, it does work. But it must be worked correctly. You can dramatically increase your influence ("the ability to move a person or persons to a desired action, usually within the context of a specific goal"—in this case, seeking out your firm) through correctly utilizing one or more of the social media platforms.

However...

If you truly want to have influence in the social media space, then please understand the following:

Your influence is determined by how abundantly you place other peoples' interests first.

Yes, placing their interests even before your interests.

Please don't misunderstand; this is not in a way that is "martyrish" or self-sacrificial but rather one that communicates to those in your social networks that your focus is on helping them; on bringing value to their lives.

After all, no one is going to retain your services because it's in your best interests for them to do so, but rather because it's in their best interests to do so. And while you may indeed be the most skilled of all your competitors, until your prospective clients know this, you won't get the opportunity to prove it.

You must set yourself apart...before you ever get to the point of engaging with them in your office for the purposes of their retaining you.

This brings us to a very basic premise, a law of business that is immutable regardless of the medium, and that is:

All things being equal, people will do business with, and refer business to, those professionals they know, like, and trust.

Yes, that is true. And the best way to elicit those feelings toward you is to communicate on an ongoing basis that every time they see you and hear your voice (video) read your post (blog) or see a post or tweet (social media) they will receive value of some sort. This doesn't necessarily mean in the form of your professional expertise—though we'll see in just a bit how that will often also be the case—but through the way you connect with them on a very human and personal level.

You see, shifting your focus from getting to giving ("giving" in this context meaning constantly and consistently providing value to others) is not only a pleasant way to operate on social media, it happens to be the most financially profitable way, as well!

So please keep in mind that while the media platforms may differ, the basic way you communicate stays the same: before clicking send, always (ALWAYS!) ask yourself, "Is what I'm about to tweet, post, etc. going to add value to this person's life/business?"

Remember that value doesn't necessarily mean your expertise but rather how you make that person feel. Have you connected in a way that says, "I care about you as a human being, not just a potential or current client?"

"But" one might very legitimately ask, "How do I do that when I'm providing information on a blog post or video, or a tweet or a Facebook or LinkedIn post that is simply informational in nature?"

That's an excellent question. The answer is that you first create the opportunity for dialogue and—and this is so key—when they click back with a question or comment...answer it in the most helpful and personal way possible.

For example, if you are an accountant, you might share a post on social media advising people to be aware that Congress passed a new law modifying the tax benefits of doing business as a corporation or limited liability company. Furthermore, that because of this new law, these types of business entities will need to take certain action within the next six months to be eligible to receive these new benefits.

When your online audience engages with you and asks follow-up questions, you do your best to respond by providing helpful answers. You share your secret sauce and do so without asking for anything in return. The idea is to provide people with value so that you become a trusted go-to resource for their future professional needs.

The same whether you're an attorney, a doctor, or whatever your profession.

Here's another powerful form of action you can take:

Let's say you're a business litigation or intellectual property rights attorney. You see a tweet from someone you don't yet know and who most likely does not know you. Their tweet concerns a legal problem they're having with content being inappropriately taken from their website and used by a third party without their permission.

First, if neither of you knows each other how would you have seen their tweet in the first place? Because on the Twitter application you are using (Tweetdeck, Hootsuite, etc.) you can place keywords in the "notifications" area so that whenever certain words or phrases are mentioned, you'll be notified.

Perhaps the person tweeted, "I can't believe this. I just saw my image and related blog post copied and used on one of my competitor's websites. What should I do? This could be a real mess."

Now you provide a helpful response, such as, "Being an intellectual property rights attorney I've seen this all-too-often. Fortunately, if you send a cease and demand letter your competitor and a DMCA takedown demand to their website host that will most likely do the trick.

Don't suggest they call you to retain you or anything else solicitous at this point. But prepare yourself for several possibilities, including the following:

1. Nothing will result.

2. The person will thank you.

3. Others will have seen your helpful tweet and taken notice of your caring and expertise, and perhaps follow you.

4. This person will tweet you back another question, which you'll respond to and eventually perhaps set up an appointment.

5. You'll begin a group back and forth with you positioned as the expert and most likely gather new followers who are now potential clients.

6. Several of the above.

You are continuing to communicate both expertise and caring, the two things that you need to do in order to be successful and profitable.

The entire point of your social media presence is to create relationships, and then develop these relationships to the point where those with whom you're connected feel so good about you personally (they know you, they like you, and they trust you) that when it comes time for them to choose someone in your profession (or change to another one) you are the only one that logically and emotionally comes to mind.

And those who are already your clients continue to be reminded of your value and are much more likely to refer you to others.

So, by all means, be on social media, create content, and most of all, engage, engage, and engage. Be that professional, and you'll find that not only are you one of the relatively few professionals "doing" social media correctly but one of the relatively few seeing lots and lots of new business coming from it as a result.

————

Bob Burg is coauthor of the Go-Giver book series including "The Go-Giver" and "The Go-Giver Influencer", and author of "Endless Referrals" and "Adversaries into Allies." He is also a highly sought-after speaker for company and organizational conferences. Burg is host of the very popular weekly, The Go-Giver Podcast. Please connect with Bob at https://burg.com

CHAPTER 3

THE KEY TO BECOMING (AND STAYING) AN INFLUENCER IN YOUR INDUSTRY

BY KIM GARST

Do you have aspirations to make a real impact in your industry?

Are you passionate and knowledgeable about your niche?

Do you have an engaged audience who looks to you for guidance and leadership?

If you answered yes to any of these questions, you may already be on your way to reaching influencer status.

According to an infographic from Social Media Today, 94% of marketers find influencer marketing effective. If this statistic is anywhere close to accurate, influencer marketing isn't going anywhere in the near future!

Whether you're already an influencer – or are on your way to achieving influencer status – this chapter will walk you through the most effective strategies for becoming and STAYING an influencer!

The key to becoming an influencer

This isn't rocket science, folks.

But it DOES require authenticity, commitment and a lot of hard work.

The key to becoming (and staying) an influencer is building trust in your industry.

Without the trust of your audience, you'll never become a real influencer.

You can have millions of fans or followers, but if they don't trust what you have to say, your opinion will not amount to a hill of beans.

So – how do you build that trust? How do ensure your current audience trusts you, and that you're continually attracting new fans, followers and blog readers who feel the same?

1. Be strategically transparent

It sounds pretty obvious, but this is something many would-be influencers fail to do.

Does this mean you need to constantly share pictures of your dog, talk about your marital issues or complain about your competitors' underhanded business practices?

A big ole resounding NOPE!! This is where the strategic part comes in.

Your audience wants to know you're a real person. They want to see your human side – not just your neat and tidy, polished, professional side.

The long and short of it is they need to know, like and trust you.

It's only when people start to see that you're a real person that trust starts to grow. People want to know:

- How and why you got into this niche or industry
- That you struggle with stuff too – no one trusts someone who always gets it all right, all the blooming time
- That you have real feelings, just like them
- That you have their best interests at heart and care about them

When all these things are in place, THIS is when you actually start to become a true influencer.

2. Know your end game

If your ultimate goal is to enact real change in your industry and to be trusted as an expert in your niche, all your social media activities should be working to this end.

This means you should have a regular posting schedule, posting no less than a few times a week (preferably much more).

It also means being careful about what types of content you post. Are you posting new, valuable info, or simply sharing funny memes? Are you freely sharing your knowledge or expertise, or are you constantly posting promotional content? (Note: not saying you shouldn't post funny memes because they DO attract people to you – just mix it up with other value-based "stuff"!)

To become a true influencer, your #1 goal should be to build trust.

Is each of your social media strategies helping you achieve this?

3. Help your audience solve their problems

To establish yourself as an expert in your field, it's critical that you give your audience tools and strategies to help overcome their struggles.

You can do this through regularly writing helpful blog or social media posts, through giving away value-packed free eBooks or guides, or by regularly doing podcasts, live Q&A's or Facebook Lives.

Regularly helping your audience in this way keeps you front of mind, builds your reputation as an expert and ensures your audience and influence keeps on growing.

4. Be responsive

Social media CAN'T be a one-way street! Using it simply to broadcast news, information and promotional content will NOT help you become an influencer.

While you may not be able to respond to each and every comment, question or mention, make a point of engaging in one-on-one or group discussions whenever possible.

Ask lots of questions, actually read the responses, and then respond – either one-on-one, in a Facebook Live or via a blog post. While you may not be able to respond to every individual question, you can show your audience that you've heard them, that you care, and that you can help them solve their problem.

What does it take to STAY an influencer?

Once you've built up a large, engaged community of people, who know, like and trust you, what's next?

The four strategies above will continue to be the foundation of your social media strategy.

However, practically speaking, it's also important to know how to act and engage in your industry - both online and offline – to continue to have influence in your field.

1. Network both online and offline

While social media makes networking so much easier and less time-consuming, it's critical to network in the "real world" to be taken seriously in your industry.

This will mean regularly attending (and preferably speaking at) industry conferences, workshops, and other live events.

It will also mean collaborating with others in your field, both online and offline.

Online, this could mean doing joint Facebook Lives or webinars or even just being part of online mastermind groups in your industry.

Offline, this could mean co-hosting a workshop with another expert in your field or simply regularly getting together to network and brainstorm with other influencers in your industry.

2. Become a thought leader

Dictionary.com defines thought leader as, "One whose views on a subject are taken to be authoritative and influential."

It's not enough to share other people's ideas or opinions – you need to develop and share your own, original thoughts to be a true influencer.

While this can (and should) be done via your blog and social media, writing a book is one of the best ways to attain and retain your reputation as a thought leader and influencer.

Live video is another great way to help your audience and showcase your own expertise at the same time. Hop on regularly and share tips, strategies and ideas that are proven to help your audience with their biggest struggles.

3. Stay on top of industry news and happenings

You can't be an influencer if you don't know what's happening in your industry. Your audience will look to you for breaking news, as well as your opinions on that news.

To ensure you always know what's going on in your field, make sure you're:

• Subscribing to and reading industry journals and trade publications
• Reading the latest books in your industry
• Subscribing to industry blogs
• Setting up alerts for mentions of industry keywords
• Following other influencers in your industry

4. Be authentic

As your influence grows, it can become tempting to put on your "influencer face" – meaning you start to act like a know-it-all or portray yourself as someone who has the answers, all the time.

I don't know about you, but this isn't the kind of person I tend to trust!

I talked above about the importance of being someone others know, like and trust. This is key to becoming an influencer and key to STAYING one!

Don't forget where you came from. Don't ignore your unique voice. Don't try to be someone you're not. Don't pretend you're perfect!

Final thoughts

Becoming an influencer in your field will afford you many opportunities you wouldn't otherwise have: opportunities to inspire, motivate and educate your audience.

But, it does require a 100% commitment to being authentic, transparent and trustworthy.

I hope the strategies above have given you a general framework for building and maintaining your own status as an influencer in your industry!

———

Kim Garst is an international best-selling author, international keynote speaker, one of the world's most retweeted people among digital marketers and a highly sought after marketing strategist. Forbes named Kim as one of the Top 10 Social Media Power Influencers. She has provided social and digital marketing advice to some of the world's top brands like Microsoft, IBM, and Mastercard as well and hundreds of influential business leaders on digital and social media business strategies. She is the co-founder of Boom! Social, a business strategy consulting firm that helps business owners create more sales using the power of digital and social media. Connect with Kim at https://kimgarst.com

CHAPTER 4

EMBRACING H2H ON SOCIAL AND DIGITAL

BY BRYAN KRAMER

Corporate jargon and robotic tones of voice – you don't have to look far to see evidence of carefully curated and restrained voices used by professionals, regardless of industry. With the myriad of ways users engage socially and digitally, it's more important than ever for professionals, brands, and businesses to connect meaningfully with their audiences, instead of using cold, calculated voices to make connections.

In a dynamic landscape of bots, AI and automation - being human is an ever-increasing novelty, instead of a guarantee. My work as a human to human marketer is based on the simple idea that we need to break down barriers, strip everything back and make marketing more emotive, vibrant and real, by appealing to other users on a human level and speak authentically to their base desires.

From B2B to H2H

B2B marketing or business-to-business marketing is about aligning with the goals of a business and communicating in a way that sells your product to their objectives. The result of this is often stale content, lacking in personality and vigor. What H2H sets out to do is to remind people that behind businesses are people. A 'business' isn't going to decide whether to buy your product (unless we're embracing AI!), it's going to be a human or set of humans whom all have their own biases, interests and complex thought processes.

With this in mind, creating marketing content on social and digital that piques the interest of the humans behind businesses and humans, instead of just 'customers,' can be the basis of a more successful strategy.

Look on LinkedIn, a lot of the social content that connects with audiences are human-based stories about journeys, vulnerabilities and opening up about testing situations. Why are they successful? Because they reflect human experience and a reader can see themselves in the stories. This can be a great starting point for networking.

Humanizing your content and prioritizing human-to-human connection when marketing your business and products will help you to make better relationships, practice emotional intelligence and use your unique human qualities to connect. As well as excellent customer experience (CX) we need to integrate good human experience (HX) too.

Jargon-Busting

There can be pressure to present a specific professional image and act in a particular, restrained way, but that stifles our creativity and lets us blend in with everyone else.

We're all trying to navigate our way through life successfully. It's tough. Also, a big part of this is trying to look like we know exactly what we're doing. Inevitably, there are areas that we don't have expertise in, so looking like we know becomes even more critical! One of the tools used to amplify our skills and show others we're on the ball is to use lots and lots of industry jargon.

Using complex terminology here and there helps to construct a vernacular disguise.

Construct a vernacular disguise? Why not just say 'helps to show we know what we're talking about.' All jargon and complex language do, it makes our language and marketing less accessible to everyone and puts up barriers. If people have to look again or consult a dictionary, you're marketing in a way that is the opposite of clear, simple and seamless.

There's a relentless desire to come across as perfect in business, but with this comes a sacrifice of humanized authenticity.

When you look to replicate the type of human complexity and emotion that your audience or customers have, you can work towards being seen as much more than your average, faceless brand.

One of the best ways to instantly practice H2H is to write how you speak – within reason, of course, leave out the 'umms' and 'erms.' When we dress up what we're saying with more formal language, it becomes distanced from how you'd naturally speak and how most humans speak too. The communication between both parties is misaligned and disjointed.

Our choice of language is, and I can guarantee that opening email marketing content that uses clear, simple CTAs, instead of convoluted, corporate waffle will generate better results. Corporate claptrap creates distance between whoever is consuming the message and the creator. Good marketing will bridge gaps not widen them.

Personality is an Asset

It's not always appropriate to use humor and a light-hearted tone in your marketing efforts, for example, if you're a charity or dealing with a sensitive topic. However, most of the time, you can use a more relaxed tone of voice to connect with your audiences.

Taking traditional copy and tones of voice that you use in your marketing and turning them on their head can be well-worth some experimentation. Testing out new vocab, phrasing, and tone of voice can garner some surprising results with how your audience reacts. Injecting personality could be one of the best marketing decisions you make and the least expensive.

Transitional, filler copy that you use to point users in the direction of a product or towards a next step might not seem like an opportunity to use your tone of voice to create rapport, but these small moments can provide an ideal way to test it out. For example, turn your website's 404 error message into something more personable. There are chances to demonstrate an H2H approach in every step of your digital output.

Connecting with your audience can also help to cushion the blow when your business inevitably makes mistakes. Mistakes are part of being human. Owning up to mistakes and working to make them better is integral.

Having a strong relationship with your audience can help weather the storm that a mistake can bring. Errors give you one of the best opportunities to show what kind of personal brand or business you are. Truthful, empathetic and determined to find solutions – that can be more human than that?

A Little Respect

If you've just met someone for the first time, you wouldn't ask them for $100. Maybe, you're lucky and stumble across a generous billionaire, but chances are, this interaction won't be successful. So you should apply the same sentiment to your marketing. Putting in minimal effort and expecting immediate results isn't realistic.

Most products need to persuade a customer to part with their hard-earned cash. And this is where the respect part comes in. Building a relationship with your customer is vital. Of course, they know that you want something from them, but not every social post you produce has to be laden with hard-sell language. Often, you can get great traction from a funny Instagram image or meme – you're not selling, but you're building a picture of the type of person or brand you are.

Build a campaign around context and creating value for your audience. The social content you put out must be cohesive, consistent and enable people to get to know your brand on a human level.

Don't expect everything to come from your customer – your relationship is mutual. By sharing, you can give people an insight into yourself or your business. Sharing is an integral part of being human.

Sharing and revealing more about what makes you tick gives people hooks and ways that they can connect with you. People are more inclined to listen to your messages or see you as a voice of reason or authority in an industry they can relate to you or feel as if they know about you.

Social Engagement

To make a splash online with your brand or business, you need proper engagement. What merits good engagement? Building a following that knows who you are, likes what you say and trusts you when you say it. Humanizing your marketing and content is part of creating a more customer-focused experience.

What are people looking for before they engage with professionals or brands? Increasingly, it's personalization and authenticity. If you can achieve this with emotive, personality-driven content marketing, then good engagement rates won't be too far behind.

Take advantage of the scalability of social media too. Reach out to your audience and followers and engage with them first, instead of waiting for interaction. You can use your social channels to build individual relationships with people and create more prosperous, longer-lasting customer relationships with enhanced loyalty. Less amplified results, but stronger relationships. Twitter chats, Facebook Live, Reddit AMAs, closed Facebook groups are all excellent ways to build communities and make loyal followers and customers central to your success.

A Fresh Approach

Taking the time to dig down and get human can be a significant change to your marketing strategy, but it can have drastic results. Learning about your audience, creating audience personas and working out how your content can be valuable and connect on a human level is time-consuming but can help you to learn about yourself and the type of business you want to be too.

In business, it's easy to lose sight of shared goals and basic human psychology. Everyone wants to feel valued like he or she belong and likes to be listened to and acknowledged. If you can build in ways to do this in your marketing strategy and content formats, then you'll generate golden nuggets of information and input from your audience for you to grow whatever project you're working on.

––––––

Bryan Kramer is a renowned social business strategist, TED speaker, global keynote speaker, executive coach, and bestselling author. He's one of the world's foremost leaders in the art and science of sharing and has been credited with instigating the #H2H human business movement in marketing and social. Bryan can be reached at bryan@bryankramer.com or through his site at www.bryankramer.com

CHAPTER 5

SEVEN PRINCIPLES TO HELP YOU REACH SUPERHUMAN PERFORMANCE ON SOCIAL MEDIA

BY MITCH JACKSON

In today's busy and noisy world, our three most valuable assets are time, attention and connecting on a human level. None of us have enough time for our family, business, and other passions. We're always being pushed and pulled in multiple directions, so it's tough to give and get the attention we all want and need. Web forms, email, text, and automated telephone answering trees make us all want more human to human interaction.

While this is all happening, and like it or not, social media, digital, and automation technologies are here to stay. You have to admit that it's never been easier to find a service provider and get a quote or set an appointment. All you need is your smartphone, and you're good to go.

If you want to learn more about your doctor, lawyer or accountant at 11 pm at night, all you need to do is visit their website, social media platforms, and online ratings. It's easy, fast, and convenient.

With all of this in mind, I'm going to show you seven ways to help you raise the bar even higher when it comes to effectively using social media to market and brand your business or practice. Using these techniques will allow you to respect the limited time and attention available to your customer, client or patient and, in the process, I'll show you how to do all of this in a very human and personal way.

I call these approaches my "Seven Social Media Superpowers," and if you use these correctly, I believe they'll make you faster than a speeding bullet, more powerful than a speeding locomotive, and help you leap tall buildings in a single bound. By the time we're done, I can't make any promises as to how you'll look in red tights, but I can promise you that it will take more than an evil villain named Lex Luther to keep you from being the next social media superhero.

The Kryptonite of Social Media

With all the content being shared 24/7, there's a tremendous amount of information and noise that we all need to navigate and digest each day. Capturing and keeping each other's attention is difficult. With it being harder and harder to grab someone's attention, never before is understanding the adage, "you never have a second chance to make a good first impression" been more true and important.

As if the issues of time and attention are not in and of themselves enormous challenges, there's a more important need we all need to understand and embrace. It's the requirement that we all engage and communicate as human beings on social media. This is especially true for all the professionals reading this book. Doing so allows us to share mutual interests and values leading to even stronger connections and relationships.

I've been in business for more than 30 years. I started our law firm when fax machines were 'the big rage' and before the internet as we know it, and social media, existed. I've watched clients and other professionals automate their services to become more efficient and to help them grow in a scalable fashion. People originally liked this. Clients, customers, and patients thought automation was cool.

Not so much today.

Recently I've watched consumer expectations change from embracing automation to coming back full circle and craving more meaningful human interaction. Smart businesses are teaching everyone on their team to do business as our grandparents did 75 years ago. That is, to embrace human-to-human relationships resulting in more meaningful experiences in business and life.

Going back to basics the Dale Carnegie way

Long before the Internet, social media and new automated digital systems, Dale Carnegie wrote the 1937 best-selling book, "How To Win Friends and Influence People." In the book, he shared valuable principles and approaches to help all of us build better relationships. Because of our new ability to instantly connect digitally around the globe, I believe Carnegie's principles of making friends and influencing people are more valuable today than ever before.

On all levels, social media substantially amplifies the value and importance of the business assets of time, attention and being human. For this reason, and using Carnegie's six principles, I'm going to share my digital version of Carnegie's teachings that has worked so well for me since putting up our first website in 1996.

Principle 1: Become genuinely interested in other people, their platforms and what they share on social.

Why do I start with this principle? The answer is simple. The truth of the matter is that being interested in other people and caring about what they say and do on social media, business, and life is a great way to earn their time, attention and respect. This is especially true with your existing and potential customers, patients, and clients.

How do you do this? Well, start off by spending about 70% of your time on social media focusing on others rather than on your own business, products or services. Show that you care by replying, engaging and sharing the content and effort of others with your digital audience.

Be genuine and don't slip in your links to self-promote. Just share and truly help others. This is where most people drop the ball. They can't resist talking about themselves, or their products and services, even when complimenting others.

Remember that in today's digital world, if your primary content is all about you, then your ultimate audience will only be you. Being human, strategically transparent, and engaging with others without expecting anything in return will earn you the time and attention of others. It will help you stand out from the crowd and allow your message to be heard above all the noise.

Now having said that, do keep in mind that once in a while, it's OK to toot your own horn. But here's the deal. If you go about these seven principles correctly, you won't have to because others will do this for you.

Principle 2: Smile, be kind, and have empathy for others.

How do you "smile" on the digital platforms? Well, my secret is to only engage and communicate on social media when I'm smiling inside and out. When I'm having a bad day, and we all do, I either refrain from engaging or let someone else in the office participate or post for me.

The key to sharing your big bright digital smile is always to try and put your best foot forward. Have a positive frame of mind and smile ear to ear while you write, record and broadcast via audio and video. I believe how you feel is often reflected in what you publish on social media.

When you create and share content while digitally smiling, people will see and feel the difference when reading, watching and listening to your content. If you're a company that's smart enough to empower your employees to share actively on social, show them how to do the same. Still, need help learning how to smile or teach others to smile? Watch this short video by Guy Kawasaki. http://bit.ly/socialmediabook-smile

One last thing. Make sure your personal and professional profile pictures display big smiles. Also remember the ancient Chinese proverb, "A man without a smiling face must not open a shop."

Principle 3: Use people's names and social media handles.

Carnegie argues that there's nothing more important than including the other person's name in a conversation. Fast forward to today, I think this approach applies when sharing content and responding in comments on social media. Try to use people's names and tag others using their social media handles.

Along the same lines, and when appropriate, personalize everything you can. Take the time to edit posts, retweets, and other content to include the names and digital handles of your customers and employees.

Ralph Waldo Emerson once said, "Good manners are made up of petty sacrifices." I'm sharing this with you because it will take a bit more time and effort to use and tag with names and social media handles. But here's the deal: the small amount of time and effort you invest in doing this (and it is an investment) will be appreciated and help separate you from your competition. It will help you get noticed, and it will help you build relationships.

Principle 4: Be a good listener, encourage others to talk about themselves and share their content.

On social media, make sure to listen more than you speak. Use your ears, eyes, and heart at all times to watch, listen to, and interpret another person's message. Slow down and actively "listen" to what is being said.

When you do post or reach out, asking open-ended questions is a wonderful way to invite an additional opportunity to listen. During video, you can learn a great deal from watching the other person's body language. Pay attention.

In my world when trying cases in a court of law, using this technique is exactly how I end up with 12 amazing jurors from a jury pool of hundreds of people randomly selected from the local community. While opposing counsel instructs and preaches, I ask questions and listen. I select my final jurors based upon their answers to my questions. Asking good questions has always been one of my keys to success in business and trial, and I think this approach will work for you too on social media.

Keep in mind that this isn't a trick or technique. For this approach to work, you must be real, genuine and truly care about the other person. Often, the other person's body language will communicate an entirely different message than the words flowing across a person's lips. On social, prior and subsequent posts may also give context to what is being said in the message at hand.

Principle 5: Talk to people about their interests and the content they share.

In his book, Carnegie shares a story about how President Roosevelt would do whatever he could to learn about the passions and interest of others. He would stay up late the night before a meeting and read all he could on the topic of interest of the person he'd be meeting the next day. He knew that the quickest path to a person's heart was to talk about the things that the other person was interested in and passionate about. You can and should do the same thing on social media.

Spend time learning about others before jumping into a conversation or approaching them with your products and services. What are her interests? What does she enjoy doing in her spare time? Engage and interact with others with genuine interest and curiosity. It's the things we have in common that bond us as human beings.

Principle 6: Be Sincere. Make the other person feel important by what you say, post and do.

Before reaching out to someone on social media, ask yourself, "What is there about this other person that I can honestly admire?" The answer to your question might be someone's personality, accomplishments, charitable interest or even the content of her blog. It may not have anything to do with business. And that's okay. Whatever it is, make sure to find it.

Everyone offers value and is special and unique in their own way. Do what you can to find out what the other person value is and then share that value with your digital audience. Make an effort to shine bright spotlight on your clients and patients.

While you're doing this, keep in mind that insincere flattery is not the goal. It's fake, obvious and will prevent you from making a connection. On the other hand, having and displaying a sincere interest and appreciation for the other, without any hidden agenda, will help you connect on a human level on social media.

Most of the time doing all of this is easier said than done. And I get that. But successful people in business and life are often those individuals who are willing to do what others are not. For this very reason, I keep this quote by Ralph Waldo Emerson on my desk and read it daily. It reads "Every man I meet is my superior in some way. In that, I learn from him."

Principle 7: Always do the right thing.

Although this particular principle is not one that Carnegie mentioned, I think it's just as important as all the others combined. What I'm talking about is leading by example. Always strive to do the right thing on the digital platforms and in your social media communities.

The ease of clicking, posting and sharing on social shouldn't result in the bar being lowered when it comes to being truthful and factual. Helping and protecting others is not only the right thing to do, it's the only thing to do. It will help you build the kind of reputation and brand that will help you and that you can be proud of.

Lead by example and always make your social media community's best interest a priority. Doing these things is not always easy but is always necessary.

Conclusion

I believe the people and businesses that understand and apply these seven principles on the digital platforms are the same individuals and companies that will earn the time, attention and respect of others and achieve success.

Embracing these principles will help you conquer digital speeding bullets and leap tall buildings in a single bound. The Lois Lanes and Jimmy Olsens of the world will cheer you on and help share your message. New customers, clients, and patients will come your way because of the brand you build on social.

Now it's time to execute and take action. Put on your red cape and digital tights, and apply these seven principles. Become the best superhuman you can be on social media.

CHAPTER 6

MARKETING TO MILLENNIALS: THE INS AND OUTS

BY DAKOTA SHANE NUNLEY

As a millennial and a marketer, I'll be the first one to say that millennials are a tough nut to crack when it comes to marketing and advertising. From the outside in, it may appear like marketing to millennials is some sort of unsolvable, constantly-changing puzzle. Yet with millennials accounting for a whopping $200 billion in buying power in the United States alone, they're also a customer base that's undeniably important to pay attention and cater to.

Here's the good news: marketing to millennials, while certainly not simple, is much more straightforward than you might expect. In fact, with just a handful of mindset shifts, some re-configuring of your content strategy and sharpening of your brand messaging, you can become an expert in no time.

In this chapter, we're going to discuss the main point to set you up for incredible success regarding millennial marketing, as well as the precise set of steps to get you there. After reading this chapter, my goal is for you to be fully equipped with the toolkit you need to not only sell to millennials, but to also build lifelong relationships with them as customers.

Let's get to it.

The Main Point

By keeping the following in mind when marketing to millennials, all of the smaller, more granular details will begin to fall into place:

Almost all millennials saw their first pop-up ad while still in grade school. They grew up with brands targeting them on social media, on their favorite blogs, YouTube channels and more. An unprecedented amount of advertising has been virtually inescapable for millennials, no matter where they are or what they are doing. As a result, they've grown numb and callous to traditional advertising tactics.

Understanding the above is important. Once you do, all other behaviors and characteristics of millennials will begin to make more sense.

Millennials being so turned off by inauthentic marketers and salesmen begins to make more sense.

Millennials having a shorter attention span than that of a goldfish begins to make more sense.

Millennials only buying from individuals they trust begins to make more sense.

Starting to see a pattern here?

Now that we've got this understanding out of the way, the next logical question to ask is what to do about it. What steps can you take today to put this mindset shift into practice? Which marketing strategies can you alter to better craft your messaging to millennials?

Those are all very good questions, and ones that we'll answer throughout the rest of the chapter. Here are the 6 shifts you need to make within your marketing efforts to fully capitalize on millennials.

#1. Add Value Before You Ask...Always

To connect with and build trust between your brand and millennials, you must never forget to add value before you ask your audience for anything in return. The value you add can take a variety of different forms, but within the digital marketing landscape, it usually translates into giving away insightful advice and guidance related to your area of expertise.

By giving, giving, then giving some more, you will naturally begin to establish trust and goodwill between your brand and those who are consuming your content. In recent years, this has become a well-circulated best practice in the marketing world, but I'm always surprised by the number of business owners and marketers who still don't apply it.

In fact, with all of the self-righteous YouTube pre-roll ads and Instagram photos with rented Lamborghinis, it seems like the amount of self-serving, inauthentic content is higher today than ever before.

Don't fall into the trap of being spammy and over-promotional. It will only get you so far. Instead, take advantage of social media platforms, email newsletters and other free channels where you can publish valuable content as much as you'd like.

Take note that when it comes to online marketing, you don't need to break down your company's messaging into a 30-second advertising spot or into 20 words on a billboard. Today, you have the luxury of taking the time that's necessary to build genuine, mutually beneficial relationships with your potential customers. Take advantage of this luxury.

For every 10 Tweets you publish, make 9 informational and 1 promotional.

For every email newsletter you send out, make 90% of the content within it informational and 10% promotional.

Add value to your audiences before you ask them for anything in return. If you don't, your marketing success will always have a ceiling.

#2. Rethink ROI (Return on Investment)

Note: To effectively reach millennials, you must effectively leverage social media. To effectively leverage social media, you must begin to rethink and redefine what it means to have positive ROI. Here's how to do that.

Once you have a solid grasp on the importance of adding value, a follow-up question you may have is the following:

But, Dakota-I have a business to run. If I spend all of this time on social media and on other marketing platforms just adding value and never selling, where does my ROI come from?

Great question. Here's the answer: social media marketing is fundamentally different than other forms of marketing and advertising. The problem is that most entrepreneurs still treat it like they would a 9–5, where an individual who puts in x amount of hours should immediately yield dollars as a direct result.

This is precisely why I always tell my clients and my readers that social media needs to be thought of more like a cocktail party and less like a sales pitch.

Let me explain.

You wouldn't attend a cocktail party, gather all of the business cards you received, run back home, send out sales pitches to those people and immediately begin to calculate the ROI of the event based on the money you receive from those individuals...or at least I hope you wouldn't.

Instead, the value of a cocktail party is strictly in the relationships and the networking you do while attending the function. If you're a copywriter, and you hit it off with someone at a cocktail party, it may be a whole year before they shoot you an email for your services because it may be an entire year before they're in need of your services.

The best bartender in town doesn't have a stopwatch to meticulously calculate the amount of time she spends talking with patrons over the number of tips she receives that night. Instead, the best bartender in town takes the time out of her busy shift to begin to build authentic relationships with those customers to build trust and keep them coming back, month after month, year after year.

#3. Social Media is a Prerequisite

The next thing you need to keep in mind when marketing to millennials is simply being active on social media is nothing more than a prerequisite as opposed to an advantage or "leg up" on your competitors.

In today's marketplace, it isn't enough to just be present on social media. Instead, you now must be present, active and producing high-quality content too.

Similar to how having a website as a business owner has slowly evolved from being an advantage to now being a requirement, social media has taken on a similar trajectory. Millennials don't just like it when they can discover you and contact you through social media, they expect it.

If you aren't present, active and creating helpful content on all, or most, of the most popular social media platforms (Facebook, Twitter, Instagram, and YouTube), then you run the risk of coming off as outdated and out-of-touch in the eyes of millennials, which can certainly damage the perception of your brand in terms of long-term value.

#4. Show Your Human Side

Because of the obscene amount of schmoozy advertisements and marketing campaigns millennials are exposed to each and every day, they have developed a huge soft spot for the "human side" of brands. They don't want to buy from a robot or a faceless logo. Instead, they want to buy from a fellow person they can relate to and has the same set of values they do.

This is why brands like TOMS shoes, that donates a pair of shoes to a person in need for every pair that is commercially sold, has resonated so well with customers around the world.

This is precisely why Wendy's Twitter account, which frequently sends insults and funny comebacks to its followers and competitors, connects well with younger online audiences.

Every so often, letting your guard down and being vulnerable to your followers will go a long way when it comes to connecting with millennials. Whether this is telling a story of the biggest mistake you've made in your career, sharing a hilarious meme or something else related, the important thing to remember is to be human.

People make mistakes, people tell jokes, and people love raw conversation-and brands should be the same way.

#5. Have Your Ducks In a Row

Now, it's time to get down to the nitty-gritty of marketing to millennials. Below are some of the most common marketing mistakes I see entrepreneurs and brands making that is damaging their image in the eyes of younger audiences. All of the tips weave in the concepts we've discussed throughout this chapter:

a.) Keep your social media automation in check. Be sure to use discretion when it comes to automating your social media. Remember, being human is critical to your marketing success, and having an auto-responder sending generic replies to all your mentions or sending spammy material to new followers via automated direct messages is not always the best way to come off as authentic.

b.) Avoid corny stock photography. Millennials will be quick to deem you cheesy and out-of-touch if all of your images look straight out of an 8th-grade textbook. Instead, use free sites like Pexels or Unsplash to gain access to thousands of high-quality, royalty-free photos.

c.) Stick to your niche. When someone selects to follow you on social media, it almost always is for a very specific purpose. If you're a photographer who's active on social media, someone probably followed you to see all of your spectacular photos. If you're an author, someone probably followed you to stay updated on all your upcoming books and blog posts. When it comes to your content, it's totally fine (and in your best interest) to publish some content unrelated to your niche- as it shows your human side-but keep most of your content centered around the reason you created the account in the first place.

#6. Follow Trends

As a final point, to expertly market to millennials, you've got to know where it is they hang out online. The most annoying part of this process is the places they are hanging out is always changing. Because of the breakneck speed of innovation today, the newest app becomes old and outdated faster than ever before.

Lucky for everyone though, there are topnotch publications online that help curate which trends you should pay attention to and which ones to ignore. For social media, I always recommend reading Social Media Examiner a couple times per week. For other online marketing trends and actionable tactics, sign up for Neil Patel's email newsletter.

If you take a few minutes a couple of times each week to keep up with the marketing landscape, you'll already be miles ahead of 90% of your competition, making relating to millennials that much easier.

In conclusion, I know trying to keep up with the interests of millennials is both exhausting and challenging. Yet, due to the pull this group has in the marketplace, it's well worth your time to invest into understanding and tailoring your marketing efforts to at least accommodate some segments of millennials. By using the tips laid out in this chapter as your foundation, you'll be in a terrific position to build long-term, meaningful relationships with millennial customers who will keep coming back, year after year. Thanks for reading and best of luck.

Dakota Shane Nunley is a globally-recognized consultant and writer on all things social media. He is also the co-founder of Arctiphi, a social media agency, and columnist at Inc. Magazine's Inc.com. Connect with Dakota here https://www.arctiphi.com

CHAPTER 7

BUILDING A COMMUNITY ON SOCIAL MEDIA

BY JOEY VITALE

If you don't have a tribe on social media, you're doing it wrong.

I'd like to introduce you to two of my friends.

First, meet Alex.

Alex just had a great idea for a new business offering. Alex is smart and a hard worker. This new offering will be super valuable.

Alex stays up all night working out the details. Hours turn into days. Days turn into months. Sketches and outlines turn into fleshed out websites, marketing plans, and lead funnels.

Eventually, Alex has everything ready. He officially launches his new thing.

Alex makes some big announcements to his contacts and on his social media feeds.

And . . . crickets.

Now, meet Barry.

Barry has a great idea for a new business offering. Barry is also smart and a hard worker. His idea is also going to be super valuable.

But Barry has something Alex doesn't have.

Barry has a tribe — a community of people that have grown to know, like, and trust Barry.

Barry reaches out to his tribe, and he lets them know his plans for this next big thing. He adds that he'll give a discount to anyone who wants early access.

By midnight, Barry has hundreds of inquiries from his community, a lot of questions and concerns that help him clarify what he should be creating, and thousands of dollars in sales from a pre-sale launch.

And this is all before Barry even starts fleshing out the details.

Here's the deal. I've been in both Alex and Barry's shoes. I know first-hand — it's better to Barry.

I know what it's like to not have a community in place that supports your business. When I first launched my business, I literally started from zero. No clients, no leads, no one who knew that my business existed except for my wife and my parents.

Within two years, I built a community in the form of a Facebook group that now has over 7.5 thousand members in it.

You might be saying, "Joey, sounds great, but I don't really want to manage a Facebook group."

No worries! Your tribe doesn't need to take the form of a Facebook group, or be on Facebook at all . . . We'll get into that.

The bottom line is, if you don't have a tribe, you're missing out. On sales. On relationships. On a deeper sense of meaning and purpose behind you and your business.

Here are 8 steps to building a tribe on social media

Step 1: Find Your Freaking Passion.

Sorry to burst any bubbles here. If you're not passionate about what you do, people will see right through you. No one is going to care about any tribe you're creating if YOU don't care.

If you're not super passionate about what your business offers, that's okay. Your community doesn't need to be squarely about your business. But connect the dots between your business and a passion of yours. This tribe you're building must be centered around something you're passionate about.

Step 2: Niche Down.

There are all kinds of online communities online. If you want to stand out, you need an angle.

The more niched your community is, the "louder" your voice will be. Imagine you're building a pool — you want this one small and deep, not wide and shallow.

Because you're putting together a group of people with such specific interests or pain points, your members will come across your stuff and be like "wow, I feel like this community is speaking DIRECTLY to me."

Step 3: Find Your Community.

You've figured out the specific type of people you want in your tribe. Now, you have to determine where they hang out online.

Are they in a bunch of Facebook groups? LinkedIn groups? Reddit or Quora forums? Are they engaging on Instagram posts?

Don't make this harder than it needs to be. Figure out where they mostly hang out. Decide on that one platform to focus on, and then join a BUNCH of the communities on that platform. That could take the form of "groups," discussion forums, or accounts who are influencers who also speak to your niche. (In fact, a great first step would be to follow the other contributors in this book.)

Step 4: Listen. Really Listen.

By now, you've identified a lot of "virtual neighborhoods" where your niche is hanging out. They might not be talking about your topic of expertise (yet), but that's okay.

You've just tapped into something amazing. You're able to see YOUR PEOPLE talking about what their concerns, hopes, and fears are. In their own words.

Pay attention. Take screenshots. Copy and paste conversation threads into a safe place.

Think about how you can translate their pain points into what you offer and the value you provide.

Step 5: Start Giving.

Here's where a lot of people get tripped up. Most people rush to sales pitching at this point.

Don't be that gal or guy.

Yes, it's time you've become an engaged member in these other communities. But be respectful. I mean, you haven't even had a "first date" with these folks yet.

Start being a part of conversations. Offer sympathy, empathy, and — where you can — value.

Don't rush into problem-solving mode. Want to know a secret I've learned? People value being heard more than they value an answer.

I like to apply the "sandwich" method here. Give your answer (the "meat") between slices of human touch (the "bread"). Create replies or responses that begin by showing you understand and can identify with the problem they are having. Then offer some help. Then finish your response on an emotional note. Show that you "get it." You understand where they're at.

Trust me here. This type of response is SO much more appreciated than a quick and dry answer to their question with a link to your website.

Remember, the goal here isn't to close a sale. It's to build a relationship.

Step 6: Build Your Space.

Alright. Now is when you can actually start creating your own space. Maybe it's a Facebook group, or a Reddit account, or a targeted email newsletter. Or even a paid mastermind like Mitch's LegalMinds Mastermind Group, which I'm a proud member of!

It doesn't really matter what "form" your tribe takes. What matters is that you waited until now to create it.

If you rush to this step first, then you really have no idea what to create that will resonate with your niche.

But now, because you've followed the steps before this, you're doing significantly less guesswork. You know your niche much better than you did before.

Step 7: Create Mirror Content.

Here's where the real magic happens. And because of the steps you've taken already, it's not as hard as you'd think. This is where you start creating your own content.

The beauty of it is you're not starting from scratch. Instead, you're just taking everything you've learned about your niche, and you're translating it all into how you can help them.

You're essentially creating mirrors. Write content that speaks to the pain points, concerns, and hopes that you've seen expressed in these other spaces.

Acknowledge and respect what you've been listening to. Then continue with how your offering helps them. For this content, the call to action should be to join your tribe to get more great tips and value.

Step 8: Love on Your Referrals.

If you follow these steps, it's only a matter of time before your tribe starts getting noticed. You'll start to build relationships with the "gatekeepers" of these other communities because you're being so helpful. And people in these other communities will start name dropping you and your tribe.

When they do, love on those recommendations as much as you can.

Thank the person who recommended you. Address people by name who have expressed an interest in you through this recommendation. Provide support and value right there, in the other community. And depending on the rules of that community, drop a link to your own virtual tribe or follow up with the people privately with a link.

This process is organic. It takes work.

But this is how you get people — again, not just numbers but actual human beings — to join the community you're building as an invested member.

There you have it! That's the 8 steps you need to build a tribe around you.

But — since I'm such a big fan of Mitch Jackson — I'm going to add a little bonus here.

Here's my list of the top 3 things NOT to do with your community.

1. Don't just think about potential clients.

If you build a community through the steps I covered earlier, you WILL get clients. I promise.

But leading a community is about so much more than getting clients. Don't lose sight of the other benefits you'll get from a strong tribe. You could find referral connections, mentors, friends, people who will never buy from you but sing your praises on a weekly basis, and experts that can help take your own business to the next level.

Remember: this isn't a community about you. It's a community led by you. Think of yourself as a guide, not a superhero. Your members arc the superheroes — you're just helping them realize their potential.

2. Don't just add to the noise or create shallow support.

In today's entrepreneurial world, the "tips" and "hacks" are trickling down more quickly than ever. I see so many business owners these days create communities, and then they fill them up with shallow prompts, goofy GIFs, and photos of their breakfast.

That stuff isn't all bad, per se. But do it in doses. Make sure that most of the conversations happening in your group are tied back to your passion and your business offering — that's why these people joined in the first place.

This is the problem with most online communities. They turn into shallow, and sometimes even toxic, spaces that members eventually realize isn't worth their time.

If you take this point to heart, respect your members, and offer value instead of noise, your community will always stay risen above the rest.

3. Don't undervalue yourself.

If you follow the steps I've outlined earlier, you will build a community of actual, skin-and-bones human beings who are interested in the topic around which you sell. That's something that you need to honor and respect — but be careful.

When I say that I have a group of 7,500 members in a Facebook community, I literally have to pinch myself sometimes. I do this to remind myself that each one of these "members" is a human being — a person with legitimate feelings and thoughts.

Each one of them has taken time out of their day to commit time and attention to this group that I'm building. While I haven't charged them anything — it sometimes feels like I do owe them something. And I do — so do you as a leader of a tribe.

You owe them to make this community worth their while. You DON'T owe them any discounted or free services.

Some of your community members might want to use this community to get the type of value from you that you charge for.

Be a giver. Charge what you're worth. Be worth what you charge.

Now get out there and build your tribe.

I'd love to support you. Send me an email at joey@indielaw.com, and let me know how things are going.

————

Joey Vitale is an attorney for thriving small businesses. As the owner of Indie Law, Joey works a variety of "creative" business owners, from social media experts and brand agencies to online course creators and handmade crafters. Joey manages an online community of over 7,000 business owners and hosts a weekly interview show on Facebook where he highlights and promotes a variety of experts who help small business owners. Connect with Joey here https://indielaw.com

CHAPTER 8

HOW PROFESSIONALS CAN SHARE THEIR 'WHY' ON SOCIAL MEDIA TO BUILD TRUST AND DO SOCIAL GOOD

BY MORRIS LILIENTHAL

If you are an attorney, it is a sure bet that you face a considerable amount of distrust of your profession. In fact, here's a statistic you may or may not know: According to Legal Ink's online magazine, a full 69 percent of consumers have little to no trust in lawyers.

An even more dismal statistic comes from a 2015 Gallup poll, which found that only about 21 percent of adults in the United States believe lawyers are honest or ethical. (In case you are wondering, nurses garnered the highest levels of trust as far as professions go). Unfortunately, this lack of trust in lawyers stems from a very few untrustworthy attorneys—by and large, the vast majority of lawyers are dedicated professionals whose daily goal (and long-term goal) is to solve problems and improve the lives of their clients.

Three Strikes?

As a lawyer, I am very cognizant of the fact that I not only have this "strike" against me, I have two more as well. The second "strike" I'm talking about is that consumers trust companies about as much as they trust lawyers—yet most lawyers work for a company, even if their firm is relatively small. And the third strike? Advertising. Yes, Americans have been so inundated with the barrage of advertising which assaults their senses each and every day, that they have learned to be distrustful of any and all advertising claims. In fact, consumers trust advertising even less than they trust companies—or lawyers.

Marketers have consistently created highly-crafted advertising campaigns with one goal—to sell. Yet we, as consumers, are well-aware of this goal, which makes us all skeptical of advertising. The bottom line is that when consumers trust a company and its advertising, they will buy their products or use their services, they will recommend the company to a friend or colleague, they will share positive opinions online, they will defend the company, and will even pay more to a trusted company. Of course, the reverse of that is that consumers will avoid the products and services of a distrusted business, will not recommend the company and will freely share negative opinions of the company—online and in person. So, I think you can see why I believe that as lawyers, we have some obstacles to overcome to gain the trust of consumers and secure the loyalty of our clients.

Don't despair—while it may sound like an insurmountable obstacle, in truth, the answer is relatively simple. The challenge is essentially to establish a personal connection with others—people trust people, not companies, not lawyers and not advertising. When others get to know you, the person, not you the lawyer—they will begin to sense your passion, recognize your expertise in your field, and realize you have the ability, the skills, and the knowledge to solve their problems. So, how do I work on creating this level of trust? I'd like to share some of the ways I work on establishing these crucial human connections through social media and my Internet presence.

Define Your Why

Your why can be personal or related to your firm—why do you do what you do? What makes you get up in the mornings? Everyone's why is different, but every human being has a story—and people care about your story. What defines you, making you the person or the lawyer you are? Are you a husband or wife, a mother or father, do you rescue shelter dogs or are you passionate about a particular cause? Did you decide to become a lawyer late in life or was it always your passion? Was it a bumpy road to get to where you are today? Are you funny, thoughtful, a hard-core athlete (or a weekend warrior)? You see where I'm going with this—let others know who you are on social media and what you care about.

What is My Why?

I want to tell you a bit about my own why. I met my wife Shannon in a small high school in Alabama where we became best friends who didn't start dating until we were both in college. We dated—long-distance—for more than nine years! Once I finished law school and Shannon and I were both established in our careers, we were overjoyed to find we were going to be parents. Our son, Will Jackson Lilienthal was born on June 5, 2009. Will had breathing issues and was in critical condition within two hours. Will's time on this earth was short—he passed away three days later from Vacterly association, which is a cluster of abnormalities. A year later, our son Wyatt Jameson Lilienthal was born (Same initials to honor his big brother). Shannon, Wyatt and I started Team Will in 2013 to remember and honor Will and help support the March of Dimes.

The mission of the March of Dimes is to promote healthy pregnancies, improve prenatal care and prevent health issues which can threaten babies. Over the last six years the lawyers at my firm, Martinson & Beason, along with Shannon, Wyatt and I, have raised over $53,000 for the March of Dimes. I share this story to tell others that we are real people with real families, interests, hobbies, and problems. I have implemented our Team Will website (TeamWill.net), our Facebook page, as well as engaging graphics and videos to tell others about this part of my life. As a result of sharing about Team Will, I have made new connections, have garnered speaking engagements, radio interviews, and television interviews. When you embrace your why as well as your other passions on social media, you connect with others who share those passions, and those people, in turn, connect with you, and by extension, your law firm.

Using Video to Connect with Others

When I include video on my website or my Facebook page, I am allowing potential clients to see my face, hear my voice, read my body language, and begin to develop trust in me, the person, Morris Lilienthal. Others will relate to what I'm talking about on my video, whether it is a 60-second tip, a life hack, information about influential leaders in our community, my new health path, a discussion about the new puppy Wyatt just got, or yes, sometimes even legal issues, and how you can deal with those issues in the best way. I truly believe that these video clips are invaluable as a method of allowing others to get to know me and to build trust. Other potentially positive videos include Question and Answer videos with frequently asked questions on a particular legal or life subject, biography videos of the lawyers in your firm which show them as real people and videos which share the goals and mission of your firm.

Social Media—a Crucial Tool

Many lawyers shy away from social media, which is really too bad because, as reported by Statista, in 2017, 81 percent of Americans had a social networking profile—a number which is expected to grow by leaps in bounds over the next two years. Facebook is definitely the market leader in the U.S., as the first social media platform to surpass one billion registered accounts, and currently at about 1.86 billion accounts. You would be hard-pressed to find someone who doesn't have at least one social media account, whether Facebook, Twitter, Instagram or another social media site. An active social media presence allows you to engage with your audience, giving them the opportunity to engage with you, ask you questions, and learn what you and your law firm stand for. As you demonstrate your passions and your skills, you are offering a transparent environment which encourages trust. Your goal is not to promote yourself. Instead, it's to provide content and information which engages your audience and adds value.

Blogging on a Regular Basis

Yes, I know, you're busy! I'm busy too, yet I passionately believe in the power of posting videos, being active on social media—and blogging. When you write blogs for your legal website, you should do your best to skip the legalese, and "talk" to those who need your help and your expertise. Show that you understand the problems and concerns facing others in today's world and that you have the skill set, the determination and the motivation to solve those problems. When you share practical information and answer the questions people actually care about, you will increase the trust others have in you as a person and as a lawyer.

So, What's the Takeaway?

When you show others you have the ability to help them solve their most pressing problems, and that you really care—that you're not just in it for the paycheck-- trust is built, video by video, blog by blog, and social media post by social media post. While my passions will certainly be different than yours—as they should—I would like to leave you with my "takeaways" for building trust through social media:

1. Be consistent
2. Be unique
3. Engage with others
4. Remember it's a marathon, not a sprint
5. JUST DO IT!!

———

Morris Lilienthal is a top-rated Alabama Trial Lawyer that has been recognized for 5 consecutive years as a Super Lawyers Rising Star and in The National Trial Lawyers Top 100. Morris has devoted his practice to representing injury victims and their families. The same competitive nature and drive that helped Morris excel as a college football player continues to help in his law practice today. Connect with Morris via email at morris@martinsonandbeason.com or through his www.martinsonandbeason.com

CHAPTER 9

UNDERSTANDING THE GLOBAL IMPLICATIONS OF SOCIAL MEDIA

BY NIKLAS MYHR, PH.D.

"On behalf of HSH Prince Albert II and as Monaco's Chief Digital Officer, I am delighted to invite you to join the Monaco Digital Advisory Council."

This email subject line certainly caught my attention. Then the skeptic inside me started thinking that this was a creative variation of the infamous Nigerian Prince scam. But just before I hit the delete key, I started thinking what if this email is real? Wouldn't this represent a glorious return to Monaco in contrast to my last visit to the Principality when I, as a 9-year-old, was refused entry to the Monte Carlo Casino?

I am no longer surprised to receive invitations to speak in places like Dubai, Singapore, Shanghai, Amsterdam, Washington DC, Skellefteå, or Munich but an invitation from the Prince of Monaco certainly stands out as very special in my book. As a marketing professor, it used to be a rare occasion to be contacted by people who didn't already know me unless of course, they were trying to sell me something.

Now, it seems as if more and more people are knocking on my virtual door. In fact, ever since I started taking social media more seriously, I do find that I experience more opportunities from around the world that I had neither sought nor have been aware of. Similarly, I have gotten used to fielding interview requests from mainstream media outlets such as the NBC, CBS, and National Public Radio, and I have also been featured in many international media and TV channels such as in Sweden, Czech Republic, Finland, and in Taiwan.

In my experience teaching business school students, coaching alumni, and consulting with executives from at least 30 different countries, I also see many other professionals who are discovering the opportunities of adopting a more global perspective. You may want to do the same. In short, if you are a professional and are not considering the potential global implications of your online presence, you are likely missing out.

I have also witnessed the stress of dealing with digital disruption, and if you are concerned that rapid change can also negatively affect you, you should know that you are not alone. Many professionals are finding that their historically somewhat predictable industries are being disrupted by new approaches of forming and building client relationships such as through social media.

Regardless, change is inevitable, and I have seen that a strong social media presence can help alleviate some of the worries and simultaneously boost professional careers. While I recognize that there are some cultural and individual differences at play that need to be respected, I also find that there are some universal social media success factors as well as some common pitfalls to be mindful about.

What the best social media strategy would be for you depends on your goals such as whether you are looking to expand to serve international markets or not. Still, the global forces of digital disruption are likely to impact you even if you choose to stay focused on your domestic market. Therefore, it makes sense for you to consider both how social media can help you withstand the threats as well as leverage the opportunities from globalization.

In this chapter, I will elaborate on some of the most important lessons related to social media of relevance to global professionals. I aim to help you find ways to use social media to grow in your profession, enhance your reputation, and develop meaningful relationships so that you can become or remain relevant and successful in today's ever-changing global marketplace. I summarize my recommendations in three steps elaborated upon in the following.

Step 1: Build a Social Media Foundation

Which social media platforms should you be on? That is perhaps the most common questions I get. In response, I usually share the proposition that social media and marketing experts, Joe Pulizzi and Mark W. Schaefer, would argue. That is, you should put your primary focus on one single social media platform at least until you get some traction and develop a meaningful following before branching out to other channels. Certainly, these arguments are persuasive, and admittedly, there are times when I wish I had personally pursued that approach as I have seen that it can work.

The other extreme would be to be present on as many networks as you can muster to keep more doors open for people to find you and, to then let the responses you get help to determine where you should put your primary emphasis going forward. Then the downside would be that you may not have the wherewithal to give each network the attention it may need for you to show up in a favorable manner.

Regardless of your approach, it is important that you keep in mind that the platform or platforms you focus on today may not be the best fit either for you or your customers tomorrow as the popularity of social media platforms changes over time. Also, if your goal is to pursue international opportunities, it will be more difficult to limit your online presence to a single social media platform.

To increase the likelihood of people abroad finding and presenting you with enticing, yet unsolicited proposals, you need to build at least a minimal global presence on at least some of the major social media platforms. In this regard, it is Facebook with its 2.2 billion monthly active users, followed by YouTube with 1.9, and Instagram with 1 billion (Statista.com, July 2018) that represent networks which are most likely to facilitate your ambitions of having a significant global reach.

If you have particular markets in mind, it will make sense to develop an online presence on social media platforms popular in those specific markets. This is particularly the case if you are aiming for the Asia-Pacific region in general and China in particular where the set of popular social media platforms are quite different from the rest of the world.

In China, WeChat with 1 billion monthly active users (Statista.com, July 2018) rules the day online and not just for social media but also for payments and many other connected services. Personally, I have barely touched the surface of what WeChat can do after I created an account and tested some functions aided by a Chinese student of mine as there is also the language barrier to consider. Still, if you are seeking more business or career opportunities in China, an investment in a WeChat presence would be advisable given its dominance in the market.

LinkedIn is a social media platform with a smaller scale with 294 million active monthly users worldwide. Still, LinkedIn could provide the key to your international success as this network focuses specifically on professional networking opportunities. This is also the platform which many buyers with budgets begin their search for qualified professional service providers.

Once you choose your social media platforms, it is imperative that you start developing a strong presence. Begin by completing your profile information to share some information about your position, passions, and objectives. The profile information is only the starting point, however, as the social connections that the platforms facilitate represent the real power of social media.

Also, for the global professional, you should focus on expanding your social network outside your regular networks and local market also to include people abroad. For example, if you want to work in Japan, wouldn't it be more likely that you can achieve that goal if you are also connected to many Japanese on social media?

Step 2: Identify New Market Opportunities

The next step is for you to identify your ideal target market and research their needs in as much detail as possible. This will put you in a position to serve them not only with quality products and services but also with social media communications that suit their preferences. While doing this, keep in mind that you'll be dealing with different languages, business customs, and time zones.

When it comes to identifying target markets, many professional services providers make the mistake of assuming that the clients that they happen to have today also represent their target market. In fact, for many businesses, the current client stock is a result of a mixture of conscious strategies and serendipitous business development, often with geographic proximity being a deciding factor.

But what if you would be better off leveraging an online presence to find a remote audience, even an international one? What if letting go of at least some of your current clients could free up bandwidth for you to serve your ideal clients with higher degrees of customer satisfaction? Perhaps you are in a unique position to serve a new audience overseas?

One litmus test in assessing whether you have the right definition of your ideal client is for you to ask yourself whether you would be excited to serve this customer indefinitely even if it would require retooling on the backend to provide new products and services as their needs change?

Similarly, would you be happy and feel well-suited to regularly create online content to be shared on social media that would be of interest to this target group? Do you currently have content that you are sharing on social media that speaks to this group? How is that content doing relative to other content that you may be sharing and in what markets of the world?

In my own case, I found it tremendously valuable to reach out to my existing social media connections from a number of different countries to choose a title, pick a winning cover design, and help crowdfund for my upcoming book, "The Social Customer Journey." Not only did the positive response I received help me decide to pursue this project, but now I also have a better sense of what countries to target with a book campaign.

Step 3: Develop New Service Offerings

A surprising number of professional services providers that I encounter consider their service offerings more or less as a given. Perhaps, it is understandable that this is the way they see it given that they have degrees, licenses, and credentials related to a specific "profession."

For example, I could forgive my parents who met in dental school for thinking that they were supposed to provide dental services, or an insurance broker for selling insurance policies, etc. Still, many professional services providers leave opportunities and money on the table as they could potentially add more services to their product mix if they re-evaluated their clients' needs.

Exploring new product and service opportunities is another way in which social media can be helpful. For example, if you are in regular contact with your prospective customers or just people in general on various social media platforms, chances are that they would at times contact you with inquiries about service offerings, some of which you may not even have considered before.

For example, a former MBA student of mine with whom I had stayed connected with for three years past her graduation thanks to Facebook and LinkedIn, told her superiors that she thought I would be a good candidate to offer a talk on diversity and inclusion in a global corporation. As a white, middle-aged male who had never spoken on diversity before, I was hesitant at first.

Still, my former student had seen me handle diverse classes on campus, organize the international travel course Business in Scandinavia, and she had also followed my adventures traveling the world as an international speaker on social media. As a result, she saw something in me that I wasn't aware of myself. I eventually agreed to share my perspectives, and before long, I found myself delivering a virtual presentation on diversity and inclusion to 2,500 employees of a global corporation.

Regardless of whether I will pursue further engagements on this topic or not, today's professionals need to at least consider expanded service offerings for continued survival because of encroaching competition, increasing automation, or changing customer needs.

Perhaps a decision to take advantage of new opportunities will require you to scramble on the back-end to be able to provide such new service offerings, but it may also be worth it if it helps preserve an otherwise valuable customer relationship. Conversely, if you decide not to serve and offer complementary services beyond your current offerings, you may lose clients who are looking for more convenience in the form of one-stop-shopping.

The key is for you to find the right balance between focusing on what you currently do and are known for versus what you could be doing in the future. I believe that you can use social media to find the right mix for you either by asking your connections or by analyzing their engagement levels related to your various offerings.

One thing to keep in mind in this regard is that your new service offerings would not necessarily have to represent a radical departure from what you currently do. At the very least, it could simply mean that you decide to emphasize some specific service offerings more and others less going forward.

Conclusion

As a professional services provider, your goal is to become and remain your clients' trusted advisor. In this chapter, I have shared some steps involved for you to continue to thrive also in an increasingly stressful and rapidly changing global market environment. In short, I suggest that you build up a solid social media foundation, stay open to new market opportunities that you may discover through social media, and remain sufficiently nimble to come up with some new service offerings when called for.

As you develop your presence with an international audience in mind, it is advisable that you stay consistent in generously sharing valuable content on relevant social media platforms. If you combine such generosity with the confidence to get out of the comfort zone of your local home market, you are likely going to be better able to remain successful at home as well as to find some international opportunities sooner rather than later. During your social media journey, keep in mind that, "the best lives are led by those who are brave and generous." - Viking saying

───────

Niklas Myhr, Ph.D., The Social Media Professor, is an author and an international TEDx and keynote speaker who teaches Social Media, Digital & Global Marketing at Chapman University in California. Dr. Myhr holds a Ph.D. in Marketing from the University of Virginia and is currently Google's #1-ranked "Social Media Professor." Professor Myhr is the author of the upcoming book The Social Customer Journey, and he has been featured in publications such as BBC, The Washington Post, Marketplace Morning Report, InformationWeek, ABC, CBS, NBC, FOX News, USA Today, Huffington Post, and San Francisco Chronicle. Connect with Niklas at https://thesocialmediaprofessor.com

CHAPTER 10

HOW TO WORK WITH A SOCIAL MEDIA AGENCY TO GET THE RESULTS YOU WANT

BY SHAMA HYDER

So you've decided to take another step in building your brand by hiring a social media agency. You've done the research, interviewed agencies, and made your selection. After months (or more) of stressing about your social media presence—what you should be doing (or not doing)—you can finally let the experts lead the way. The agency will do the heavy lifting, set the pace, and gauge progress. You can relax and turn your attention to "the real work" piling up in your inbox and on your desk. Right?

Well, yes and no. You can breathe easier. You've accomplished the monumental task of identifying and hiring an expert. You're on a new path towards great results. But you should prepare to press in, not take off—especially in the first 90 days.

The process of working with an agency is collaborative and custom. That's because building a brand doesn't happen overnight. It takes perseverance and patience, trust and teamwork. If you want to be pleased with your results, you need to be clear about your goals and expectations. Most importantly make sure that your expectations are reasonable. Furthermore, if you build a brand strategy with your agency that you don't have the resources to maintain, you'll end up unhappy with the results.

The good news is—you now have a guide. You've partnered with an expert who has the creative and technical expertise to get the results you want. But to be successful, you must commit to a sustained, collaborative process. In the beginning, you're the only one who knows your business goals, your audience, and your voice in the industry. You're the expert when it comes to your business, and your social media team has a lot to learn from you.

Start at the beginning

The first thing you need to do with your agency is taking a minute and discuss foundational aspects of your company. Your "brand" encapsulates each of these, directly affecting your social media strategy. Covering these points with your agency early on will save you time down the road.

Your mission—the heart of your business.

The core. The glue. This is what you want your audience to associate with you when your name comes to mind, or your logo pops up on their screen. You should be able to sum up your mission in a sentence or two—it's who you are, what you do, and how you do it. Lots of brands sell shoes, but TOMS gives away a pair of shoes for every pair sold. It's the company's distinctive mission. Your mission should be the subtext of every message you create.

Your audience—the connected consumer.

When we refer to the "connected consumer," you may initially think of a young, hip, digital native Snapchatting their favorite Spotify playlist. But today's connected consumer is so much more than that. It's a baby boomer couple researching their next cruise. It's a Gen X dad searching for videos to teach his toddler all about colors. With more than half the world now using mobile devices to connect, communicate, research, and purchase, the connected consumer is diverse in identity, yet homogenous in many of their needs.

These empowered consumers have knowledge, choice, and high expectations of companies they choose to do business with. They aren't looking for just simple and fast. They are asking for personalized and proactive, and the companies which can deliver will have the numbers and market share to show for it.

Now that you know you're talking to the connected consumer, it's time to work with your agency to figure out specifically which connected consumers you want to target, what you want to say to them, and how to best reach them.

Your goals—the results of your efforts.

Your business always should have plans to stretch, grow, and change in particular ways. Maybe you want to reach a larger, but more specific audience. Maybe you want to use your advertising dollars more efficiently, or even attract employees with certain types of experience or values. Your goals should be tangible and measurable. Once reached, you should be able to maintain them and grow your business in new ways.

Your culture—your company's distinctive values, personality, and style.

Each of these is reflected in your product or service, your work environment, your customer relations, and your messaging. How do people to feel when they come into contact with your brand? How do you want them to feel? Underlying your mission, does your business promote wellness? Social responsibility? Advocacy? Some of that depends on whether you're selling smoothies, handbags, or legal services. Whatever your cultural focus, it should permeate every aspect of your business.

Your tactics—the to-do list that supports your goals.

Share your business goals - both as they stand and as they evolve. By doing this, you give the agency the tools to be a strategic partner and help you get where you want to go. Once the agency understands your mission, audience, goals, and culture, they should present you with a written plan outlining a strategic, creative approach.

If you've found the right agency, your team will guide you in communicating what you're all about. But at the same time, prepare to speak up. The more energy you invest at the beginning of the process—to engage, educate, and clarify—the happier you'll be with the results.

Setting the pace

I was watching the show "Love it or List it" on HGTV the other day and noticed the homeowner's straightforward remarks about each home the realtor showed her. As they walked up the driveway of one home, she said, "This neighborhood is way too suburban. I like that it's closer to my job, but I hate feeling like I'm living in the suburbs." Once inside, she said, "Those black kitchen cabinets are definitely not my style!" To some people, her comments may seem abrupt, perhaps even a little rude. But as someone who's spent hours in client meetings, I thought her transparency was fantastic and refreshing!

When clients meet with Zen Media, we want to know exactly what's on their minds. We invite feedback, as should any other service-based business. Yes, of course, speak with civility and kindness, but don't be shy. Let us know what you love, what you feel indifferent about, and what you disagree with. Whether it's Zen or someone else, you need experts who will receive your criticism, listen to your concerns, provide honest and realistic feedback, and make necessary changes.

The right agency will provide you with a media plan in writing and encourage you to make adjustments before you approve it. Set dates on your calendar according to the timeline of your plan, and follow up when needed. When your agency contacts you, don't let the emails languish in your inbox. Be responsive, and avoid assumptions. Your creative team should actively collaborate with you to make sure you get the results you want within agreed-upon parameters.

Staying on course

After the first 90 days of establishing your expectations, your media plan, and your rapport with your agency, you should be well on your way to a successful partnership. You and your social media team should be ticking things off the to-do list that's been defined by your audience and your goals. You should have processes in place to evaluate your progress and discuss changes that come up. If everyone's doing their part, you will see results over time. It's kind of like wellness and weight loss. The consistency of good nutrition and frequent exercise, day after day, eventually adds up to inches lost, muscle gained, reduced stress, and more energy. These things won't happen overnight, but eventually, the right changes will yield results.

After you find a routine for communicating with your social media agency, contact will probably become less frequent. You've established a working relationship with your point person, and you've gotten familiar with one another's communication styles. You've set up tools for measurement and accountability, and the upkeep should be lower maintenance. However, make sure you keep the agency up to date on any changes in your goals. New leadership in your company, changes in revenue, and a public crisis of any kind are all examples of change that will shift your social media goals. As you communicate changes to your agency, you should see them reflected in your social media strategy.

You can say that again

In short, here's what to expect as you start working with a social media agency, and how you can help build a strong partnership to yield the best results for your business.

What you should expect from your agency:

- A written plan that accounts for your goals, timeline, and budget
- Clear communication about what you need to provide to stay on schedule
- A responsive client success representative you can reach out to when you have questions
- Periodic meetings to evaluate progress
- A process for measuring results

What's needed from you for the best outcomes:

- Clear communication about your goals, timeline, and budget
- Timely responses to agency inquiries and approvals of deliverables
- Clear communication about changes in company leadership, goals, brand, crises, etc.
- Straightforward feedback about marketing strategy, creative, etc.

As your social media agency learns who you are and what you want, communication gets easier. As you start to relax and turn your attention to the "real work" piling up on your desk, remember to stay closely acquainted with your messages and feedback on social media. Responding to your audience has become "real work," now, too. But that's another topic altogether. Ask your agency about it.

———

Shama Hyder is a visionary strategist for the digital age, a web and TV personality, a bestselling author, and the award-winning CEO of Zen Media – a global marketing and digital PR firm. She has been named the "Zen Master of Marketing" by Entrepreneur Magazine and the "Millennial Master of the Universe" by FastCompany.com. Connect with Shama here https://zenmedia.com

PART II

HOW TO USE THE SOCIAL MEDIA PLATFORMS

————

CHAPTER 11

BLOGGING FOR PROFESSIONALS: BRING SOMETHING TO THE PICNIC

BY CHRIS BROGAN

I can quite honestly say that blogging (and later making video and audio) brought me every significant business success in my life. I've met and interviewed celebrities and billionaires like Sir Richard Branson, gave advice to the CEO of General Motors, presented to a princess, went on the Dr Phil show, published a New York Times Bestselling book (and 9 others), keynoted over a thousand events, and did a whole lot to help others thrive along the way.

I started blogging in 1998 when it was called journaling. I had just left Ma Bell, the old phone company. I was 28 and a relative nobody working in a new wireless telecom service provider. My first blog posts barely reached anyone. I remember telling my friend Becky McCray how excited I was when I got my first 50 subscribers to my blog. It took me eight years to get my first 100 subscribers (mostly because no one even knew what blogs were back then) and then I went on to have the #1 marketing blog in the world for a time (according to the Advertising Age Power150 rankings).

How did I do it? And much more importantly, what can YOU learn from all this? That's why Mitch asked me to write some of his book for him, so I'll show you.

Blog is a Stupid Word

More than half of what you'll be asked to do in this book comes with a dumb term or phrase that makes you want not to do it. Blog is no exception. It comes from a mangling of "web" and "log" that became "weblog," and then shortened more to "blog." So even though it sounds like the sound you make into a trash can after too many martinis, just ignore that. I say "I write online" or "I publish an online magazine." There. We're past the first hurdle.

Why Should You Blog?

The act of blogging is a mix of self-expression and creativity, but it only matters if you create material that helps the people you're hoping to serve others in some form or fashion. If you want to write to prove to the world how smart you are, that will likely get you nowhere. If you seek to create because you've heard it's cheap advertising, the feel of your work will be as you wanted it, cheap.

Why should you blog, then?

Your goal with a blog is twofold:

1.   Create material that helps a prospective buyer know they should work with you and that serves them whether or not they choose to buy what you sell.

2.   Create material that educates and informs potential buyers on topics that are your subject matter of expertise, especially if you can help someone learn and grow from your efforts.

But wait, Chris. Mitch said you'd tell us how to get all famous and stuff by blogging. Oh indeed, good reader. That's what I'm doing. Teaching you how to be famous "and stuff" from blogging.

It's not what you think. The goal is to connect and serve, not tell everyone how amazing you are. As it turns out, precious few people in your life care whether you're famous or not. But the number of people who are looking for help and service? Endless. I've not yet run out.

Seems Like a Lot of Work

Blogging isn't as easy as putting out an advertisement. Ads are just a tiny bit of copy, usually with some kind of sale, and you pay for them to be placed in a paper or magazine or a little pop-up or banner ad online. But of course, no one's looking at ads. Online, there's software to block them.

And blogging is only a lot of work if you don't have simple systems in place to make the work a little less painful for you. Don't get me wrong. Blogging is like running. The more of it you do, the better you get.

So let me share some of those systems and ideas with you, okay?

The Very Basics

Make your blog posts brief. I prefer 300-500 words on a typical post, with the occasional massively informative post reaching 1500-2000 words. Remember that people aren't reading as much any longer. The US Department of Labor and Statistics reports that the average person reads only 19 minutes a day total, including texts, emails, etc.

The goal of every post MUST be to help the people you serve and to remind people you're there to help further. Any post that doesn't accomplish both goals is a waste.

Don't worry as much about keywords as you worry about attracting attention. Keywords don't hurt, though. Think of what someone might Google to find your information.

Also, if you're going to include links, check them before you publish. Broken links will earn you lots of the annoying type of interaction instead of leading to new opportunities.

A Simple Blogging Template

I've shared versions of this template since probably as far back as 2006 (Remember, I started blogging in 1998, so 2006 was nearly a decade later.) It's not that difficult. I'll walk you through it.

• Start with a great title - 80% of blogging is getting someone to want to read, and if you can't get past the title, you're doomed.

• Add a photo - I do not mean stock photos. Post something you took yourself. It's okay if it's not very professional, provided it matches the intent of your business.

• Lead with a personable paragraph - the first paragraph, I use to try and connect with the people I'm trying to reach. Give them some kind of setup for the post that helps them see why they want to read it.

• First subheading echoes the subject line - after the lead in paragraph, I get right to business. Put the meat at the beginning.

• The next two or so paragraphs are meat - fill in whatever needs further explanation as clearly as possible.

• Finish with a next action or call to action - when you hit the end of the post, invite a next step of some kind. It might be to contact you for a consult, or it might be just seeking replies and perspective. But never end a post without inviting the reader to a next step.

And there's the template I've used on almost every post I've written since around 2006 or so.

How to Find Blog Topics

First of all, I should say that if you google "blog topics," you'll likely run into my most popular blog post of all time, "100 Blog Topics I Hope You Write." Feel free to use those topics all you'd like.

Here are a few more ideas for you:

• Turn any reasonable question into a blog post. If one person has the question, it's likely that others will, too. You don't have to mention the person who asked the question, especially if that might embarrass them.

• Look around for FAQ for your industry on other sites. Turn any questions there into topics.

• Look at Quora.

• Think through the mindset of your buyer's world. Where are they right now? What do they want?

Another way to get more topics is to walk through the customer experience journey. Here's my simple little map for it:

• An Event Happens.

• Awareness - buyer looks for a product or service to suit their needs.

• Evaluation - buyer considers between products, and/or not to buy at all.

• Purchase - the actual exchange of money for the product or service.

• Onboarding - what happens immediately after the purchase and thereafter.

• Retention/Referral - after the sale, do you need to work to keep the customer, or should you be seeking referrals.

What would a buyer of yours need at any part of the journey? How can you make them more prepared to work with you? What else will equip your potential buyer for success whether or not they choose to work with you? Sometimes working through your buyer's journey will help.

My Secret Favorite Two Methods for Finding Blog Topics

I do these two actions more than any others to find the topics I want to write about:

• I take pictures of randomly interesting things I see out and about during my travels.

• I read voraciously outside my own industry, looking for parallels and juxtapositions.

Steal these two ideas to get even further with topics.

The Blogging Practice: How to Be More Consistent

I have three ideas for you here:

1.   Write five new topics a day into a file on Evernote or OneNote. Use something you can access anywhere instead of a paper journal. The topics are blog post titles. Your list should grow and grow, and you'll never have a free moment to write without having a topic to consider fleshing out into a post.

2.   Set a weekly publishing schedule and stick to it religiously, BUT also stack the deck and write two posts a week instead of one, storing the others for future publication. Write and publish a post on your scheduled day, but also write and schedule a post for the week after. You get bonus points once you hit one month ahead of yourself. (And don't forget, you can shift the schedule around if you find you need to write something timely instead of going with a stored post.)

3.   Set a timer (I use a physical ladybug timer - http://cbrogan.me/ladybug) for 20 minutes at a pop and write on your topics. Everyone thinks they don't have enough time. You can find 20 minutes of unused time for this. It might take you as much as 40 to get a post written. Maybe more. But like running, it gets better with practice.

And when you finally start feeling comfortable with writing textual blog posts, get ready to jump into video.

Videoblogging - No, Really. You Can Do This

Remember when I said people read 19 minutes a day? YouTube reports that people consume over 1 billion hours of video content every day. While not apples to apples, a billion hours a day tells us something. Also, YouTube says 100 million of those hours are shown on a set-top box (meaning on the TV). It means that every day, 100 million hours of mainstream TV is being replaced with YouTube.

What does it take for YOU to get started making a video and posting it on the web? If you have a smartphone, you already have enough equipment to start.

But why video, Chris? Because video shows people a sense of who you are outside the written word. It allows people to relate to you in a way they can't through text. And it allows people to see your earnest self-unfiltered by well-edited words.

So what does it take to make a video blog? I'll give you a very first step and then a next level. How's that?

Videoblogging - Set Up

Start with a smartphone. Click to the camera app on your phone and find the video setting. Start recording. Aim it at something for a bit. Get a sense of how to start and stop it. Realize that you can turn the camera to face away from you or have it and the screen face you. Easy peasy.

YouTube accounts are free. You can upload the video easily. Or delete the first few because they're garbage.

There you go. You've got all it takes, technically, to start putting video on the web.

Level 2? Use editing software like iMovie on Mac or Sony Vegas on a PC and slice the videos up a little. Make transitions. Maybe even layer in a little bit of music underneath if you're feeling cheeky (I use a site called epidemicsound.com to source my music).

Level 3 is something I cover for free at chrisbrogan.com/startvideoblogging/

Videoblogging - What to Say

The same effort you brought to topics and writing goes into video making. Only, you don't have to write the entire text out. Just bullet up what you want to cover in the same framework as I gave you above and you can walk someone through video content just as easily as you did the blog post.

Speak into the camera. Make eye contact with the lens. Talk as if you're addressing one person in conversation. Speak just a little louder and a little more animated but not a lot. Speak just a bit slower than you think you should, and enunciate. Kapow. You're practically a pro.

Blog Like It Matters

I have only one challenge to you as I wrap up my time with you in Mitch's book. Don't blog just because someone told you to. Don't throw junk out there. There's already plenty enough clutter and garbage. Write as if you have something you want to share with someone and write from a place that serves both you and your buyer. Blogging has brought me mountains of success, almost all of it, and it can definitely do something great for your career, as well. I wish you success with it all.

———

Chris Brogan is president of Chris Brogan Media, offering business and marketing advisory help for mid to larger sized companies. He's a sought after keynote speaker and the New York Times bestselling author of nine books and counting. His next book is "Be Where They Are. Go Where They're Going: Share, Sell, and Serve Your Customers From Their Side of the Story." Connect with Chris at ChrisBrogan.com

CHAPTER 12

FACEBOOK- THE SOCIAL NETWORK THAT EVERY PROFESSIONAL NEEDS

BY STEPHANIE LIU

As a professional and entrepreneur, you don't have a lot of time to spend on social media. You've bought this book to help you prioritize and get ramped up fast, and you might have even been hoping that you could skip the chapter on Facebook.

Well, don't.

Any statistic we put here will be outdated as soon as the book is published. Suffice it to say; Facebook is the largest and most popular social network on the planet and a highly effective platform for growing your business.

We're going to quickly get through the basics of setting up a successful Facebook Page for your business - which will help you whether you have an existing Page or not - and then jump into specific strategies and tactics you can use to raise awareness, drive demand, and boost sales.

Have an Optimized Facebook Page

Your Page makes your business discoverable to a broad audience and provides an opportunity for you to have one-on-one conversations with your customers. Think of your Page as an extension of your business—if customers came into your store, you want to capture their attention as soon as they step inside.

Here are a few things you should add to your Page to make it helpful:

1. Useful details about your business
2. Your products and services
3. A call-to-action button

Provide Useful Information About Your Business

1. Show your brand identity with a creative cover photo or video.

   Pro Tip: If you don't have a video editor on staff, you can easily create a cover video with paid tools like Animoto or Wave. Alternatively, design a static image using Canva.

2. Provide information for the About section to make it easier for customers to discover and learn more about you on Facebook. Highlight your expertise, company achievements, and link to your website and other key social media profiles. Providing all of this information can also enhance your presence in search engines.

Pro Tip: Add your hours of operation, so customers know when you're open. This is super handy especially when existing customers tag you in posts and prospects click on your Page to find out more.

3. Enable ratings and reviews by customers to appear on your Page. If you select the Local Business category when you create your Page, customers can rate your business and write reviews.

Getting ratings and reviews on your Page is an effective way to help people to trust and choose your business.

Pro Tip: You can organize your Page so that Reviews appear at the top of your timeline. Simply go to your 'Page Settings', then go to 'Edit Page' and then dragging the Review widget to the top.

Promote Your Products And Services

Sections let you highlight what your business offers. Depending on the Page category you chose, you can add different sections:

1. Promote products with a Shop Section

2. Display services with a Services Section

Shop Section

The Shop Section is where you can showcase and sell your products — whether it's clothing and accessories or handmade furniture — directly on Facebook. Your customers can subscribe to your Shop, or call you right from your Page. Facebook designed this feature so you could create and manage Shops without needing to work with a third-party partner.

Pro Tip: Entrepreneurs, promote your affiliate products and tag your products in posts!

Services Section

The Services Section lets you list all of the services you offer. If you're a CPA, for example, you can add a variety of offerings for your target audience — such as accounting, consulting, or tax services — and detail what's included, how you approach each client or project, pricing, and more.

When deciding what information to include in this section, always keep the customer in mind. The better they understand your offerings, the more likely they are to get in contact with you.

Select a Page Call To Action (CTA)

Right under your cover photo, you can add a call-to-action (CTA) button to encourage visitors to take a specific action. For example, a CPA can feature a "Book Now" button, encouraging customers to schedule a consultation call.

Use Your Facebook Page to Grow Your Business

Once you've gone through the initial set up and optimization of your Facebook Page, simply review it once a year to ensure that everything is up to date, leaving you free to focus the remainder of your time on growing an interested audience.

To stand out and engage both your current and potential customers, use your Page to connect, communicate, and provide customers with what they're looking for.

You can share text, images, or videos. You can pin posts to the top of your Page so that they're the first thing a visitor sees when coming to your Page. You can create targeted ads, as well as partner and cross-post with other businesses.

Facebook Pages can also create and "sponsor" Facebook Groups which are great for fostering and engaging with a larger community. (That community might be geographic or interest-based, depending on who you're hoping to reach.)

As you start publishing content and growing your audience, you may wonder what type of posts people are most interested. The Page Insights tab will provide you with detailed analytics on how your posts are performing in terms of reach and engagement. You can also see demographic data about your audience and when your audience is on Facebook so you can time your posts perfectly.

Other tools like Messenger Bots or Social Media Management apps can help you and your team stay engaged with your audience in real-time.

So what's the fastest and easiest way to raise awareness, drive demand, and boost sales?

Hint: Combine the power of video with Facebook retargeting.

Quick Refresher on Retargeting

You may have experienced Facebook retargeting without realizing it.
For example, have you ever visited a website to research a product, left without buying, then come across a Facebook sponsored post in your feed that says, "Hey, remember that service you were thinking about purchasing? Check it out again."

That's retargeting, and it's one of the easiest and most cost-effective means for closing potential customers.

In fact, all you have to do is add a tiny snippet of code to your website called a "Facebook Pixel" to take advantage of retargeting.

However, what if you don't have a ton of traffic to your website, can you still take advantage of retargeting?

Yes, you can!

This is where video comes in.

Facebook Loves Video And You Should Too

There are a lot of statistics and evidence regarding the use of video on Facebook, ranging from how much video is consumed to how much better video content reaches audiences.

However, for a professional business, there's only one statistic that matters:

Viewers retain 95% of a message when they watch it in a video, compared to 10% when reading it in text. (Wirebuzz)

When you couple the effectiveness of video content with the powerful reach Facebook gives you, that's a winning formula.

Plus, Facebook gives you several options when it comes to creating and sharing video content.

1.   You can upload pre-recorded videos.

2.   You can broadcast a Live video and engage with viewers.

3.   You can broadcast a Live video with guests. Unlike personal profiles, you'll need to use the Facebook Creator app or a third-party tool like BeLive.tv to bring on another guest.

As with any content you create, video should be entertaining, educational and engaging. But it doesn't have to be a variety show or even highly produced. Some of the most effective videos are simply one person, broadcasting from their smartphone, and sharing their story.

You can do that.

Moreover, the more often you do it, the easier and better at it you will get.
The key to a successful video is to get your viewers engaged with the video and

make sure that they know up front what it is that they'll take away from the video - then deliver.

Getting people to watch as much of your video as possible is the key to being able to leverage that video content later. Also, that's where the money is.

Why "Pay To Play" Is Actually Awesome

Over the years, as organic - read "free" - reach on Facebook has declined, businesses and marketers have decried the fact that they increasingly have to pay <gasp> to reach their target audience.

While you can create a Facebook Page for free, to really reach and convert your audience, you're going to have to invest in Facebook Ads. But here's the good news:

With the rights ads in front of the right people, your business will make money.

So let's talk about what that means.

Reach The Right People With Custom Audiences

When creating a Facebook Ad, aside from the ad itself and the budget you wish to spend, you will also tell Facebook who you want to show that ad to. You can choose from options like:

1.   Saved Audiences - People who match a particular set of characteristics.

2.   Custom Audiences - People who have engaged with your business (e.g., website visitors, installed your app, engaged with your Facebook or Instagram Page, signed up for your email list).

3.   Lookalike Audiences - People who are similar to your existing customer database – making them highly likely to convert as well.

You can also use the video content that you've been creating!

Not only does Facebook pay attention to who watches your videos, but Facebook also tracks how long viewers watch your video. Drill down in the "Create Custom Audience" section to find the details.

This means you can retarget people that viewed your videos and move them further along your marketing funnel.

To make things easy, focus on viewers that watched 10 seconds of your video and viewers that watched 95% of your video.

Here's why...

Those 10-second viewers are potential customers that have now seen your brand, and you're now in their awareness. While those viewers that have watched 95% of your video are now really engaged with your brand.

Custom audiences - which you can create within Facebook Ad Manager as an audience to target - allows you to nurture those relationships and keep your brand top of mind.

You can create content and ads specifically designed for each of those groups, and use your new custom audiences to drive interest and engagement accordingly.

Retarget viewers that only watched 10 seconds of your first video with other content that highlights your expertise, while folks that have watched 95% of your video are prime for pitching.

Sell To The Right People With The Right Ads

The reason why all of this works so well is that, once you get the hang of it, this becomes a system you have in place that can constantly work in your favor.

Create videos and blog posts and landing pages that sell your services - they target people who are familiar with your brand and what you do and are ready to engage you professionally.

Create ads that target your most engaged video viewers to drive them into those high-converting destinations.

Create videos and live videos that bring more and more people in that are higher up the funnel and target those people - the ones who are just getting to know you and haven't watched much of your video content yet - with more great, educational video content.

As you create more videos over time, Facebook will keep your custom audiences up-to-date automatically, feeding into your advertising system. (And don't forget that you can use those videos to create blog content and on other social platforms, so all of this work isn't solely for Facebook.)

Wrapping Up & Ramping Up

Creating content and growing an audience - and building sales systems - doesn't happen overnight. It takes time and patience and investment of creative energy - but ultimately it will become a tremendous growth engine for your business.

Start with the optimization steps outlined above, then create your first post. Then your second, one step at a time. When you're ready, work on your first video. Talk to your audience and get a sense for what they're interested in, then work on your second video.

Whether it takes you days, weeks or months, it doesn't matter, as long as you're moving forward.

———

Stephanie Liu is an energetic online marketing strategist, live video trainer at LightsCameraLive.com, and self-proclaimed 90s beat scholar. She has been implementing the psychology of human behavior in the advertising industry for more than a decade. Connect with Stephanie at https://www.lightscameralive.com/

CHAPTER 13

HOW TO USE FACEBOOK ADVERTISING TO BUILD YOUR PROFESSIONAL BRAND AND PRACTICE

BY AZRIEL RATZ

You knew it was coming. As you read through this book, learning about how to use video, how to use Facebook groups, Instagram hashtags, YouTube search, etc. you knew that eventually, you'd get a chapter on Facebook ads, and you probably were planning to skip it.
DON'T!

At this point, you likely think that Facebook ads aren't for you, Facebook ads are for businesses with big budgets, Facebook ads are too risky for your business. You're better off working on the organic side of marketing first before you are willing to spend money on social.

However, the truth that most social media managers don't tell you is that Facebook ads can be powerful and, you don't need a giant budget to start using them. By the time you're done with this chapter, you'll have a good understanding of how to use Facebook ads the right way to build your professional brand and practice.

Over the last seven years, I have run ads for just about every niche from small local businesses to large online publications, to business coaches and amusement parks, music festivals to non-profits, and many others in between. What I noticed when running successful Facebook ads for so many different types of businesses is that the first $500 per month you spend on Facebook is likely targeting the same audience no matter what your business is. This means you can pay only $10-15 per day to get great results, especially if you are doing the other things in this book correctly.

Ready to learn more? Good, let's start at the beginning.

Every Facebook profile has a Facebook ad account connected to it. What that means is that all you need to do to get started is create a Facebook page, and you can start running ads.

To create your first ad, go to https://www.facebook.com/adsmanager/manage/ and click "Create."

From there you need to set up three things: Ad Campaign, Ad Set and Ads.

Think of the ad campaign as your business objective. What do you hope to achieve with the money you are spending? Do you want people to learn about your brand, want more traffic to your website, or have a video you think everyone should see? Each business objective has a different campaign optimization you can use.

In the ad set, you choose the budget, the targeting and the placement of the ads. When creating ads, I suggest creating different advertising sets for each category of person you want to target. If someone knows you well, put them in one ad set (email addresses, phone numbers, FB likes.) If they know of you, put them in a different ad set (website visitors, video viewers, page engagement.) Finally, if they are don't know you, put them in a separate ad set (lookalike audiences, interest, and geography-based targeting.)

The last step to finishing your ad campaign is setting up the ad. Here is where you write the copy, choose the image or video, and place the link and call to action. My suggestion here is to create multiple ads within each ad set. Choose 3-4 different images to test or a video with a few different thumbnails to allow Facebook to choose the one they believe will perform best.

Now that you know how to create an ad let's talk about strategy.
When building a marketing funnel, I focus on four key stages. The method is called ATTS, which stands for Awareness, Transformation, Taste, and Sale.

We will get into each stage later, but a general breakdown of each step is as follows:

Awareness – Who are you? Why should your audience care? What makes you different than everyone else in your space?

Transformation – Don't focus on giving over information, focus on how your service will improve their lives, relationships, businesses, etc.

Taste – Give over one simple, practical step your audience can take today and see results.

Sale – After your followers have experienced the taste, create a product that allows them to get the most out of your knowledge to get the full experience and the best results possible.

Now that we know what each step looks like, let's walk through building out the entire experience. Instead of starting from awareness, where you will be targeting audiences that do not know you, start with the sale, targeting your best five audiences first: (1) Your email list; (2) Your website visitors; (3) Your Facebook likes; (4) People who have engaged with your Facebook page in the last 365 days and (5) People who have engaged with your Instagram account in the last 365 days.

If you have been on social media for a while, you are likely reaching a nice amount of people between these five audiences. These are the people to run ads to first. Let's be honest; if you can't sell to them, you usually are not going to be able to convince a stranger to pull out their credit card and hire you for professional services.

The people in these audiences already know you, they likely know what your business does, and many of them may be a nice fit for your target market.

Organic reach on Facebook is challenging. The same applies to many other social media platforms and even email marketing. For example, even if you have the greatest email newsletter in history, you probably are not getting above a 40% open rate, with only a fraction of those people clicking on any of the links.

And sticking with email for a section, taking the above into consideration, this means that 60% of the people that are most interested in hearing from you probably didn't even see your email in their inbox, and 90% never got to your website or landing page to read more about that new service your business recently announced.

Facebook Ads allow you to find these people, your best people and spend just a few dollars a day reminding them why they signed up for your email newsletter in the first place. That's why I'm such a big fan of Facebook advertising.

Remember, these people already know you, so the ad doesn't need to go into details about who you are or what your business does. It just needs to focus on the offer you have for sale. For most businesses the ad must only take about 45 seconds to read or watch and can look something this:

"Hey, this is Azriel Ratz. I have been working with high ticket coaches for a long time and have created a perfect product for coaches looking to scale their businesses without spending a ton of money on ads. For just $5-10 per you can reach your entire audience making sure they know about any new product or service you have for sale. If you are looking to book up, let's schedule a call. All the details are on the landing page, so click below to learn more, and I hope to speak to you soon!"

That's it! The goal is to move them off Facebook and on over to your website or landing page as quickly as possible. Once these ads are up and running, you will be driving your best audiences to your practice.

From here, we want to take one step back in the funnel, to the "Taste" section. The best example I have for the taste step happens to apply to sales coaches.

Let's pretend you're a sales coach. As part of your program, you have a suggested a sales script that you tell clients to use. This script has helped you generate over $500,000 and has helped your clients do the same. That means this single sales script has helped generate over $1,000,000.

What if, for only $25, you offer this sales script plus 3-4 videos of sales calls where you have successfully used the script? Your follower takes the script and closes 3-4 deals and generate $5,000. That means they invested $25 and walked away with $5,000 within a pretty short period of time.

Now, you offer these people a 90-day sales optimization program. A program which helps them streamline and optimize their sales process as much as possible. They have already seen massive results from your products and so purchasing your high-ticket program for $3,000 no longer seems like a high price. It's now an obvious purchase.

If they made $5,000 after spending $25, think what kind of returns they can get when they have taken the full course. The Taste offer is an alley-oop, you're placing the ball (potential customer) in the perfect position to score a point (get a purchase). Taste Sale is the ideal combo for helping potential buyers see the worth in your services and purchasing. This approach can be applied to almost any kind of product or service you offer as a professional.

Let's shift our focus to the top of the funnel, the "Awareness" and "Transformation" stages. In these stages, the people you are reaching do not know who you are. Being honest, to them you are just like everyone else on the internet. Why should they care about you? What makes you different from the thousands of others advertising? These are the questions you need to answer for them to care about anything you have to say.

The solution? Focus on the 2-3 most important features of your business that they desire the most and show them how you are the best one to help them achieve these things. Show them the promised land!

Give your audience a clear image of what you have achieved for you or your clients. Create an image in their mind that allows them to experience and put into words what it is that you have. If they can easily picture it, then they will connect you for your solution.

Next, shift into their problems. The main reasons why they have not fixed their problem. What is holding them back? Find their most significant pain points and press into them. This may be connected to their personal life, their relationships, health, or business. The goal is to lay on the table the key reasons why they are failing today.

Finally, present the solution. Explain clearly how you/your clients have been through these issues and that you were able to help. This process allows you to show the consumer that you have created the perfect solution to their professional need. In the end, you're the solution to their problem.

To go through all these stages, you will likely need several minutes, but if you follow this formula, you will keep the attention of the highest quality users while weeding out potential clients, patients, and customers who are not a good fit for your practice.

Finally, let us discuss the Transformation stage. Most content creators online are creating what I call "informational value." This breakdown of ATTS is informational value. It is usually the easiest thing to talk about. What I mean by this is that by focusing on the "how to," you can teach potential buyers something new.

Understanding this, you'll soon learn that the issue is that most people don't buy after learning how to do something. Yes, it will likely position you as an expert, but it will not get them excited to purchase from you. It will not get them to pick up the phone or swipe their credit card.

If you want people to take real action, you need to stop focusing on informational value and start creating "transformational value." If you are like most of my clients, you're probably asking, "what is "transformational value?"

Let me give another example. Imagine you are a fitness coach. If you are like most fitness coaches online, you are creating workout routines, healthy eating guides, information on new vitamins, or a 7-day challenge of some sort. All these things are information. They are great and do have their place to help grow your audience online but are not the best for creating purchase intent.

You want to use what was already built up from the Awareness stage and show them how they will transform over time. Show your audience how they will feel when it's over. In 6 months, how their pants will be too big, how they will wake up with more energy, how they will have better relationships, be able to run around with their kids in the park, how their lives will be dramatically better overall if serious steps are today to make that happen. Show them how they will improve their situation by following what you say.

Only after they understand the transformation will they be a qualified lead. If you skip this step, you will be missing out on what is likely the most significant driver of high-quality purchasers into your business.

For all the professionals reading this chapter, think about how you can help your client or patient and with your help, how much better their "situation" will be in six or twelve months. Share that final transformation in your Facebook advertising. That's what will separate your professional practice from everyone else in your community.

Once you have built out the ATTS method for your business, you will be able to target cold audiences based on interests or lookalikes. You will be able to persuasively show them who you are and why they should care. Doing this will allow them to understand the transformation they hope to achieve, then give them actionable tasks they can do today to begin seeing results. After they have done this, they will be ready, and excited to buy whatever you sell.

Moreover, the craziest part is that you can begin this entire process for just $5-10 a day.

————

With seven years of experience in Online Marketing, Azriel Ratz has perfected the skills to find the most effective ads and best target markets to promote company sales. At only 26 years old, he became the CEO of Ratz Pack Media, created the "Facebook Ads Mastery" course in 2017, and wrote the eBook "Find, Engage, and Optimize" in 2018. You can learn more and connect with Azriel and Ratz Pack Media at https://RatzPackMedia.come

CHAPTER 14

LINKEDIN- LEARNING THE LANGUAGE OF CONNECTION

BY CHRIS HARGREAVES

Writing a chapter of a book without knowing what's in the other chapters is like trying to buy wedding presents without a gift registry – there's a good chance the happy couple is going to end up with 13 toasters but no steak knives.

I don't promise steak knives, but I'll try for a toaster that doesn't burn things.

I want to avoid writing something here that will be useless when LinkedIn next changes its user interface, so a lot of what I'm going to recommend is strategic rather than tactical.

We also need to give a nod to the fact that attempting to summarize an entire book into a single chapter is... hard.

Is LinkedIn Right For You?

There's little point in driving yourself to a networking event made up of 18-year-old singles if you're a divorce attorney.

Sure – you might find someone who knows someone that might be interested, but it's hardly a good use of time.

Before leaping into the fray, it's worthwhile asking whether the people you serve as a professional are likely to be on LinkedIn at all.

Given its positioning as a "professional networking platform" there are obviously going to be a lot of professionals: lawyers, accountants, engineers, architects and so on.

While I could try and list every industry on LinkedIn, your best bet is going to be to jump on yourself and do some recon – find out if a critical mass of the "right" people are using the platform.

If you don't know how to search...

Master the Platform

There's no point in having any tool that you don't know how to use. That goes for social media, circular saws, and toothbrushes. To achieve the desired result, you need to know what you're doing.

So the first and most important thing you can do with LinkedIn is master the platform.

You probably know how to share a post. But what's the character limit? What picture dimensions work the best? Can you upload video natively? If so – what's the best resolution to use? Portrait or landscape? Where do you find the analytics for your posts and what do they mean?

Less than 30 minutes dedicated attention would give you all this valuable information and more. Of course, I tell you all of the current answers to this stuff, but then this would be out of date before you can say "platform update."

Mastering the platform will ultimately save you time, give you more valuable information, and form the foundation of greater success on LinkedIn.

Mastery doesn't just come with consuming information though. It comes with practice.

Dedicate the Time

If you're reading this, you're probably a busy professional of some kind. Telling yourself repeatedly "I really should do more on LinkedIn" isn't going to move the needle.

To use LinkedIn effectively, you need to diligently set aside productive time during which you are performing useful activities.

Speaking of useful...

Premium Accounts

The most frequent question I get about LinkedIn is "do I need a premium account" so let's get that out of the way.

A premium account will not magically propel you into LinkedIn success. Premium accounts open some advanced options for searching the platform and finding new connections, as well as tracking your "leads." You certainly don't need one to use LinkedIn profitably.

I suggest you develop good habits with a free account first. If you're doing well and feel that you'd benefit from a premium account, then get it later.

Company Pages

Being a platform designed around personal connections, LinkedIn company pages are a bit of a strange creature. They tend to be less engaging, less interesting, and ultimately less useful than your personal profile (although often this is because of the poor approach taken by brands to their pages). The main exception here is if you want to do paid advertising, in which case you'll need a company account.

Since my view is that the best and highest use of LinkedIn is for personal connection, everything I'm about to say is more relevant to personal accounts than company pages.

Nothing's Really Changed

While the tools in the world of professional services marketing have changed dramatically over the last few years, the underlying philosophy hasn't changed at all: "All things being equal, people do business with people that they know, like and trust."

Nowhere is this more apparent than on LinkedIn, where (IMHO) you have a prime opportunity to tick off the entire trifecta.

Why? It's because...

That's What People are There For

We tend to visit different social media platforms for slightly different reasons. We go to YouTube to learn how to do something. On Instagram, we like living vicariously through the adventures of other people. And on Facebook, we keep up with the lives of the people we don't telephone.

On LinkedIn, you have a distinct advantage – people are already there in a professional mindset.

That means, they are there to:

1.   build their own networks;

2.   receive useful information;

3.   have a chuckle* now and again.

*Yes – I consider chuckling a professional activity. Not guffawing, or raucous laughter, or snickering – but chuckling.

Of course, there are exceptions to every rule. Many people on LinkedIn are there to build their networks and be cheerful participants in the process alongside you. Others are there to spam you until you disconnect.

So which kind of person do you want to be? And what are you going to use LinkedIn for?

Permission and Value

Let's run with the assumption that you want to be a decent human being, and not a walking advertisement.

From that, you can start to see the opportunity LinkedIn gives you for a constant cycle of human connection and relationship development.
Here's LinkedIn in a nutshell:

1. Find the right people (being a well-defined and understood audience).

2. Get permission to be a part of their lives.

3. Use the platform to offer them value.

I could end there, but let's make things a little more specific.

Who Are You Looking For?

It's quite challenging on LinkedIn to target multiple audiences. If you try, you'll probably end up with generic fluff on your profile that won't be attractive enough to any audience that they think "wow – this person is exactly who I want to get to know."

For that reason, I recommend identifying a specific group of people that you're looking to connect with. That doesn't mean you're limiting your practice. It just means that, for now, your profile and your strategy are focused.

So how do you pick and define which set of people to go for? The easiest place to start is to ask these questions: who are the people I love working with, and who I can help the most?

If you're lucky, that will be the same answer. If not, then at least you've got two good places to start.

From there, many people (myself included) recommend writing a "persona" that describes your client in detail. The trick is to use enough detail that you're describing a real person, their desires and their fears. Doing this right will help inform the future decisions you make.   Here's a rough example of what I'm talking about:

"Janice is a 37-year-old mother of two. She runs an online business from home that helps people do DIY interior decorating for their homes. Her husband works. She'd love to get more people to help with her business but can't afford it now. She's worried that the time spent on her business will hurt her relationship with her kids as they grow up but hopes that she can avoid having to go back to work if she can get her business running well enough beforehand."

Lay the Foundation

The question for every profile section is the same: if Janice was reading this, would she think "this person is exactly who I need" or not?

Creating a good LinkedIn profile is a detailed process, so this is going to be the highlights.

Your picture should be a headshot only, smiling, in focus, and looking at the camera or just slightly to one side.

Your headline is not a job title, and it's not an industry. "Senior Accountant" is not a good headline. If Janice is your target client, then perhaps your headline is "Helping Online Businesses with their Legal Needs," or "Accounting Solutions for Mums Who Work at Home." Bear in mind that your headline gets cut off sometimes, so you want to place your most important words at the start.

Your summary is where most people fail, usually by cutting and pasting the third-person marketing drivel that goes on most professional websites.

Your summary should be in first person because third-person summaries make you seem weird. Here's a simple model for writing a semi-decent summary:

1. An opening paragraph designed to either ask a question that provokes interest or summarize your expertise in a few words (like a second stab at a headline).

2. Make a personal connection – say a couple of things about yourself, focusing on the things that Janice might care about.

3. A sales line – why you're the solution to problems that Janice has had in the past.

4. How you've helped people like Janice in the past.

5. Call to action with your contact details.

How's that look in practice? Something like this:

"I help large construction companies resolve major disputes quickly, efficiently, and effectively."

"I understand the disruption that litigation can have on a company that wants to grow. Disputes can distract from your overall strategy, take time from your key staff members, and take you off your main game."

"My job is to help you finalize your dispute and get back as quickly as possible into what you do best. Along the way, I ensure that you're fully informed about what's going on and what's happening next. That way both you and I can guarantee your dispute is managed in a way that minimizes disruption to your business."

"In one major dispute recently we reached a fast resolution, recovering more than $2.5m for our client by ensuring we made good, strategic decisions right from day one. Happy client, happy lawyer."

"If that's the kind of lawyer you need, feel free to reach out directly to me on 555-5555-555 or connect with me on LinkedIn."

Your picture, headline, and summary are the key pieces of your profile, so with them in place you can flesh out the rest of your profile in whatever way makes you happiest.

Next comes our cunning three-step plan.

Grow your Network

LinkedIn has a powerful search tool that allows you to find new people to connect with – use it.

It's not hard to find Janice and people like her. You'd search for business owners, in your local area, in an "online business" type industry. If that doesn't narrow it down enough, then you can go right ahead and start refining it even further by the available search terms (these will vary depending on whether you have a premium profile or not).

Once you find people – send them a connection request. Please for the love of everything personalize it – it takes all of 20 seconds to say "Hey Janice – I'm looking to expand my connection with business owners in the Bay area, and your name came up in my searches. It would be great to connect if you're open to it".

Of course, you can also connect with anyone you meet, engage with or where you can find a meaningful reason to do so.

Listen to People

Depending on how well you already know your audience, this step might take different amounts of time. The ability to connect with people involves learning what they care about. Then you can start to use the language they use, address questions they have, and help them avoid the pitfalls they fear.

LinkedIn is an excellent place to listen. What do your connections talk about? What questions do they have? What posts do they like?

Of course, you listen to your current clients too. They have common questions, fears, issues and desires that you help them with.

Over time, you'll notice patterns, common issues that people mention over and over. Your job is to find out how you can connect your expertise with the things they care about.

Engage with Value

Value takes many forms. Sometimes a brief, kind comment is valuable ("Janice I'm sorry to hear that you've had a rough time with all the Windows updates – I had exactly the same thing!").

Sometimes you might share an article, a video, a note.

In each case, though your question is the same: is this valuable to Janice?

If yes – carry on. If no – rethink.

It really is that simple – 3 steps, Connect, Listen, Engage.

What About Content Types?

When it comes to engagement, LinkedIn has an array of content types. Long blog posts, shorter "thought bubbles," images and video are all natively supported.

What should you contribute?

I suggest you go for a mix. Remember, people might not always have time for a full article but might manage to read a 2 sentence post or enjoy a fun quote before they log off.

If in doubt though, do what you're best at.

The 15 Minute LinkedIn Strategy

Using our 3 steps, here's a simple strategy that you can replicate to get kick-started.

First, commit at least 15 minutes a day to the platform. If you can't, then invest 15 minutes every other day, or every three days, or whatever – but commit to something and put it in your diary. What you get out of LinkedIn will be directly related to how much you put into it – much like everything else, really.

Now run through a simple process:

• 5 minutes – growing your network. Whether through searches, people who have commented on your posts, or others you have met recently, this is the time to connect with them. Find their profile, personalize your invite, and send out as many connection requests as you can inside 5 minutes.

- 5 minutes – engaging and commenting. This is the only time you'll spend in your news feed. Scroll, read, like and comment. If you comment, say something meaningful to demonstrate you read/watched/listened to the thing on which you're commenting. Be kind, generous, helpful and engaging (just like I'm sure you are in real life).

- 5 minutes – sharing. This is where you might share a short post, record a 3-minute video and post it, or share a piece of curated content from somebody else with a meaningful comment on it.

Simple, right?

Think about this though – what are we doing? Our first 5 minutes is expansion – known. The second 5 minutes is relationship – liked. Our final 5 minutes is where we demonstrate our expertise – trusted (with a bit of liked thrown in).

Known, liked and trusted. In 15 minutes a day.

But the Main Thing

The main thing is to do something regularly.

It's the people who show up regularly on any platform that generally succeed the most.

Now it's your turn to show up. You can start by connecting with me!

———

Chris Hargreaves is a digital marketing consultant and lawyer from Australia. He offers a no-nonsense approach to digital marketing and helps lawyers build their practices using digital tools. You can find him at https://amodernprofessional.com

CHAPTER 15

HOW BUSINESS OWNERS CAN BUILD THEIR BRAND ON TWITTER

BY NANCY MYRLAND

It was shortly before 10:35 PM ET on September 6, 2008, when it happened. I was sitting on my mom's couch all by myself with my laptop up in South Bend, Indiana. It was a moment I will never forget, which is why I can write about it so clearly today.

I was watching presidential election coverage on CNN with Rick Sanchez, an early adopter of the use of social media in the newsroom. I looked up from my laptop and watched this full-size backdrop called a Twitter Wall moving rapidly behind him. My heart was probably racing because that Twitter wall was full of people...real, live people from all over the world who were talking to Rick and to each other!

There was no turning back. Right then and there, I knew I had to be a part of it for more reasons than one. The news was no longer news being reported by one person sitting behind a desk but by people all over the globe at the same time with little more than a keyboard and monitor in front of them.

It is no secret that I am a businessperson and a marketer. I have come to discover that intense interest in these tools that help people communicate is a part of my DNA, so I immediately wanted to know more about Twitter.

I also remember that Rick Sanchez was making a statement comparing the presidential candidates that were as far from an apples-to-apples comparison as any statement could be, and I wanted to let him know about it, by golly! Why not, right? Suddenly, it was effortless to do so. This wasn't about politics, which I don't tend to touch publicly, but rather about his lack of accuracy in communicating about a topic that was important.

I knew then, as I do now, that the chances he would see and comment on my Tweet were pretty slim, but that didn't matter. In an instant, I was a part of a global conversation. I had an outlet to connect with people all around the world.

Think about that for a minute. THE WORLD was now at my fingertips, and it was easy!!!

My First Tweet

Here was my 1st Tweet:

"Take care of my mom who had open heart surgery three weeks ago."

I know…kind of serious for a 1st Tweet, right? I feel pretty good about it, though, especially after discovering that Twitter Co-founder and CEO Jack Dorsey dipped his toe lightly into his own product two-and-a-half years earlier with this tweet:

"just setting up my twttr"

I believe I was already on LinkedIn and Facebook, but not "all-in," if you know what I mean. I had joined Facebook because it was a good way for me to stay in touch with what my nephew, Sean, was doing. LinkedIn just made good business sense, as it still does today, so I was already there. Even though I am most often invited to train professionals on the use of LinkedIn, I regularly tell people that Twitter was my 1st social media love…if there is such a thing. I use all of the platforms in many different ways on a daily basis today, not just to stay close to my family, but that is an added benefit, of course.

From Followers To Relationships to Friendships

The best part came after that when I met and followed people I knew, and people I didn't. I don't remember all the details about the relationships I made, but I do remember finding professional colleagues Kevin O'Keefe and Gerry Riskin early on. We have since strengthened our relationships and are connected in many ways on several platforms. We have spoken on the phone, met in person, shared family stories, and offered professional advice.

I don't dare go down the path of naming all of the other friends I connected with in those early days as there were too many, and I will feel terrible if I leave someone out. Suffice to say I am thankful for the relationships I've built that I would consider real friendships, many of those with my co-authors in this book. I am writing this and the voice marketing chapter because of the relationship Mitch Jackson and I developed via social media. Don't ever think Twitter and other social media aren't extremely powerful relationship builders. I know for a fact they are.

Does Twitter Matter?

Yes, it matters…a lot. Because of Twitter, I've virtually attended conferences and met attendees. I've stayed ahead of world, national, local, professional and industry news. I've learned more than I imagined I could, and hope that I've shared a bit of knowledge along the way, too. I've grown my business, and I have also built close relationships with people I first met in-person. Because of Twitter, the world is very close.

Should Professionals Use Twitter?

Yes, I believe Twitter has merit for many professionals, and I enjoy discussing how to integrate it into existing marketing and business development strategy. I say integrate because that's how we should approach all of these tools and tactics we call social media and social media marketing. They complement and support those marketing goals we're already thinking about.

I am often asked what I like about Twitter. One of the comments I always share is:

"Twitter helps to peel back the layers of unfamiliarity that exist between professionals and their potential, and sometimes current, clients."

It is that unfamiliarity, those often awkward, getting-to-know-you moments that Twitter can help peel back.

Twitter can help accelerate the removal of those layers, so that you can find and get to know your clients, potential clients and target audiences much quicker, and more thoroughly, than if you had to wait for face-to-face meetings to do so, which can take a very, very long time.

Setting Up Twitter For Business

Before you begin using Twitter to communicate with others, you need to lay the foundation by setting up your profile.

You rarely get a second chance to make a good first impression so spend time making sure your profile is complete. Twitter does a good job of walking you through the setup process, but the most important parts you need to pay attention to are your Twitter name or "handle," which should be your name. If the name others know you by is no longer available, use one that is as close as possible, possible adding your professional credential.

You then need to add a professional photo you are proud for others to see, and that represents you. Don't use a playful picture or your firm's logo as people are here to connect with people, not logos.

You then need to craft your bio to let people know what you do and for whom you do it. You don't need to add hashtags to your bio as Twitter will search your bio for keywords when delivering results to those who are searching. Hashtags are not necessary for discovery and can make your bio look disjointed and even unprofessional.

The exception is if you have a branded hashtag that is used for all of your content and clicking on it in your bio would keep visitors on your content. For example, mine could be #LetsAskNancy. Within your Twitter bio, you will want to add the URL that is most important to you, as well as any other information that is critical, including a location or hours, for example, if those are among the most important pieces of information you need to communicate.

Next, design a banner image that is consistent with your brand and what you do for a living. If you don't have access to a graphic designer, head over to canva.com where you can create beautiful graphics in every size. Canva will show you the size to use for Twitter, as well as other social media banner sizes. Be consistent between all of your social and digital media accounts, including your website, as well any traditional communication you send to your clients. Feel free to include any words you would like others to see that reinforce what they are reading in your bio.

10 Twitter Tips For Professionals

Everyone is different, but here are Ten Twitter Tips I hope you find useful.

1. Use A Twitter Management Tool To Help Prioritize Your Time

As early as possible in your Twitter career, use one of the many tools available to help you prioritize your time on Twitter. Create lists of the followers you want to observe or interact with the most as this helps you find them quickly when you only have a few minutes on the platform.

The tools vary but the features you will find most valuable are being able to view the activity of those who are the most important to you, and those tools that offer analytics and team-sharing. There are also aggregators that combine your notifications from all of your social networks into one platform. Those can, indeed, be helpful, but make sure you remember how important it is for you to interact with others that don't show up in your notifications, meaning you need to spend a little time on the site, not just the aggregator, to continue to grow and nurture your network. Some of the tools to help with these activities are Twitter itself, Hootsuite, Agorapulse, and Sprout Social.

2. Set Up Searches on Twitter Using The Title Of Your Blog Posts

It is easy to miss the kindness of others who share, or Retweet (RT), your content on Twitter. If you miss these gestures, you miss the opportunity to discover who finds your content valuable. People don't always include your Twitter @name when RTing your blog posts, so set up a search in the exact name of the title of your blog post so you can monitor blog post activity for a few weeks. When you find your blog post being shared, reach out and let them know how much you appreciate the gesture.

3. Use Conference Hashtags When Attending or Presenting At Conferences

A hashtag is simply placing a hash mark, #, known to many as the pound sign, in front of a word, which then causes this word to become an active link that anyone can click on to find all Tweets with that same hashtag. This is a way of discovering like-minded people or issues.

When you know you will be attending or speaking at a conference, set up a column in TweetDeck or Hootsuite, or a search directly on Twitter.com (or any number of tools) for that hashtag, then interact with attendees ahead of time-based on their use of that hashtag. Hint: You don't have to attend a conference to observe or interact with those using that same hashtag. You never want to hijack a discussion or one-up the speakers or host, but it is perfectly okay to join the conversation.

4. Create A Twitter Moment

There are many uses for Twitter Moments but suffice to say they help you and others collect and curate content on a particular subject. For example, I am involved in the Legal Marketing Association's Ethics Advisory Council. One of our projects this year has been to help advocate for change to several outdated Model Rules of Professional Conduct as they pertain to advertising.

During a recent victory, I created a Twitter Moment to collect Tweets that were related to this decision by the ABA House of Delegates. This not only helped our committee find this activity quickly, but it also notified those whose Tweets I added to my Moment that their Tweet was being added to a Twitter Moment by @NancyMyrland. These are the foundations of relationships.

5. Earn The Right To Promote

Don't jump on Twitter and start promoting yourself. I tell my clients they have to earn the right to be promotional. This is no different than walking into a chamber of commerce business after hours talking about all the wonderful things you do. You might be quietly shunned as this is pretty obnoxious behavior.

You first need to spend time getting to know people and promoting them. This type of behavior prompts others to want to help promote your news when it's your turn. Remember, Twitter and all social media are much more about others than about you. Again, these are the foundations of relationships.

6. Use Your Head

For most of you who have been around a while, you know how important it is to think before you confront or attack someone in a public forum. Remember that you can't take back what you Tweet.

In essence, too many of your followers, you are what you Tweet. The personality you show when Tweeting is how others will come to know you. Unless this is your personal brand that you want to become known for, don't attack others. Don't say anything you might want to delete later. Don't jump to conclusions. Also, don't cause client conflicts. Respect ethics and confidentiality. Understand your words are discoverable.

7. Set Up Search Columns and Create Lists of Your Clients

Twitter is a gigantic search engine. For those of you who rely on establishing and nurturing relationships with your clients and prospects, search for them, their staff, alumni or anyone else you've identified in your Marketing and Business Development Plan and place them in a search column all of their own on Twitter so you can quickly check in on their activity. Within Twitter, you can easily set up lists to do this. You can even set alerts and notifications if you'd like to quickly see what they are sharing.

Share their content. Talk to them. Comment about something they said. Ask them a question. Introduce them to others they might like to know. Tag them if a news item might be of interest.

8. Use Visuals

One recent study suggests a 200% increase in engagement when photos are added to your Tweets. Video trumps that in a big way. Human beings are becoming more visual by the day, and the content that caters to that appetite will catch the eye of others. Post photos or video of speakers at your seminars, of your staff cleaning up a local park, of moving-in day for a new colleague or partner in your office, or of one of the events you sponsor.

One of the most under-utilized but most effective tools that exist on Twitter is the ability to reply using video. When you tap on the camera, tap the video camera and record a short comment to that person. They will be delighted to see and hear you, and you will stand out among others, I assure you.

9. Create Separate Twitter Accounts For Teams With Fast-Moving Developments

Let's say you have a Government Affairs Team, a Tax Incentives Team, or an ACL & Meniscus Tears Group. There is a lot going on every day in each of your practices, and in the community that cares about the topics you represent. You can't send out an email or newsletter 10 times a day with the current vote on House Bill 8562, or on the current caution regarding a radical new therapy that has gone viral on the Internet, but you can instantly Tweet developments that are important to your clients, right? Remember that you now have a platform to communicate your messages very quickly, and one that media visit on a regular basis when looking for experts.

10. Remember That Twitter Is A Contact Sport

Twitter will never make sense if you only worry about yourself and what you have to offer. It is not a one-sided sport. It takes at least two to make Twitter work because it is all about building awareness and relationships. The best way to build relationships on Twitter is if you follow people, get to know them, spend time on a regular basis nurturing your relationships and looking for ways you can be helpful. That is how you become memorable to your followers.

Bottom Line:

Don't over-think this. There's no magic sauce. There are guidelines such as those I've shared with you in this chapter, and many more, that will help you get up to speed quicker. The most important practice to remember is to just be human and get to know people. Help them understand what you are like to do business with by showing them you are more than a name and a tiny avatar on a platform, and that you are a valuable person to get to know. Before long, this unfamiliar territory will begin to feel like a community you like being a part of. As with any new experience or relationship, it takes time. It takes proper care and feeding to grow.

Remember, as author and marketing expert Seth Godin wrote in the Foreword to Steven Pressfield's book "Do The Work"

"And here's a keyboard, connected to the entire world. Here's a publishing platform you can use to interact with just about anyone, just about any time, for free. You wanted a level playing field, one where you have just as good a shot as anyone else? Here it is. Do the work. That's what we're all waiting for you to do --- to do the work."

———

Nancy Myrland is a Marketing, Business Development, Content, Social and Digital Media Speaker, Trainer and Advisor to lawyers, legal marketers and law firms, specializing in helping you grow your firm and your practice through the understanding, creation, and integration of marketing and strategic plans with content, social and digital media. You can connect with Nancy here http://www.myrlandmarketing.com

CHAPTER 16

TWITTER CHATS

BY MADALYN SKLAR

I've been a digital marketer for 23 years and got hooked on social media in its early days. Then, Twitter happened. It was love at first tweet. This was in 2008. I was drawn to the 140 character count. Concise and to the point was exactly my style.

One day I discovered Twitter chats. I was immediately hooked. There is something mystical about connecting with a group of people through short, concise tweets. Conversing for an hour with like-minded people was incredibly appealing.

At the time, I was running a large online community called GoGirlsMusic. We were on a mission to support, promote and empower female musicians worldwide. In 2011, I decided to start my first Twitter chat and launched it for my music community. I called it #ggchat. It was the start of my journey to connecting amazing people together through tweet conversations.

In 2015, I launched the #TwitterSmarter chat. At that time, my #ggchat was so big and popular that I was running it twice every Thursday, one chat in the afternoon and another one in the evening. We had so many people around the world that wanted to participate, we needed to add the second chat so we could reach more time zones. I added the #TwitterSmarter chat to my Thursday afternoon schedule.

This is what my Thursdays looked like:

1pm - #TwitterSmarter
3pm - #ggchat
9pm - #ggchat

Today, I no longer run #ggchat or my music community. My focus is teaching people how to harness the power of Twitter for their business, especially with Twitter chats.

What Is A Twitter Chat?

The simplest description of a Twitter chat is a group of people coming together on Twitter during a set time each week to have a conversation that revolves around a predetermined hashtag. As long as people include the hashtag in their tweet, they're part of the conversation.

A Twitter chat is a way for people to meet up and have a conversation about a topic they are interested in. It's bringing like-minded people together at a scheduled time, usually running for an hour.

Imagine you're at a networking event with hundreds of people. In an hour you have the ability to walk up and say 'Hi' to everybody. You can have concise 280 character HELLOS to everyone there and make great conversations, great connections, in a very short period of time.

A typical Twitter chat has one or more hosts and one or more guests. While some chats do not have a guest, the most common type is one host with one guest. For example, my #TwitterSmarter chat is every Thursday at 1pm ET. You participate by monitoring and following along the hashtag.

My chat runs for one hour. Most people leave after that time. Some linger around either because they came in late or they are enjoying the conversation so much, they don't want it to end.

Twitter chats are free and open to the public. This makes it appealing because you can get educated on a topic while networking with amazing people.

Everything revolves around the hashtag. You participate by using the chat's hashtag to listen in and be a part of the discussion. You must include the hashtag in your tweets in order to be seen by the group.

You can learn a lot from participating in a chat. I always encourage people to chime in and share their own expertise.

Chats are a great way to meet like-minded people with similar interests. It's akin to a giant cocktail party where you connect and network with lots of people.

When you're a regular on a Twitter chat, it's like you're Norm from the TV show Cheers, where everybody knows your name.

Why Participate In Chats?

There are several reasons why participating in Twitter chats is a great idea. One is the connections you make. There are so many incredible people that you will meet on a Twitter chat. I could probably name at least a hundred colleagues of mine that I've met from a Twitter chat. It's that powerful.

Another reason to participate in a Twitter chat is the education you get. For example, my #TwitterSmarter chat is a great resource for learning new ways to use Twitter to market your business. We share things like Twitter tips, great resources for learning, advanced strategies to implement, and the tools we use that help us manage Twitter better.

But chats aren't limited to just Twitter or social media. Whatever industry you're in or topic that resonates with you, there's probably a chat out there that you'd be interested in.

How Does A Chat Work?

I best describe a chat as everyone being hyper-focused on a hashtag for an hour. We are not looking at anything else. If you do not put the hashtag in your tweet, we do not see you. You do not exist.

A Twitter chat is not a place to sell or promote. It's a community of people. We are there to connect. Listen and watch before jumping in. Pay attention to what's going on. I recommend you attend several different chats to get a feel for how they work.

There are a variety of formats for a Twitter chat. The most common is a Q&A style where you have a host and a guest. The host will tweet questions to the guest as well as the participants.

Some chats simply throw out a topic at the beginning of the chat and the participants run with it. This is less structured but can make for a great discussion. This method works well when you have a good number of vocal participants who like to chat.

Every Twitter chat has their own set of rules, but most encourage an open discussion so that everyone is free to chime in their answers to the questions. It's all about the dialogue.

Keep in mind every chat is different and some may frown upon you giving unsolicited advice. Make sure you get a feel for the chat and be mindful of their rules and practices. If you're ever in doubt, you can always reach out to the host and ask them.

Here are some practices:

- Be respectful of everyone.
- Introduce yourself at the beginning.
- If it's a Q&A chat, answer with A1 for question 1, A2 for question 2 and so on.
- End each tweet with the chat hashtag.
- The point of the chat is to be social.
- Engage and have fun!

How Do You Find Twitter Chats?

You can find Twitter chats through Google, word of mouth in your community, and, of course, by searching Twitter. A few years ago I put together my own list of the Best Twitter Chats for Social Media & Marketing, MadalynSklar.com/chatlist. I keep it updated as I find new chats.

What Tools Do You Need?

You can participate in a chat at Twitter.com or the mobile app by typing the hashtag in the search bar and following along with the conversation. The most important thing you want to do is put the chat hashtag in every tweet you post. During the chat, everyone is hyper-focused on viewing tweets that have the hashtag. If you forget to tweet the hashtag, no one will see it. Always keep in mind that the conversation revolves around the hashtag. A rookie mistake is forgetting it in your tweets.

The best way around this is to use a tool like TweetChat.com. It's a great platform for participating in chats. You log in with your Twitter account, put in the chat hashtag, and you'll have access to a page that shows all the tweets with the hashtag in it. It will be in reverse chronological order showing you the most recent tweets at the top of the page.

Also, at the top of the page there is a box for you to compose your tweets. It will automatically add the hashtag in for you so you don't have to remember to do it every time. This is great for beginners!

However, Tweetchat isn't just for beginners. I use it myself when participating in chats because it's an easy way to consume all the tweets. But that's not all I use. I also have a tab open to Hootsuite.com to monitor my notifications that way I don't miss anyone who's tweeting me during the chat. I have another tab open on Twitter.com to monitor the host's Twitter account so I don't miss the chat questions. And if I'm hosting the chat, I'll have a tab open to the guest's account so I don't miss their tweets.

A popular tool that many marketers use is TweetDeck. This can be used in place of Hootsuite. Personally, I prefer Hootsuite. They are both very similar.

I recommend experimenting with these tools and find what works best for you.

Should You Start A Twitter Chat?

There are many great benefits to hosting your own Twitter chat.

It's a great way to:

• connect and engage with people in your industry
• get seen as an expert & thought leader
• help you build authority
• be identified as an influencer
• boost your brand awareness

Twitter chats allow you to be a connector in your community.

Hosting a Twitter chat allows you to be the leader of the pack. All eyes will be on you as you lead the discussion each week (or however often your chat meets). You'll be providing a platform for yourself and your participants to discuss topics that are important to the community.

Starting a Chat

Your Twitter chat needs to have a purpose.

Are you filling a need or niche? Are there others doing the exact same thing? It's okay if they are. Just do something different. Set yourself apart. Find a new angle.

Research Chats

Are you familiar with Twitter chats in your industry and/or niche?

If not, take the time to uncover the chats and participate in them. Connect with people and get yourself known. Introduce yourself to the host. Do these chats stand out? Discover what makes them unique. This will help you figure out how to make your chat incredible.

Your Chat Hashtag

Make a list of 5-10 hashtags that appeal to you and your community. Once you have a list, do some research. You want a hashtag that is not being used. Or if it is, it's not being used often (no more than a handful of times each week). If it's an actively used hashtag, move on to the next one until you find the right one for your community.

Find the right hashtag that clearly communicates what your chat is.

Back in 2013, I was actively seeking a hashtag I could use to help promote a new online Twitter course I was developing. I researched a variety of names and first settled on #TwitterRockstar. It was being used but not in a consistent way. And it certainly was not being used for a Twitter chat. But I realized it was not the right hashtag for me.

I conducted additional research and settled on #TwitterSmarter. It was barely being used. Just a few tweets here and there. I staked claim to it by using the hashtag daily. You cannot own a hashtag but you can stake claim to one by using it regularly.

While most chats have the word "chat" in it, you don't have to do that. But it may help differentiate your chat from generic hashtags.

Are You Ready To Chat?

As you can see, Twitter chats are a great way to bring a community together. You can boost your brand awareness while engaging with your target audience.

Twitter chats are a great way to connect with your avatar and get noticed above the noise.

Twitter chats are an excellent opportunity for you and your business because you can easily get connected with like-minded people in your industry. You can share your experience and expertise.

And above all, you'll have fun and fall in love with Twitter.

———

Madalyn Sklar is a serial entrepreneur, community builder and leading Twitter marketing expert. With 23 years digital marketing experience and 14 years social media marketing under her belt, it's no surprise she's ranked the #1 Social Media Power Influencer in Houston. Each week Madalyn hosts the #TwitterSmarter Twitter chat that brings together hundreds of people in an active one hour discussion revolving around Twitter marketing. Since launching three years ago, it has reached over 6 billion impressions. Connect with Madalyn here https://madalynsklar.com

CHAPTER 17

HOW TO GROW YOUR FOLLOWING AND BUSINESS USING INSTAGRAM

BY SUE B. ZIMMERMAN

Let's get this out of the way right now: It's not too late for your business to get started on Instagram. Not even close. So, if you are eight years late to the party don't worry!

Instagram has now reached over one billion monthly active users, and it hasn't shown any signs of slowing down anytime soon. And why not? The image-first platform is continuing to evolve and redefine itself as the go-to platform for businesses and brands of all sizes. Do you have a brick and mortar store or private practice? Are most of your clients virtual? Or maybe you're a small business, solopreneur or creativepreneur trying to expand your customer client base?

Perfect because your audience is already waiting for you on Instagram.

But with so many creative options, there's one type of content that really has professionals and social media marketers buzzing: video. Instagram Stories, LIVE, and IGTV are now an essential part of any social media marketing strategy. If you are feeling overwhelmed, don't worry. I am going to walk you through everything you need to understand Instagram video content and embrace it as part of your Instagram business strategy.

Why is Instagram the perfect platform for your business?

Before we talk about the different ways you can create Instagram video content, let's cover the basics of Instagram and why it's important for your business. At this point, you probably have a vague idea about Instagram. Maybe you even have a personal Instagram account that you update periodically. At its face value, Instagram is a social networking app that is designed to share photos and videos from your smartphone.

Pretty straightforward, right? But when you dive deeper into the tools, analytics and other options available on Instagram, it becomes clearer that Instagram is truly an all-in-one business marketing tool. From Instagram Stories to Live to IGTV, the newest app update, Instagram continues to reinvent itself as one of the most relevant, impactful business marketing tools.

If you are promoting your brand on Instagram, one of the best ways to amplify your profile is by switching to a business account. While many people rely on vanity metrics, such as "likes" and comments, having a business account will only help your brand grow. Rather than making assumptions about who your audience is and how much money you should spend on ads, all the data is right there on Instagram. With access to analytics and other features unavailable in a personal account, it's one of the easiest ways to turn Instagram into an effective marketing tool.

Really, it's not surprising that Instagram has seen exponential growth. But Instagram isn't just a platform where people come to passively gaze at their favorite brands, businesses, and online educators. Instagram has one of the highest engagement rates of any social platforms, three times more engagement when compared apples-to-apples with Facebook. If that wasn't enough to convince you of Instagram's importance, take a look at these stats:

- Instagram clocks up 3.5 billion likes every day

- On an average day, over 80 million photos are shared

- Of the top 100 brands in the world, 90 percent have an Instagram account

- Over a third of Instagram users have used their mobile to purchase a product online - making them 70 percent more likely to do so than non-users

The truth is that even with its high engagement, you need to think strategically about how you share videos on Instagram. Engagement is great, but unless it helps you build stronger relationships with your potential customers, you're probably missing the mark. To save yourself from wasting time and money, you need to have a comprehensive video strategy planned out. Here's what I recommend.

Instagram Stories

Stories are now becoming an indispensable tool for businesses and brands trying to create engaging content while also meeting their business goals. Introduced in 2016, Stories allow people to post the highlights of their day, whether it's a quick 15-second video or photo. Unlike the normal grid, these Stories are found at the top of the feed. With a bunch of creative tools, like "type" modes and GIFs, Instagram Stories encourages users to push their creative boundaries outside of their perfectly curated feed.

But why does this matter to business owners? Because brands and businesses of all size are taking notice! According to The State of Instagram Marketing 2018, 64 percent of businesses have recognized the power of Instagram Stories and plan to create more stories this year. Plus, over 200 million people use Instagram Stories. That's an enormous amount of eyeballs that can see your content.

With all of this creative flexibility and opportunities to share more content, how can you use Instagram Stories to build relationships and grow your business? Here are a couple of tactics.

Drive more traffic to your website

To achieve long-term engagement, you need to funnel people to your website. One of the easiest ways to do that is by including a link for people to "swipe up." However, this is feature is only available to accounts with over 10,000 followers. If your account doesn't have the swipe up feature, you can still use Stories to encourage people to click the link in your bio. Tell them exactly what you want them to do – no guesswork!

Check your Instagram Direct Messages

I always say that the conversations in Instagram Direct Message are golden. There's no better way to get feedback on your Stories than to go right to the source. Make sure you're scheduling time to periodically check your DMs when you have an active Story. When you take the time to respond, people take notice. You're demonstrating that Instagram Stories isn't just a one-way communication platform for you, and you're invested in the relationships it takes to grow your business.

Instagram Live

I know, the idea of being on video, let alone going live, is enough to make people's stomach flip. But here's the truth, people want to know the face behind your brand or business. As followers turn more to video content, Instagram Live's instant connection can help you stand out from the competition.

Let's put it this way: with the new Instagram algorithm, over 70 percent of Instagram posts aren't seen. That's why it's important that you share content, like live videos, that encourage greater engagement and connections with your followers.

If you have some Instagram Live jitters, here are some ways to prepare and make the most of your broadcast.

Promote your Live broadcast beforehand

How can you expect people to tune into your broadcast if they don't know when it is? Let people know across your Instagram account, on your feed, and in Stories. This is your opportunity not only to tell people what you'll be talking about but why it's worth their time. If you make it clear that you are offering valuable content, people will feel like it's a can't-miss opportunity.

Host a dual broadcast

One of the most exciting features of Instagram Live is the option to add another person to your broadcast. Whether you want to invite another expert in your field, a satisfied client or an influencer, this individual should add value and relevance to your broadcast. Even better, double the reach of your broadcast by making sure your guest shares the Live details on their Instagram account.

IGTV

Even with all of its creative video tools, Instagram recently unveiled a feature that could disrupt the traditional TV experience. IGTV offers Instagram users a more modern, mobile experience. This update comes at the perfect time when people are demanding more and more video content on the go. By 2021, mobile video will account for 78 percent of total mobile data traffic.

For now, videos can be 10 minutes for most accounts, and up to one hour for larger accounts, but Instagram has already said that eventually there might be no time limit. You can view IGTV videos in the Instagram app, in the standalone IGTV app, or by tapping the IGTV button on someone's Instagram profile. There are a few other perks to using IGTV:

-    Shareable link: This makes it much easier to share your IGTV channel in Stories or on other social platforms

-    Live links: People will actually be able to click on links in your IGTV video descriptions and be taken outside of the Instagram or IGTV app

-    Hashtags: Just like in your Instagram posts, hashtags for your IGTV episodes make your videos more searchable and likely to show up in the hashtag hub

Here are some ways you can leverage IGTV for your brand.

Make sure your videos are vertical.

Unlike Youtube, IGTV is all about vertical videos. You could technically upload a horizontal video, but that's not a user-friendly experience. One reason for the vertical-only push is because it's more mobile-friendly.

Instagram wants you to create content right on your mobile device. While this might seem like a challenge at first, especially if you're used to cropping videos horizontally, this more mobile-friendly experience can actually help your viewer retention rate. The easier it is to watch your IGTV content on the go, the more likely people are to keep tuning in.

Curious what your followers think? Look in the comments.

You don't need to guess what your followers are thinking about your IGTV. Just scroll down and take a look at the comments. While there are bound to be some random comments, you might be surprised by the meaningful conversations happening right below your video. If you see something particularly interesting, don't be afraid to reach out in the DM.

So, what are you waiting for?

In today's noisy digital landscape, most people just want to be heard. That's why using videos to build authentic relationships on Instagram is more important than ever. Instagram doesn't need more people adding to the noise, it needs more brands and businesses like you that are focused on how they can turn Instagram into a two-way channel of communication. In doing so, you can meet your business goals and grow your Instagram reach.

———

Sue B. Zimmerman, also known as The Instagram Expert, has built her career empowering entrepreneurs and marketing professionals to utilize the power of Instagram to get tangible business results, including creating her highly sought after Instagram business courses: "Insta-Results" and "Ready Set Gram." Connect with Sue here https://suebzimmerman.com

CHAPTER 18

HOW TO USE PERISCOPE
TO BUILD YOUR BUSINESS AND BRAND

BY ALEX PETTITT

I happened to be at Twitter's office in London, England doing something for the UK elections. It was 26th March 2015, a cold day outside but inside, things were heating up with excitement. "Alex, I have a heads up for you," said the local head of video. "We launched 'Periscope' today. Be one of the first people to use it."

I jumped onto my iPhone and opened the App Store. Within minutes I had downloaded the Periscope app and was exploring it guided by one of the technicians. "Guys, come on then. Let's go live on Periscope", I said pushing the head of video and the techie together in front of a view of London as a backdrop. "I am going to interview you about Periscope and what it's all about."

Looking back, I was at the right time and place for my first live stream. That very first stream changed the direction of my life. Immediately in those first few minutes, I felt the potential of the app. Over the next few days, I could not put my iPhone down and learned all there was to Periscope. I wanted to share my knowledge and went live daily with all the tips and tricks I was learning. "Scopers" would follow me to get my next stream but also would share me out to their followers. In live social video (as with all social media) content will always be King. My following grew from 0 to over 65,000 in 3 months, to over 250,000 in just over 12 months. In the past 3½ years following my first Periscope live streaming has given me so much and many incredible experiences and opportunities.

Before its launch, Periscope was acquired by Twitter. It was the first Live and Interactive platform from a social media giant. The first release back in March 2015 was only for iPhone. You could go live and stream from your front-facing camera, and your followers received a notification. Your followers using their own iPhone Periscope app with wifi or good mobile internet connection could watch and listen to your stream from anywhere in the world. Live streams were also listed in the app, so any Periscope user could also discover your stream. The streams were interactive in real time because viewers could type comments that everyone could see and by tapping on the screen give a display of hearts if you liked the content.

Periscope was true Live, Interactive and Mobile social video. Periscope's founder and CEO Kayvon Beykpour had a vision to show the world through other people's eyes, and this was it. People were live streaming from incredible places all around the world and by using the comments you could ask questions about what you were seeing and learn from those that lived there. Take a trip through the canals of Venice on a gondola, or check out the New York skyline at midnight, or be guided through the narrow streets of ancient Jerusalem. Well, that was the first envisaged intention for Periscope and worthy it was.

Twitter has endlessly committed resources into Periscope, and today the product is technically far beyond anything imaginable when I did my very first stream on launch day. Both audio and video is of high quality and stable with wifi or a decent 3G or 4G mobile signal. The Periscope app works on all Apple or Android phones and tablets devices. Additionally, you can also watch on the Web with a browser or on Apple TV. On your phone, you can stream in both Portrait and Landscape modes and switch between front and back facing cameras with a tap.

Periscope remains an app in itself but is also fully embedded into Twitter enabling you to live stream from your Twitter app too. Your Periscope followers and your Twitter followers can receive a notification when you go live. If they can't make it, the streams are stored under your Periscope profile and can be replayed any time by anyone. They are also stored as Tweets and fully viewable within your Twitter timeline, and you may "pin" any of them.

At the end of 2016, I was privileged to do the world's first live interactive 360° broadcast using Periscope, and it attracted over 250,000 views with 24 hours! Viewers can drag their screen left, right up or down and get a full 360-degree view of any live 360° stream.

Besides showing us the world with the main phone camera scopers create a face to camera conversation with viewers using the back camera. This technique is popular, and face to camera Periscopes pop up from the office, on the beach, anywhere in fact (because this is true mobile streaming). The topics are endless and sometimes controversial. But if used in clever ways they can also be very powerful marketing tools so more on that later.

Did I mention all the above is free for scopers and viewers? On Periscope, no live stream or replay has any ads either. You can scope from a drone, and there have been many amazing and beautiful streams. This remote camera concept led the way to the biggest game-changer for brands and professionals – Periscope Producer. Instead of using the camera on your phone or tablet you could now use an external high-quality camera and microphone. Indeed more than one camera can feed into a vision mixer so your live broadcast can be TV style and quality.

You can mix in pre-production graphics or even whole pre-recorded segments or live Skype calls. The equipment you can now use to produce content range from budget to the highest quality. The same goes for the software to control the live production and output the stream directly to the Periscope servers. OBS is by far the most commonly used software and is still free! Your Periscope Producer live stream is still viewed precisely the same over Periscope with all the comments and hearts engagement. What's changed is the high production value and the variety of show format and content you can use. My whole Alex.Live agency arose and evolved around consulting, producing and directing branded and professional, highly creative, live and interactive streams. We now multicast simultaneously across all the major social media platforms including Twitter and Periscope.

Periscope led the way in many of the key developments for mobile streaming, but it now has strong competition from the other major social media platform. Facebook Live, YouTube Live, Amazon's Twitch and now Instagram Live all saw the potential of Periscope and the power of live interactive streaming and wanted in.

I have tried streaming from all the platforms and indeed work with my clients on all of them. A lot of live streamers have said to me, and I agree, that Periscope still provides the best experience when going live from a mobile device. It's the interactive element that scopers and viewers like. The way comments appear on the screen and move upwards and how the hearts (the likes) flow continuously up on the right side. There is a comfortable feeling about this engagement with viewers and enhances the conversation between scoper and viewers better, in my opinion, than any of the other platforms.

As a professional or a brand, you have knowledge and expertise, a message to share, and a service or product to promote. In many cases, Social Media is or should be the most important element of your marketing mix. Your potential client base is getting more and more tech-savvy using a smartphone daily. Cord cutting is now the norm, and we are consuming our selection of news, entertainment, and sports from apps on the go wherever we are.

I read and write more emails on my phone than my laptop, and the same goes for most of daily tasks. You need a strategy that targets your market on their mobile devices with the right content for a mobile audience. You may already be tweeting on Twitter and posting pictures and mini videos to Facebook and Instagram. You may already be creating and editing a polished YouTube every so often. So if you are a professional looking to build your brand and grow your practice what can Twitter's Periscope do for you?

Well on Periscope you can authentically engage with your audience, having a two-way conversation and building up a relationship with viewers turning them into a loyal following. When you go Live on Periscope, be authentic and be yourself.

Face to camera streams can be powerful if you have a theme to the broadcast and you answer questions while at the same time, allow yourself to be guided by real-time questions in the chat. Give a lot before you ask anything in return. Of course, you want everyone who comes into your stream to follow you and share out the stream to their followers but asks when you see positive comments after you have given out nuggets of free and useful information.

Livestreaming face to camera is more akin to having a real-time conversation with your audience. Once you have done a few, you will get better and better at it, and your followers will look forward to your streams. Building a loyal following is crucial in social media for two main reasons. Firstly they will help to grow your base by sharing your streams and re-tweeting them. Secondly, you can ask them to say good things about you on their social media or to refer you if they can think of anyone that may benefit.

Like most things in business, you need to spend time on your social media or pay some else. Periscope is no different from every form of social media in that being "discovered" is the main quest. If you already have a good and engaged Twitter following powering up Periscope inside the Twitter app and going live will give you a starting audience. Otherwise, it's a slow burn approach doing regular scopes.

Being discovered is not easy, so you can consider targeting your audience with Twitter paid promotion or working with influencers with large followings. If you chose an agency to help, make sure they have proven experience with Live. Many have little.

I can't emphasize enough that content is King. Plan your broadcast writing down what the key areas and points you want to cover. The questions and comments can easily take you on a tangent.

Be interesting or controversial and start with the title. If you are a property lawyer, you may want to start with something like, "My 5 top tips on reducing legal fees when selling your home." This kind of catchy title may turn a few heads and attract attention. Remember you are competing with hundreds of other live streams. Periscope will list your stream as live, and you will have new people come in. The only way to retain them is to have great content.

Viewers arrive and leave throughout your broadcast. It is like a revolving door. You need to know a series of retention techniques, one of which is to re-introduce and re-cap every so often. Pre-promote the live and then post-promote the replay and get your loyal followers to re-tweet. Remember RETAIN and MULTIPLY should be the result of your live social video strategy.

If you are involved in an event, make sure to livestream it. Everyone involved should pre-promote the stream beforehand including a link to your account and include a hashtag. Depending on your budget, the broadcast could be just a mobile phone may be on a tripod with an external microphone. Or it could be a Periscope Producer broadcast with vision mixed multiple cameras and graphics and live poll.

To see some of the accessories I use, and for a link to my streaming kit and video, please visit https://alex.live/kit

Hopefully, after reading this chapter, you now have the background and flavor of live streaming with Twitter's Periscope. There are many tips and tricks to help you along the way. I have briefly mentioned but a few. If you'd like more information, I recommend http://petestewart.co.uk/the-live-streaming-handbook/ as a good guide.

_____

Alex Pettitt is a tech broadcaster, interactive live producer, consultant and speaker. Connect with Alex via email at alex@alex.live and through his website http://alexpettitt.tv

CHAPTER 19

YOUTUBE FOR BUSINESS OWNERS AND PROFESSIONALS

BY ROBERTO BLAKE

In the landscape of social media, YouTube seems to the gold crown, and the most challenging platform to gain traction in. YouTube is much like its parent company Google, it is a one-stop destination for anything you want to learn how to do.

The difference between Google and YouTube is that one is a search engine, and you are required to create content for the search engine to find. By contrast, YouTube allows you to upload content directly to its platform, which can be found by both Search Engines and distributed or embedded in other platforms.

YouTube is the single largest online video hosting platform in the world, and the second largest search engine and currently the second largest trafficked website in the world. Competing with YouTube for the number one spot, is its parent company, Google.

Unlike other like other social media platforms, YouTube prioritizes the media aspect over the social aspect. YouTube essentially begins and ends with the content itself. Rather than acting as a communication platform with media sharing options like Facebook or Twitter, YouTube is a media hosting platform with limited communication features built in. This is one of the things makes the context and culture of the platform different and makes it more challenging to master. You can't grow on YouTube without prioritizing quality content above all else.

YouTube Benefits

The benefit of YouTube to professionals is that it is a video-driven platform that allows them to host recorded or live videos. A professional now has the opportunity to produce their own show or series in the new media equivalent of television. Unlike broadcast media before it, digital media exist as an on-demand archive, and this where YouTube and its power as a search engine for video content really shines.

Professionals who take advantage of what the platform offers have the opportunity to put their skills, expertise or opinions on the record, and reach an audience that wants what they can provide. Anyone can showcase their abilities and slowly but surely reach an audience. Unlike paid marketing, the content doesn't disappear, and there is no real barrier to entry, only a barrier to reach and relevance, and that is predicated on communication skills, access to technology and a basic understanding of the platform.

The ability to reach an audience via traditional media broadcast was never accessible to the small business owner or even the average person. YouTube and social media overall, is an equalizer. However, do not mistake accessibility for ease. Just because anyone can do it, doesn't mean everyone can do it well.

Something I have learned over the past 5 to 6 years of being part of the YouTube community is that YouTube is a unique experience and you get out of it what you put in, much like entrepreneurship. There is no one size fits all version of success or no secret formula, there are however best practices. YouTube itself tries to educate users regarding this as best they can.

Things To Keep in Mind

With that in mind there are a few things that stand out in the context of being on YouTube as a business owner or professional:

- Narrow your niche as much as possible
- Initially focus on growing your audience on the platform before growing your email list or driving traffic to your website
- Not every video can or should be a sales video or a video where you pitch the audience
- Consistency in uploads and in messaging matters the most
- You can't take shortcuts when it comes to representing your brand
- ROI doesn't happen overnight or the first 90 days. It takes time
- There isn't a real downside to having video content to represent your brand on YouTube
- Content doesn't need to be overproduced or over the top
- Your content should provide value for your target client/customer base
- Don't be afraid of the comments section, you can filter or curate the comments
- YouTube offers robust analytics and data that can help you understand your audience
- With paid advertising on YouTube, you can reach a targeted audience at as low as $0.01/view through the Google AdWords for Video Product
- YouTube ads can also work for remarketing campaigns
- Building a content strategy that relates to your business goals and aligns with audience interest and attention is the key to success on the platform for professionals
- YouTube can be used to educate potential clients and generate leads
- Through the YouTube Live feature you can host live videos and training events such as webinars, and by making the videos Unlisted, you can require an email sign up form using appropriate software and services
- YouTube videos can be embedded into your website pages to help you generate content

As a professional, your YouTube channel will probably not appeal to the main demographic of YouTube which is under 18 years old. Your target market in most cases will typically be older, and you will be relying more on YouTube's search engine than on the more traditional methods of building a YouTube audience.

When a viewer decides to commit to your content on YouTube, they have the option to subscribe to your channel to receive more videos from you. While this is usually the method by which YouTube creators measure their growth and success on YouTube, there are some things you should consider as a professional.

For business professionals, YouTube subscriptions are not like subscriptions to an email list. YouTube will not notify 100% of your subscribers that you have uploaded a video. They will notify a portion of those subscribers and typically the most active ones, as well as those who have activated notifications. Therefore you should not use your view to subscriber ratios as a measurement of success or impact the way you would open rates within email marketing subscriptions.

Regarding measuring success, consider your engagement metrics such as the feedback from those who view the videos, as well as the viewer retention rates on the videos. Also, you should focus on using your video marketing strategy on YouTube as a way to demonstrate your value to potential customers and put your expertise or the value of your products on the record in a way that is accessible and search engine friendly.

Keep in mind that videos on YouTube are also served as video results within Google searches. You can also use the free video hosting on YouTube to place these videos within your own website or blog to enhance the content there and communicate valuable information to your customers or clients.

What YouTube Wants From You:

- Watch time
- Session time (binge-watching)
- High click thru rates 2-10%
- Retention rates (50% or higher)
- Optimized metadata (use TubeBuddy)
- Low session ends (keep people on YouTube)
- Frequent uploads (3-5 times per week)
- View and watch time velocity (first 24 hours)

The list above is merely a guideline but is ideal to maximize YouTube growth and channel potential. The important thing is to communicate your value through your videos and be relevant to the needs of your audience.

Concerning overall strategy, a great place to start in terms of making content would be to create videos that either explains the jargon of your industry or provide useful information to educate your clients prior to them engaging your services. If you can be the introduction to understanding a complex issue, it not only builds awareness but trust as well.

When a brand uses content on YouTube to educate clients, it is more likely to translate to sales down the road. It can take several interactions to get a commitment, creating more videos means you have more touch points in the customer experience and also more opportunities to win them over.

Have clear calls to action within your video, whether that means subscribing to the channel, joining your email list, or making a direct product purchase.

Your goal is to ideally become the "Netflix of your niche," and have a library of content that makes you an authority, vanity metrics are irrelevant in this context, though many use them as an indicator of success, at best they are an indicator of market demand or interest. By themselves they are not an indicator of the quality of your content, the feedback from those who view the content is a better indicator of the quality of experience.

Strategies for YouTube Growth and Success

- Launch short web series of 4-10 episodes
- Run a continuing series or vlog with episodic content
- Structure your titles to have your branding at the end
- Use gateway content like tutorials or product reviews
- Maintain a consistent upload schedule for your viewers
- Make videos with playlist in mind of filling out a playlist of 5-10 or more videos
- Make enough ever-green search-friendly content to create a view/sub funnel
- Create hero videos to generate mainstream attention
- Activate high levels of engagement with your audience and encourage video shares of your content on Twitter, Facebook, and Reddit.

While YouTube is the second largest search engine and the largest overall video platform, you should also consider repurposing your video content outside of YouTube. Using video on platforms like Facebook and LinkedIn can be useful as well.

You can distribute your videos from YouTube on these platforms; however, you can also choose to directly upload video content there as well. Using YouTube for your business, you don't have to worry as much about uploads to other platforms competing with attention on YouTube since your focus is to gain brand awareness through your videos wherever possible. You are not trying to be a successful "YouTuber," you are trying to grow your personal brand or business.

Prioritize making your videos creative and stand out in your niche, be consistent in your overall message and visual branding, as well as focus on creating context around your brand for viewers who discover you. If you follow these principles, you will be able to use the YouTube platform to become more successful and deliver value and represent your brand well to your audience.

———

Roberto Blake is a Creative Entrepreneur helping businesses, brands and individuals market themselves effectively with engaging visuals and compelling messages. He has over 10 years of experience commercially in design and marketing and has helped brands, both large and small achieve their goals and reach their audiences. Roberto's work has been recognized by Forbes, Huffington Post, Adobe and Photoshop Creative Magazines. You can connect with Roberto Blake at http://robertoblake.com

CHAPTER 20

PODCASTING TO EXPAND, INFLUENCE AND ATTRACT

BY NICOLE ABBOUD

People launch podcasts for many reasons

Some realize podcasts are "hot" right now, and they want to get in on the action. Others see the business development and marketing potential in having a podcast that supports their brands and brings in clients.

And a select few simply have a message and a story they want to share with their communities, and audio is their medium of choice.

Whatever your personal and professional goals are, you'll find that a podcast can help. By the end of this chapter, you'll have the knowledge and insight about what makes podcasting such a powerful platform for professionals. You'll also gain the confidence to go forth and begin planning your own podcast.

Before we get started with reasons to launch a podcast, let's take a look at the state of the podcasting industry. In fact, let's explore the state of audio overall.

According to the Infinite Dial 2018 report from Edison Research :

- 64% of Americans are familiar with podcasts – that's approximately 180 million people (up from 60% in 2017)
- 44% of Americans have listened to a podcast
- Listeners consume an average of 7 podcasts per week
- An estimated 48 million Americans listen to podcasts weekly, up 6 million from 2017
- 80% of listeners hear all of most of each episode they listen to
- 69% of podcasts are consumed on a mobile device
- 51 million Americans own a smart speaker in their home, either an Amazon Alexa or Google Home

This upward trend in audio, and specifically podcasting, is reason for optimism. But for me, podcasting goes far beyond just listener trends and statistics. Launching my podcast changed my life. My podcast gave me the courage to leave my job and launch my own business. That, in and of itself, made it all worth it and remains until this day one of the best decisions I ever made (and I've made my fair share of good decisions; befriending Mitch Jackson being one of them).

Now, let's get to the good stuff. Why is this medium so powerful, and how can it help you professionally?

Create convenience of consumption for the listener

One reason podcasting is gaining in popularity is the ease of consumption on the listener's part. People are always looking for ways to get more done during the day. Time is valuable (and seemingly scarce), and thus, any type of content consumption that allows for multi-tasking will win over the hearts of consumers. Podcasts are on-demand, (available whenever the listener wants to listen), and available on the go (i.e., while driving, walking the dog, riding the train, doing the laundry, etc.). Listeners can listen to podcasts when they want, where they want, and how they want. That makes them appealing.

Take a moment to think about the person on the other end and how likely it is that they would prefer audio over other types of content. If it's highly likely, then a podcast is indeed a smart decision.

Build trust in an intimate and authentic way

We've all heard the saying – customers need to "know, like, and trust" you in order to do business with you. Well, I believe that "liking" you is no longer sufficient. Now, it's a matter of "loving" you. Is that a tall order? Sure. Is it possible? Sure is...with a podcast.

Podcasts by their very nature are intimate and personal. As the podcaster, you are essentially whispering into people's ears. It doesn't get much closer than that. Through voice, listeners are able to decipher a podcast host's personality, feel their spirit, and assess their trustworthiness.

Your voice can go a long way in helping you establish trust with the listener because it's difficult to "fake" being yourself on a podcast, at least not for a prolonged period of time. You're forced to show up as your authentic self because, unless you've got an acting degree, it's going to be difficult to sustain being anyone but yourself. That authenticity is what will help you build relationships with your listeners and eventually convert them into customers.

Showcase expert knowledge and build thought leadership
You're good at what you do. You understand your industry well. You have experience. You know your stuff.

Great.

But do others know that you know what you know?

That's where a podcast comes in.

A podcast is your platform and your permission to showcase what you know. It's your way of highlighting your knowledge and demonstrating your expertise in a subject matter. Because of the periodical nature of a podcast, you will constantly show up on your show and discuss topics that are related to your field or your business. The more consistently you show up as someone who is knowledgeable and competent, the more regarded as an expert you will become.

Here's the cool part about hosting a podcast: even if you don't consider yourself to be an expert or you're wary of giving yourself the label of "thought leader," you will become more comfortable in that role over time because you'll realize that by virtue of keeping up with your industry's latest trends or through the wisdom transferred to you by your guests, you too become an expert.

Podcasting gives you the confidence to stand in your greatness, whether it already exists or is still being developed.

Expand your network and sphere of influence

Attending networking events can be awkward and time-consuming. Networking through your podcast can be fun and time-efficient!

As a podcaster, your network will increase exponentially. This happens in a few ways. First, if you decide to host an interview-type of show, you will need guests to fill the spots on the other end. These guests are people you might already know but likely will be people you've never met before. By inviting guests onto your show to interview them, you're able to meet new people and broaden your network.

Because of your show, you will be able to reach out and connect with heavy-hitters in your industry; folks you never thought you'd have a chance at ever meeting. You now have a platform to offer as a way to begin building relationships with power players and acquaintances in your industry.

The second way a podcast helps you expand your sphere of influence and network is by allowing you to build a community of listeners who tune in with each episode to hear you speak. You are the star of your show, and your listeners are people who trust what you have to say and believe in your mission.

Over time, you will learn more about your listeners and develop a relationship with them. Your message will resonate with the right people, and they'll want to reach out and talk to you. In some instances, they'll even want to work with you.

If you nurture the relationship with your listeners correctly, your listeners become your brand ambassadors. They will promote you and your show to their friends and networks. That's how you expand your own network and sphere of influence.

Your Podcast Planning Considerations and Checklist

If my words above convinced you that a podcast is the right platform for you and your professional aspirations, then below is a checklist of things to consider before you get your show up and running. Use this as a checklist and accompanying examples to work through some of the finer details of launching your own show.

Creation

• What is your topic? Will it be narrow or broad? Some podcasts are broad in their subject matters, like the show Online Marketing Made Easy with Amy Porterfield which covers an array of online marketing topics. Others are more narrowly-focused with a focus on a niche area, topic, or audience base. A great example of that is the Maximum Lawyer podcast with Jim Hacking and Tyson Mutrux, which focuses on marketing and business development for lawyers specifically.

• How long will each episode be?

• What format will it take? Many hosts rely on the wisdom of their guests in an interview/Q&A-style show like Lewis Howes's The School of Greatness, where he interviews inspiring individuals to learn how they built successful lives. You can choose to host your show on your own and create your episodes solo. You can choose to have one or more co-hosts who help you create the show. A wonderful example of a well-produced co-hosted show is the Inclusive Education Project podcast which is focused on equal opportunities issues in education and hosted by special education attorneys Amanda Selogie and Vickie Brett.

• Will it be only audio or will you want to record a video too?

• Will you rely on a general talking outline or script?

• What are your scheduling mechanics – how will you schedule guests and how often will you record/publish?

• Gather your show music, openers, and closers

• Select and clear availability for show title/name

• Create cover art

• Select a launch date

Technical

• Purchase your necessary gear: Hardware – microphone, headphones, a mixer if necessary, pop sockets/filters: Software – recording software (Audacity, Adobe Audition, Garageband)

- Consider production + post-production: Editing, Show notes and episode description, Uploading process, Media host, Promotional material (like social media graphics)

Marketing

- Set up distribution to directories (Apple Podcasts, Google Play, Stitcher Radio, etc.)

- Pay attention to SEO for each episode

- Use social media

- Publish on website/RSS feed

- Promote your show as a guest on other podcasts

Monetization

- Advertising

- Sponsorships

- Sell your own products/services

- Subscriptions

- Patreon/listener donations

- Affiliate commissions

- Media kit

The benefits of launching your own podcast are innumerable. In this chapter, I shared several reasons why a podcast is an important and powerful content creation platform. I also discussed a few ways a podcast can help you grow your brand, connect with a wider community, and establish your thought leadership.

In a world where content is king, and attention spans are short, it's important to carve out your own space online to share your message. I hope this chapter proves to be helpful in helping you take the next step in launching your own podcast.

———

Not one to shy away from risk, Nicole Abboud quit her law practice in 2017 and launched her social media and content marketing strategy and consulting business working almost exclusively with lawyers and law firms – Abboud Media. She documented her entire journey from being an unhappy attorney to a new entrepreneur through insightful interviews on her award-winning podcast, The Gen Why Lawyer. Using content marketing and social media, Nicole has built a powerful brand and now travels the country as a speaker and trainer. You can find out more about Nicole and her services at www.nicoleabboud.com

CHAPTER 21

TO LIVESTREAM OR PRE-RECORD VIDEO? THAT IS THE QUESTION

BY JENNIFER QUINN

With a whopping 85% of all content consumed online being video, and 59% of executives stating they would rather watch a video than read a blog with the same information, it is no longer a question of Should I include video in my marketing strategy? it is now Which type of video should I include in my marketing – live or pre-recorded?

The good news is, there's no wrong answer! While livestreaming is how I began my video marketing journey, both pre-recorded video and live video have a relevant place in every business marketing strategy.

In 2012 when I gave presentations on social media, without fail business owners would ask me, "What's the ROI (Return on Investment) for social media? I would tell them, "The ROI is that you get to still be in business in five years!" Today, I say the same thing about incorporating video in your marketing strategy – doing so will ensure that you will still be in business in five years.

You see, people do business with people that they know, like, and trust. Video is a tool that catapults the "know, like, and trust" factor like nothing we've ever seen before. Whether it's on-demand video (pre-recorded) or live video (livestreaming), video truly is the next best thing to being there.

Digital marketing has changed the way we do business. Having your company ranked #1 on Google isn't enough anymore. Whether someone is referred by a friend, or discovers a business via a Google search, 70-80% of consumers report that they also do additional research on businesses by looking at their social media profiles. When your prospective client is comparing you and your competition - all other things being equal - your videos will give you a measurable advantage.

Video allows your future clients to get to know who you are, what you stand for, who you serve, and what problems you solve, all before even calling your office to schedule an appointment.

To many prospective clients, the idea of reaching out to a professional can be intimidating. New clients don't know what to expect for the first visit, who they are going to meet with, and what they are going to experience when they arrive. Video gives you the opportunity to put those concerns to rest. A simple introductory video on your Facebook profile or YouTube channel can be very comforting and inviting to new clients.

Top benefits of a well-planned video marketing strategy:

- Demonstrate your expertise and authority
- Build credibility and trust
- Educate your clients on who you serve and the problems you solve
- Top-of-mind awareness with regularly posted videos
- Strategically show your personal side
- Be relatable by sharing your humanness
- Highlight your community involvement

The most important things to do regarding video marketing are to GET STARTED and DON'T QUIT.

Thanks to recent technology advancements, getting started is easy. I teach my clients to avoid most newbie mistakes by paying attention to L.A.V.S.

What is L.A.V.S.?

Lighting: Good lighting is essential and one of the easiest components of video to achieve. Daylight is the best, so simply sit in front of a daylit window, with your device or camera in between you and the window. If you need to use artificial lighting instead, use options such as a mini smartphone clip-on lighting ring, a large mobile "diva ring" light, or studio-grade box lighting.

Audio: Perhaps one of the most important aspects of good video is excellent audio. If you are recording or broadcasting from a quiet location and are using a recent model smartphone within 1-3 feet, the smartphone's built-in microphone will work great. In other situations, consider earbuds, an external mic, or a laptop/desktop USB mic.

Video: Recent model smartphones already have HD capability, which works great! Just clean the lens with a microfiber cloth so your image is not fuzzy. If you record from your laptop/desktop, get a USB camera made for video. A good entry-level camera is the Logitech C930. As you advance in video production you will want to consider a DSLR (Digital Single Lens Reflex) camera.

Stability: Shaky videos will cause you to lose viewers quickly! This is easily fixed with a simple tripod or gimbal stabilizer. (For quick equipment and gear recommendations go to JennyQLive.com/Resources)

Most Common Question regarding Video Marketing

Whether discussing live video or on-demand video, one of the most common questions I get is, "WHAT DO I TALK ABOUT?" Here's a list to get you started!

Top 10 Content Creation Picks for Professionals

1. Behind the Scenes - Show how things work - process, system, etc.

2. Q & A – Answer commonly asked questions or allow live-video viewers to ask questions they would otherwise need to book an appointment with you for answers.

3. Educational / How-To - Teach a how to do something, or an unusual skill.

4. Interviews – Interview experts in adjacent fields that would interest your viewers and prospective clients.

5. Newsjacking - Insert your unique perspective into a breaking news story by doing a livestream broadcast about it. (Take care to not exploit disasters or violence to promote your business or brand.)

6. A Day in the Life– Show a behind-the-curtain moment of what you do, or how you prepare for a speech, trial, or presentation.

7. Rant - Go on live video to rant about something. (Be mindful of how this aligns with your brand and represents your business.)

8. Recycle – Existing content from previous writing, blogs, vlogs, videos, etc..

9. Live Events – Capture footage – at a conference, grab a speaker for a quick interview, or a musician for a back-stage interview.

10. Highlight community events and organizations you support.

Perhaps the most important thing to remember is that all social media interaction, including video marketing, is about building relationships. While sales are made, and clients are contracted via these modalities, the long game - and the real ROI - is based on creating, developing, and nurturing relationships. Add value, inform, educate, and entertain your viewers - they will keep coming back for more, and it is you that they will reach out to when they need your product or service.

Live Video Benefits and Platforms

Being able to interact with viewers in real time is the quickest and most effective way to build digital relationships, which can then, when it makes sense, be parlayed into offline relationships.

Why should you consider incorporating livestreaming and on-demand video into your marketing strategy?

- 80% of people would rather watch live video from a brand than read a blog
- On average, people watch a live video more than three times longer when it is live compared to on-demand video
- People watch 42.8 minutes for live video content versus 5.1 minutes for on demand
- Viewers spent eight times longer with live video than on-demand
- 82% prefer live video from a brand than social posts

Livestreaming is like a magnifying glass on life. If you are a great person, your company has an amazing mission, or your product serves people in a way that changes lives, it's going to show up on live video infinitely greater than what you can portray with a simple ad, image or text alone.

Which Platform Should You Livestream From

The good news is that the skills acquired in livestreaming on ANY platform transfer to livestreaming on ALL platforms. That being said, the most important thing is just to choose one and get started.

The most used and viewed live video platforms are:

1. Facebook Live
2. YouTube Live
3. Instagram
4. Twitter/Periscope

From the list, ask yourself: Which platform does my business or brand already have the most engagement and/or the most followers? This answer will more than likely give you the best starting point where to start livestreaming. But, it's important to measure both the follower count AND the current engagement. For example, if you have a large number of followers on Instagram, but not much engagement (likes, comments, etc..) and have a smaller number of fans on your Facebook business page but a very active community, you might consider starting your live video presence on Facebook, even though Instagram has a greater number of followers.

Viewer Engagement Skills

There are a few basic skills you can learn that, once mastered, will put your livestreams into a higher league than all other beginning livestreamers (and many experienced ones!). Remember, the purpose of livestreaming is to build relationships by increasing the "know, like and trust" factor. With that in mind, let's cover some basics.

The thing that sets live video apart from on-demand video is the ability for you to engage with your viewers in real time, and an opportunity for them to spontaneously engage with you and participate in the broadcast. Personal connection happens during a live broadcast, and profound personal connection happens when the broadcaster is also skilled at engaging. Remember this basic truth about human beings and your livestreams will create magical results: People want to be seen, recognized, and validated. When you are able to meet those needs on your livestreams, you've made real human connection, even when you can't see your viewers.

So, how do you make that livestreaming magic happen? As with any new skill, engaging with your viewers is going to take practice, and lots of it. Here are some basic skills you can start implementing with your broadcasts:

1. Eye contact with viewers – look into the lens of the camera for at least 70% of the broadcast

2. Bring viewers into your world – be vulnerable and real. Share personal stories and anecdotes. Give them a glimpse of your world.

3. Don't assume they know what you know – in other words, over communicate, over explain, and over demonstrate. Share street-level information. It will feel very basic, but the easier your info is to understand for those outside of your field, the better results you'll have on live video.

4. Do not wait for people to join the broadcast – immediately start into your content instead of waiting for a certain number of viewers to join. A good rule of thumb is to say a quick hello to the live viewers and the replay viewers, then move into the content you are there to deliver.

5. Welcome people by name – People love to hear their name, and what better way to make someone feel seen, recognized, and validated, than to welcome them to the broadcast by name!

Remember, people want to connect with you, be recognized, and be seen! They want to learn from you, they want to buy from you, but they won't be able to do either of those if they don't feel validated. When they can resonate with you—your energy, vulnerability, approachability—then they will connect with you, and they will be able to trust you enough to open their minds to first learn, and then open their pocketbooks to buy.

Pre-recorded Video Benefits and Platforms

I tell my coaching clients that if you don't want to engage with your viewers in real-time, then don't do livestreaming. On-demand videos (pre-recorded) are still very much an effective marketing tool and offer different benefits than livestreaming, one of them being that you can edit them before sharing. This fits very well for many people's time availability, temperament, and marketing strategy.

Also known as on-demand video (think Netflix, YouTube, etc.) pre-recorded video is the more familiar form of video marketing. There are many benefits from a production standpoint.

Benefits of on-demand video:

• Batch recording – create several videos in one studio session to be distributed at future times
• Editing to remove errors can be done post-production
• Subtitles, branding, and logos can be added in editing
• More platform options for video content
• Great for creating short form videos – often called "snackable" content for quicker consumption

Which Platforms are Best for On-demand Video?

The top pre-recorded video platform is undeniably YouTube. As the world's 2nd largest search engine, with optimized titles, descriptions, and tags, not much can beat the discoverability function of YouTube. However, that does not rule out the huge value that comes from other social media platforms, as all of them strongly favor video.

Top Pre-recorded Video Platform Options for Businesses and Brands:

1. YouTube
2. LinkedIn
3. Facebook
4. Instagram (short form video)
5. IGTV (Instagram TV – long form video)
6. Twitter

With livestreaming I suggested choosing the platform in which you had the most engagement to determine the platform to use, however, with recorded video, you can share the same video on multiple platforms. The culture of the platform will also determine where you'll upload certain videos. For example, a video that is more lighthearted and playful could do well on Facebook or Instagram while a professional or "how to" video might perform better on LinkedIn or YouTube.

Horizontal or Vertical Orientation?

For both livestreaming and pre-recorded video, the best orientation depends on which platform you're broadcasting from or uploading to. For example, when uploading a video to IGTV the user experience is better when the video is created in portrait (vertical) position. When broadcasting live on Facebook, the best option is landscape (horizontal) position.

However, since video marketing is evolving so rapidly, don't get too hung up on orientation. Here's why: If I had written this chapter just six months ago, my recommendation would have leaned strongly toward horizontal video with vertical being the exception for some platforms. Since the introduction of IGTV vertical video appears to have taken a leap towards being not only more acceptable, but quite possibly a preferred viewer experience. Currently over 60% of video views coming from a mobile device making the argument for vertical video even stronger. Even YouTube, which has traditionally favored horizontal videos, incorporated a feature that allows a vertical video to be automatically optimized on a mobile device for the most positive user experience.

Your Next Step in Video Marketing:

At I mentioned earlier in the chapter, the most important things you can do are:

1. Get Started
2. Don't Quit

Yes, it's scary – because it's new - but like everything else you've mastered, you will get better at creating video the more you do it. My virtual door is always open – if you have any questions on your specific situation or circumstance, please feel free to send me an email at JennyQ@JennyQLive.com

Here's to your video marketing success! You've got this!

———

Jennifer Quinn "JennyQ" is a livestreaming expert, coach, and trainer. Her book, "Leverage Livestreaming to Build Your Brand: Start, Master, and Monetize Live Video" debuted as a #1 Amazon Best Seller. Connect with Jennifer here https://jennyqlive.com

CHAPTER 22

SNAPCHAT (SNAP) AND CREATING ENGAGING REAL-TIME ON THE GO CONTENT

BY CHRIS STRUB

Disruption has become cliché in the social media industry – lately, it's tough to go a full day without being notified of a cataclysmic announcement, a landscape-shifting acquisition, or a "major update."

The hyperbole of a 24-hour digital news cycle tends to dampen the effect of legitimate major shifts, one of which occurred in October 2013, involving an app heretofore shunned by the general public as a sexting platform for teenagers – Snapchat.

The app itself had been around for two years, but in Oct. 2013, the Snapchat team launched the 'Stories' feature, which allows users to compile photos and/or videos into a rolling 'Story,' where each piece posted is available – either to Friends or the Public – for 24 hours.

The ephemeral nature of this short-form medium gradually spurned a whole new generation of storytellers. Prescient artists like Shaun McBride – better known to the world by his nickname, 'Shonduras' (inspired by a visit to Honduras) – seized upon the opportunity to create Snapchat stories for some of the world's most popular brands.

As its Stories exploded in popularity, Snapchat quickly found itself in an identity crisis – one that, in many ways, still looms over the app to this day: is Snapchat, at its core, an app for Storytellers, like McBride? Or are its roots too deeply buried in its user-to-user messaging capabilities?

For several years, Snapchat embraced, and profited wildly, from that newfound imbalance. Snapchat "influencers" popped up everywhere, spurning a gold rush of sorts: analytics companies, like Delmondo, to provide insights into this walled-off world where data was hard to come by; influencer agencies, like PopShorts, which helps pair attention-yielding creators with attention-craving brands; even paraphernalia factories, like PopSockets, which are glued to the back of one's phone, to facilitate seamless video storytelling.

Snapchat's Stories feature was an enormous, industry-shifting success – and Facebook founder Mark Zuckerberg knew it. Although never officially confirmed, Forbes reported that Facebook offered Snapchat CEO Evan Spiegel $3 billion to purchase Snapchat in late 2013 – an offer that Spiegel rejected.

Having been shut out by Snapchat, Mark Zuckerberg had to resort to a Plan B. Facebook knew that Stories were an enormously value asset, but instead of buying out the competition, they'd now have to go about things the hard way.

For years, the Facebook team worked behind the scenes to develop tools that would mimic the magic that Snapchat had tapped into. This would require a top-to-bottom re-examination of the structure of each of their suite of apps, up to and including the Facebook app itself.

In August 2016, they pulled the trigger.

When Instagram Stories were launched, in many ways, the bell was tolled for Snapchat. Little did we know at the time that Instagram Stories were just the first prong of a four-headed approach; in the months ahead, Facebook also introduced 'Messenger Day' and 'WhatsApp Status,' which implanted stories atop of its two popular messaging apps; and Facebook Stories, bringing the Stories feature front and center to its flagship's one billion monthly active users.

In one of the largest A/B/C/D testing concepts of all time, Instagram Stories, WhatsApp Status, Facebook Stories and Messenger Day each had their own quirks, but each medium was essentially the same – a mechanism where users can share limited-life photos and/or videos to a rotating carousel for 24 hours. (Messenger Day was eventually merged with Facebook Stories.)

In late 2016, Snapchat rebranded as Snap, Inc., calling itself a 'camera company' and unveiling sunglasses with a built-in camera, which they called Spectacles. As of the latest available data, Facebook Stories has 150 million daily active users; Instagram Stories has 300 million daily active users; WhatsApp Status has 450 million daily active users – totaling 900 million DAU's between Facebook's three channels.

Snapchat claims 191 million daily active users – just 70 million more than they claimed in late 2015.

My Personal Experience

I was invited by Mitch to share a bit of my own experience with using Stories 'on the go.' The idea is to show professionals how to use apps like Snap so share your personal and professional story while out and about and, embrace a new, temporary, short story medium.

Setting up Snap is easy and anyone can Google the steps. What I want to do is dive a bit deeper and give you the feel of the platform, share what works, and in the end, the tools you'll need to create your own Snap stories on the go.

Let's get started.

I've been on Snapchat since December 2012, and remember experimenting a bit with Stories for the first time in 2014.

It was in 2014 that I came across content by a gentleman named Mark Kaye, a disc jockey based in Jacksonville, Fla. Mark hosted a show called 'Talkin' Snap,' where, using a few clever technology hacks, he would interview popular Snapchat creators around the world in a fun and exciting way.

I watched how Mark was using Snap and I decided in early in 2015 that this storytelling revolution was real. Snapchat was becoming all the rage, and although I was no Mark Kaye, I felt extremely comfortable sharing stories. I also knew I was comfortable road tripping around America, but if I was going to go again, how could I give meaning to the work I was doing?

I made the bold decision to go around the country, again. This time, though, to all 50 states – and this time, I was going to visit nonprofit organizations in every state.

And this time, I was going to Snapchat it all.

By the summer of 2015, the aforementioned age of the 'Snapchat Celebrity' was fully upon us. Artists and storytellers were accruing huge followings – which portended to huge money.

I had a vision; I had a plan; and I had a car. What more could a young bachelor need?

My trip would take me first to Charleston, S.C., and then clockwise around the lower 48, with a week- long jaunt to Alaska and Hawaii in the middle. I was going to visit nonprofits in every single state, each with one common theme: youth.

I climbed behind the wheel of my 2007 Honda Accord – that's right, I ride in style, my friends, and set out Eastward toward coastal Carolina. With the previous summer's experience under my belt, I both had no idea what to expect this time, and every idea of what to expect.

The journey was incredible. I met and interviewed hundreds of the nation's top nonprofit thinkers, from Ed Guthrie, the outgoing CEO of Opportunity Village in Las Vegas, to Robin McHaelen, the bold visionary behind True Colors in Hartford, Conn.

The onset of both Snapchat and another parallel storytelling revolution – mobile live-streaming – were both a blessing and a curse. I was able to capture and share the stories of all these organizations at the touch of a button – but I also boorishly set a terrible example by recklessly using these tools while driving, often 70+ or even 80+ miles per hour, across America.

According to Teensafe.com, distracted driving accounts for 25 percent of all motor vehicle crash fatalities – a number I'd unfortunately expect to continue to rise as our devices become increasingly inseparable from our hands.

Thankfully, I survived a summer of dangerous driving habits, and now take every possible opportunity to remind our community to stop distracted driving. (Please visit EndDD.org for more information on the dangers of distracted driving.)

Putting aside the inherent dangers of my habitually Snapchatting while driving – an unchangeable aspect that, again, I am far from proud of – the idea of using an app like Snapchat to share stories on the go had now become part of my modus operandi.

In his book 'Real Artists Don't Starve,' Jeff Goins emphasizes how successful artists 'Practice in Public,' and that's exactly what my road trip had been: a 100-day learning experience, that helped me not only sharpen my Snapchat skills, but also introduced the format to scores of nonprofits around America. By the time the trip ended, I could hardly imagine going a day without walking, talking and sharing the lessons I'd learned in that state.

Of course, the journey was much more than just a 100-day how-to-use-Snapchat course – in my book, "50 States, 100 Days: The Book," I dive deep into all the lessons the trip taught me about America, about road tripping, about nonprofits and about myself. It's worth a read, but I digress.

And while '50 States, 100 Days' was officially over, my propensity to travel was just beginning. In 2016, while working in upstate New York, I accepted a contract role with Humana in Louisville, Ky., which led me to visit nonprofits in southeastern cities like Tampa, New Orleans and Knoxville.

In 2017, I launched 'I Am Here, LLC,' a solopreneurship that brought me to speaking engagements, workshops and event hosting roles in San Diego; Las Vegas; Dayton, Ohio; St. Louis; Atlanta and more.

I was tapped to represent The Salvation Army as a National Red Kettle Ambassador during their 2017 Red Kettle campaign, which raised more than $44 million. In the style of '50 States, 100 Days,' I took a solo, 25-state, 38-day road trip – this time, of course, without the behind-the-wheel content creation – spotlighting the organization's everyday heroes who sustain the Army's Fight For Good 365 days a year.

This broad variety of career experiences has been emotionally fulfilling, but accumulating these professional experiences in this particular field, in this decade, has felt almost mildly paradoxical.

The acceleration and mass adaptation of these mobile technologies has simultaneously advanced our ability to share stories from anywhere, with just our phones. It's also dramatically reduced the lifespan of each specific memory: 24 hours after sharing, that moment is gone, theoretically, forever.

What doesn't disappear like clockwork, however, is our ability to communicate with one another about specific stories. The fungible lifespan of our conversations – from a one-off style, 3-am "U Up?" to a years-long 'Snap streak' (when two users Snapchat each other at least once a day for an indeterminate period of time) – shows how the two sides of these Storytelling/Messaging hybrid apps exist in diametrically irreconcilable ways.

That Snapchat lives with (what I believe to be) a fundamental flaw does not mean that there isn't an enormous amount of benefit to be gained from the app; nor does it mean that Facebook's forced adaptation of the Stories concept is misguided.

Snapchat's five-year run since introducing Stories has been extraordinarily profitable, brought exposure to scores of highly successful mobile storytellers and artists, and brought immeasurable enlightenment about the world around us to its tens of millions of users.

From a personal perspective, I've made nearly ten thousand connections on Snapchat alone, not to mention the positive externalities of developing a recognizable brand that cuts through the noise in our industry.

But as this infantile industry begins to mature, the model for success is shifting, from determining which artists can accumulate the largest followings and view counts, to who among that group can most effectively lead a community tied together by the bonds they share.

Not surprisingly, Facebook has been on the forefront of this community-based approach: both digitally, through the growing appreciation and algorithmic shift toward Facebook Groups; and in real life, as the company, following in its CEO's footsteps, has started dispatching representatives to real-life meet-ups around the country and theoretically around the world.

And while it may seem like it's "too late" to get started with Stories, that couldn't be further from the truth. Five years may seem like an eternity in the current news cycle, but for customers who have been with your brand for years or even decades, seeing that your brand is now using Stories is the perfect way to keep their attention. And this five-year grace period has given millions of storytellers the chance to perfect their craft – if capturing video of yourself isn't your thing, social media conferences, digital publications and even your real-life network, like Mitch Jackson, are sure to know a great storyteller who could be the perfect fit for your brand in 2018.

This chapter has been a winding road to get to one overarching point: *authenticity is everything and telling your story in real-time is everything.*

While thousands of employees at Facebook, Snapchat, and many other of the social media conglomerates work tirelessly to figure out the perfect Stories formula, way too many of us "super- users" get caught up in the chaos. The answer is so much simpler than we often seem to realize.

Be you. Be authentic.

The very core of what Snapchat's Stories feature accomplished, was to wash away the unhealthy, and ultimately unattainable, facades that social media was forcing us to develop. Stories were designed as a stark slap in the face to perfectionism.

I began my Storytelling journey chasing perfectionism. I began '50 States, 100 Days' hoping that my digital interviews would be the next 'Talkin' Snap.'

It wasn't until long after that trip ended that I'd accomplished exactly what I should've been after in the first place: understanding exactly who I was.

I'm grateful to Mitch to have been asked to share some of my story with you, but ultimately, it's not about my story – it's, hopefully, about how this story inspires you.

I can preach about Maslow's Pyramid and achieving Snapchat Self-actualization all day long, but knowing that this book will be read by many savvy businessmen and women, I recognize the importance of putting this into dollars and cents.

If you're reading this book, I surely don't need to sell you on the value of social media itself. For too many practitioners, success on social media is still defined by views, impressions and followers– all numbers that can be easily gamed and, yes, then passed up the chain to marketing heads, board chairs and CEO's.

The older I get, the deeper I question the meaning of conventional success. What I've learned and share with you today is that in today's world, if you're not innovating, you're dying.

Think for a moment about the acceleration of machine learning and artificial intelligence. Ask yourself for a moment if a computer can set up a Facebook ad, or post five inspirational quotes a week, the way that you can. Now think for a moment about the one thing that a computer can never possibly take away from you, the one thing that technology can never disrupt, your ability to be your authentic self.

Stories all may seem like fun and games, but there's a billion-dollar reason they sit atop your Facebook and Instagram apps. Give yourself permission to be yourself. Truth be told your audience wants to see you and your brand's, imperfections. Give them what they want in the form of real-time "on the go" stories using platforms like Snap, Instagram, and Facebook.

Ready to get started? Good! Remember, while the best time to get started was five years ago, the second-best time to start is now.

Disrupt away.

———

Chris Strub is the CEO of "I Am Here, LLC" and the first person to live-stream and Snapchat in all 50 U.S. states. He is the author of "50 States, 100 Days: The Book" and "Fight For Good Tour: The Book," and the creator of the online course "Live-streaming for Nonprofits." Chris is an award-winning international keynote speaker and when he's not on stage educating and entertaining, he's worked or working with companies like Humana, Big Brothers Big Sisters of America, the Community Foundation of Louisville and live-streaming app Live.me. Find Chris across all social media platforms via @ChrisStrub and learn more about Chris at www.teamstrub.com

CHAPTER 23

THE POWER OF CHATBOTS

BY RYAN STEINOLFSON

Chatbots are changing everything. They make relationships, marketing, and sales faster, easier, and better. Before I dive into what chatbots are and, how to use these new tools, I'd first like to take a minute and put my excitement into context.

Saying Hello to Your Prospective Customer

Before I started my digital marketing agency ten years ago, I was in Biotech sales. During this time, there was always a "healthy tension" between marketing and sales. Sales would say marketing needed to provide better leads, and marketing would argue that salespeople had to sell to the marketing leads better.

When I moved to the digital marketing world, I was challenged with setting up marketing funnels to generate the type of leads that salespeople wanted. Building marketing funnels always seemed a little foreign to me as a salesperson who always focused on building relationships and trust through the art of communication before throwing that right hook to close a deal.

I always believed, and still do, that quality communication ultimately came down to having a meaningful conversation with a qualified consumer. The digital marketing approach always seemed very disconnected to me with the email sequences, tags, opt-in forms, etc.

I never really understood why people put up with filling out forms on a website (to start down our marketing lead generation funnels) with nobody there to greet them or even say hello. In the real world, I believe that's the equivalent of a prospective customer being asked for their name, email and phone number thirty seconds after entering a store in the mall. Then, sending that potential customer quickly on their way. The communications are then done by text or email every other day until that customer reaches out to you to make a purchase. I can't imagine how anyone would think this kind of interaction would be a good thing.

I believe the best time to greet somebody, say hello, and make a great first impression is when they first walk into your practice or visit your website. In the digital world, chatbots allow you to do just that.

Leveraging Body Language with Video Chat To Increase Conversions

It's often reported that about seventy percent of communication happens via body language. If all you're using is text and email to try and communicate your message, how effective can you be? Increasing the chances of sending a clear message is where the power of chatbot related video comes into play.

Getting Basic Questions Answered

Some people visit your website to get basic questions answered quickly without the commitment of talking to somebody on the phone, watching a webinar, or getting an entire email sequence. One of the best things about chatbots is that if they are programmed correctly, they can intuitively answer prospects questions just as well, if not better, than a real person.

Can you imagine the impact you will make with your leads, and the increased conversions you will get if your chatbot immediately greets your leads and gives them instant answers? When you join the conversation with your chatbot (from your phone or desktop), you can quickly see exactly what the leads questions and concerns are from the chatbot conversation.

Add video to your chatbot, and things get crazy! Your potential client is now getting answers to their questions while watching your body language. To your potential client, the impression is that a human to human connection is being made. That's a powerful business asset that you can put to use 24/7.

How Fast are You with Responding to Website Leads?

A Harvard Business Review study was conducted to find out how quickly 2,241 companies followed up with web-generated leads and what happened the longer the companies took to respond. The results were shocking. "Although 37% responded to their lead within an hour, and 16% responded within one to 24 hours, 24% took more than 24 hours—and 23% of the companies never responded at all. The average response time, among companies that responded within 30 days, was 42 hours."

The good news is that chatbots can solve the delay problem. They deliver instantly and if you add video into the mix, are incredibly useful. Firms that tried to contact potential customers within an hour of receiving a query were nearly seven times as likely to qualify the lead. For those companies that waited twenty-four hours or longer to have a conversation with a new client or patient lead, the firms that acted quickly (within an hour) were sixty times more likely to close the deal.

Time is everything when it comes to engaging with potential clients and patients. Even with good chatbots, I believe it's still imperative that you have a dedicated person "staffing the digital booth" to take over within 5 minutes of the chatbot starting the conversation.

Types of Chatbots

There are two main types of chatbots. One is designed to start chat conversations from your website, and the other is intended to begin discussions on the social media platforms.

When it comes to choices, I've found that Drift is an excellent example of a web-based Chatbot. What makes Drift different than other types of web-based chat is that you can program the chatbot to take people down a different conversation path (and answer specific questions) based on their responses.

A social media-based chatbot is designed to start conversations from social media platforms like Facebook, Twitter, and others. If you'd like to see a chatbot in action, please feel free to visit http://www.m.me/RyanSteinolfson to start a conversation with my Messenger chatbot. One significant aspect of social media chatbots is that you can program them to provide value while making them interactive and fun.

Although I like how easy it is to send audio and video using a chatbot from my phone, I don't like the fact that I am building my list of chat "subscribers" on a social platform that I do not own and can be kicked off of at any time. I have heard stories of colleagues getting bounced from YouTube for no apparent reason or having their Facebook Page shut down without any warning.

The great thing about web-based chatbots like Drift is that you have three main metrics or Key Performance Indicators also known as KPI. These metrics include (1) conversations started, (2) emails gathered, and (3) appointments scheduled. The platform allows users to build an email list that you own. You or team members can then focus on scheduling appointments from the conversations that are taking place in the chats.

What I've noticed with using chatbots is that you will typically convert about 1% to 3% of unique website visitors into scheduling an appointment. Another 7% to 15% of unique visitors to your website will start a conversation with your chatbot and someplace between 40% to 60% of the people that begin chatting will leave their email so you can follow up, answer questions and add value. Keep in mind that 70% of these numbers are entirely from a chatbot doing all the work and that's the power of this emerging technology.

My strategy is to typically let the chatbot go as far as it can before a team member, or I jump into the conversation. In my experience, most of the 1% - 3% of unique visitors that are converted into appointments are appointments that would never have been scheduled if we did not have a chatbot on our site.

Pro Chatbot Tips

To leverage the power of chatbots, use video. The sooner you can leverage video into the chatbot conversation the better.

Think about the most common questions you are asked each month from clients and patients. Next, create detailed answers to each question. Share your secret sauce. Don't hold anything back. Next, add your answers into the chatbot system so that they are distributed via your chatbot or with you or staff member clicking a button.

The power of saved messages and answers is that they make the communication process more efficient, give your team a more consistent message, and allow you to improve your conversion rates more quickly because you have a process of what is being communicated. Creating answers to common questions and then adding them to your chatbot process can make you a chatbot rock star.

I believe chatbots can help save you time and increase conversations and sales. They'll also add value to help create a better client or patient experience. In the end, more website and social media visitors into paying clients and patients.

————

Ryan Steinolfson is the CEO and founder of Accelerate Marketing, Inc., a digital marketing agency in San Diego that has grown over 500% in the last 4 years. You can connect with Ryan at https://ryansteinolfson.com

CHAPTER 24

HOW CAN PINTEREST HELP YOU DRIVE REVENUE GROWTH?

BY ANNA BENNETT

So you're thinking WIIFM? Pinterest can help you drive new revenue growth by; 1) dramatically increasing the amount of qualified buying traffic visiting your website or business and 2) helping you rank on the top of Google when someone searches for your type of goods or services.

Context:

1.5 million businesses currently use Pinterest to help them rank higher on Google; increase traffic volume to their websites & blogs; rapidly get new customers; increase sales and profits; build brand awareness; automatically grow their email databases; collect market intelligence for competitive advantage

What is Pinterest?

For businesses, Pinterest is a giant marketing platform. For consumers, it is a massive online shopping platform.

Most people think that Pinterest is a social media network, it is not. It is a search engine like Google for people who are looking for ideas, services and things that they can take action on.

Whether it's to learn something, buy something, or to save an idea for a future project, there are 175 billion images and videos for people to explore. More than 75% of the content is from businesses. The consumers and shoppers who use Pinterest love that because they are in the market shopping for something. What that means to you is that you have the opportunity to connect with your target audience in a new medium or meet new customers you might otherwise never have met.

Pinterest is a marketing platform where businesses have a "page" and they fill that page with content about their goods and services as well as helpful information their target audience would love.

How is Pinterest Different from Other Social Media Platforms?

What makes Pinterest different from other socials is that users have a planning and buying mindset when they are on the platform. It's their natural behavior.

People don't share selfies or post stories about what they ate or where they went or what they are doing. They don't check what their friends are up to like they do on Facebook or they don't have conversations like they would on Twitter. They are primarily there shopping and looking for new ideas, inspiration, products & services they can add to their lives.

There is some social aspect to it since Pinterest allows you to engage with other users through group boards, community boards, sending messages and commenting on pins.

Who Uses Pinterest?

As of 2018, over 250 million people use Pinterest each month to; shop, look for suppliers, discover new ideas. Their ages range from 18 to 65+. Therefore, all types of businesses can benefit from leveraging Pinterest from B2B, professionals, e-commerce, and brick and mortar.

Pinterest reaches 83% of all women aged 25-54 in the US, "Deciders" as Pinterest calls them. That's more than Instagram, Snapchat and Twitter. That's significant because they're responsible for 80% of household buying, and they control more than 50% of the wealth in the US. 85% of deciders views Pinterest as an integral part of their lives where they look for helpful information compared to Facebook 53% and Instagram 44.3%.

Deciders plan big moments like building their dream home (architects, home builders, interior decorators, furniture suppliers, craftsmen you need to be here while they are researching) planning a vacation, getting cosmetic surgery, etc. Smaller moments matter too including; finding healthy recipes, seeking inspiration for a kid's first birthday party, easy outdoor entertaining ideas and finding smart ways to save and invest money. They rely on businesses and what they post on Pinterest to help them make the best decisions about what they need and what to buy.

What makes Pinterest so appealing is that the users take action on the; ideas, products, and services they discover & save on Pinterest. Meaning they buy goods and services based on the research they do on Pinterest. It's not like Facebook. People are not sharing their lives, they are on Pinterest shopping and looking for new ideas.

How does Pinterest work?

People go onto Pinterest and type in a keyword or phrase to start looking for something that interests them. For example; farmhouse home designs or quick fitness workouts or how to start a business or golf clubs. Just like how you use Google.

Users share and collect their favorite pictures and videos based on their interests. The sharing of these pictures and blogs with other users on Pinterest is what gives your business more exposure.

Pinterest offers free tools for businesses to help users to search and learn more about the things they want to buy or do. This includes the Pinterest Search engine, Pinterest Lens and Shop the Look.

The Pinterest Search Engine

Think of what you do on Google, you go to a search box and type in keywords, things you are searching for right? That is the same behavior Pinners engage in on Pinterest, they go to a search box and type in keywords or phrases of things they are looking for. Next, Pinterest will show you results that are related to those keywords.

When Pinterest users find the content they are looking for they save those images or videos to their "boards." When they are ready to take action or to learn more, they click on the image which then takes them to the website where that content came from. That is how you can get massive traffic from Pinterest.

The Pinterest Visual Search Tool

Pinterest rolled out its first visual search tools called "Lens" in 2015. It's a real-time visual search tool embedded in the camera of the Pinterest App. It allows you to discover products and services anytime you point your Pinterest app & phone camera at something.

What's the big deal about the Lens?

Did you ever spot something you loved but couldn't find the words to describe it? Pinterest has solved that problem with the Lens. Let's say on your last trip your eye was drawn to the lighting fixture in the hotel lobby. You thought to yourself. I love that! I gotta have it! Well, all you need to do is open the Pinterest app on your mobile device and tap the camera icon in the search bar. Next, pinch to zoom or tap on a specific object to focus your camera on, tap the button to snap a picture and voila Pinterest will show you pages of images of those exact or similar objects.

Shop the Look

Another ambitious visual search tool Pinterest has produced is called Shop the Look, and it is specifically designed for fashion and home decor pins. Shop the Look pins have white dots hovering over the different parts of an outfit or a room. When people tap on the white dots, Pinterest will show the exact or similar products featured in the pin. When they're ready to buy, your customers can click through to your site to check out. That is how you make more sales on Pinterest.

Why Should It Matter to You As a Business?

Millennials are expected to overtake Boomers in population by 2019. Half of all the Millennials in the U.S. (those born between 1981 and 1996) use Pinterest every month. Pinterest is the number one destination for 18-34 year-olds outranking all other services and apps.

If your customers and those you want to attract are the Millennials or moms, then you need to be on Pinterest. That's important because they comprise the fastest-growing consumer segment in America and according to Accenture Millennial; these buyers are projected to spend an annual $1.4 trillion by 2020. Don't you want a piece of the pie?

Pinterest is Indexed by Google

What I especially love about Pinterest is that it can help you rank on the first page of Google. What that means to business people is getting more traffic and a better quality of traffic because they are self-selected. Plus it's free. Imagine if your website ranked # 1 on Google when people searched for type of product or service.

Regardless of what business you are in when you learn to operate Pinterest correctly your business will also eventually get found on the first page of Google too. As a B2B business owner myself, Pinterest has helped me rank on the first page of Google under my keywords "pinterest marketing expert" and "pinterest expert." Pinterest set-up correctly can help you rank # 1 on Google without buying ads.

Search Engines Are on The Rise

According to a 2017 report, there's been a significant shift in how websites receive their traffic. Search engines (Google and Pinterest) overtook social media sites like Facebook and now drive more traffic to all types of business websites.

I suggest that you take a hard look at Pinterest. Marketers and business owners should continue to invest in platforms driven by search engines and keywords instead of by social referrals. Pinterest is business friendly, and its users are in a shopping mindset.

Blogging Helps Consumers Get to Know, Respect and Trust You

You need a blog. If you don't want to write it, then hire someone. A blog is an essential marketing tool in today's digital world. This is especially important for business professionals like; lawyers, doctors, CPAs, cosmetic surgeons, architects and so on. If you're in the business of solving problems for your customers, then you need to have a blog. You need meaningful content that your target audience will consume, so you become their trusted advisor.

On Pinterest, blogs continue to work for years long after you post them which increases your odds of engagement, and that could mean more click throughs. This doesn't happen on other socials where content only lasts for a few seconds to a few hours.

Pinterest users are looking for information that will help them improve and build their life. They are hungry for knowledge – maybe it's about how to live debt free, start a new career or where to seek legal advice.

If you have content that inspires people to take action, you will stand out and drive revenue growth. So, a core principle of Pinterest marketing for business is to feed that hunger for knowledge. Remember no problem = no sales. Help people solve problems, and you can make more sales.

How to Get Started on Pinterest

I offer a free training course for people who want to leverage the power of Pinterest to drive more revenue growth. You will learn how to: 1) set up a free business account, 2) integrate the right tools so your content gets found by more buyers, 3) write your profile, 4) identify the right keywords for your business so you get found on top of the search engine ahead of your competition. Everything you need in an easy to use blueprint format that will guide you on how to get your business set up on Pinterest.

Unfortunately, without the right knowledge or roadmap to success, many people effort to use Pinterest, struggle, fail and quit too soon. Pinterest is a mixture of science, business savvy, and art. It is worth investing the time or resources to learn or get someone else to manage it for you.

In Summary:

Hundreds of millions of people are shopping on Pinterest every month, go where your buyers are. Many of them are your target audience.

If you fail to have a presence there, you leave sales on the table for your competitor.

Blogging is essential to your success.

Learn how to set up and manage your Pinterest account correctly or hire an agency like mine to do it.

———

Anna Bennett is the owner of White Glove Social Media and co-founder of True North Marketing. Her 30+ years of experience in retail operations and business coaching is the rock-solid foundation for her dynamic Pinterest marketing and training services. Anna is one of Pinterest's Business Elite Experts chosen by Pinterest themselves. She is the author of "Pinterest Marketing For Business Master Online Course" and "How To Become A Pinterest Account Manager" and has been featured in Forbes Magazine Investor's Business Daily, American Marketing Association, and several other publications. You can connect with Anna here https://www.whiteglovesocialmedia.com

CHAPTER 25

HOW TO USE COMMUNITY MARKETING AND SOCIAL MEDIA TO EARN LIFELONG BUSINESS

BY ANNEKE GODLEWSKI

Sharing Kindness and Gratitude through Community Marketing

For most professionals, clients only need them when they have a problem. There is something that the client can't get on their own; they are, in a way, forced to find help from an expert. Desperate parents want to legally adopt a baby they have grown to love, a working mother is struggling through recovering from surgery after being t-boned by a truck, a single father is anxious for joint custody of his child, a grieving son is fighting with his siblings over fulfilling mom's last wishes, an immigrant is wading through a maze of paperwork simply to work toward his American Dream.

Most clients would rather not have the problem they are facing; they don't want to need you, so, by extension, they have no reason to like you. This also means it is hard to gain their trust. In "real" life outside of the office, the general rule is that if you are a human who is likeable and honorable and who thinks about others instead of yourself, you will make friends and be a trustworthy companion.

What if that "general rule" was extended to professionals? What if you were an attorney who made a concerted effort to give back to your community by giving away bicycles, instead of putting money and effort into empty TV ads that ran every hour? What if you were a doctor who spent the 28-minute drive home chatting with the patient you treated two days prior, just to learn more about the cancer awareness 5k he mentioned his granddaughter was organizing so you could highlight it on your Facebook page?

Chances are, you will be portrayed as a professional who doesn't care more about his pocket than the client's problem and, by extension, the client will trust that the issue causing them to lose sleep at night is being handled in the best way possible, with no strings attached.

Handling a legal case, treating a patient, or securing investments for a client is no different than simply removing someone's fear/pain/worry through the methodical steps you take as an expert in your field. But how is a potential or first-time client to know that you are really are different than the other guys and that you really do care about the outcome of their case and not just the money to be made from it?

It is important to give potential or first-time clients (i.e. strangers) something to alleviate a bit of that anger/fear/worry/doubt/stress in their minds – well before you have a chance to prove firsthand that you are trustworthy – so that the potential client has no doubts when they pick up the phone to contact your office. On the same note, it is important to give your top referral sources proof they can share with others to show that you really are as awesome as they claim you to be.

But if talking about yourself is tacky and outdated, how do you provide that proof?

That's where Community Marketing comes in.

For this type of outreach to work, one must:

- Embrace the fact that you will not be talking about yourself.

- Believe that giving without expecting anything in return will yield faithful followers, referrals, repeat clients, and more business.

- Be willing to celebrate others, share it on social media, and encourage a ripple effect of good will that often comes when kindness is brought to light.

What is "Community Marketing"?

Efforts to help the community your business is a part of through programs specifically aimed at your target market can be done in a variety of heartfelt and attention-grabbing ways. Just a few examples of what firms all over the country have done include:

Bicycle giveaways - Giving bikes to children who have done something positive in the life of someone else makes for awesome stories and happy families.

Student of the Month contests - When kids hear that their hard work in the classroom or in the hallways doesn't go unnoticed by teachers, life paths can change.

Teacher Appreciation Videos - Tears of joy from simple :60 videos of kids telling the camera which life lessons will stick with them forever can be career-changing for an educator.

Videos for the Armed Forces - Inviting the loved ones of overseas soldiers and sailors into the office to make heartfelt videos at no cost is social media gold.

Bike Helmet Giveaways - Protect some noggins, team with an organization that focuses on traumatic brain injuries and give people something for free: the trifecta of news-worthiness.

5k Races as an Office - Group training, cool t-shirts, and goal-setting together for a big race are perfect reasons to involve your clients, too. (Bonus: a healthy staff could mean lower health insurance premiums!)

Biggest Loser Contests - Use health and wellness as a reason to reach out to doctors, grocery stores, gyms, and nutritionists for help getting the community off the couch and on your weight-loss team.

Nominate Your Favorite [INSERT TOPIC HERE] - Choose a topic that is near and dear to your company's heart. Are you an attorney fighting for the rights of the elderly? Ask people to nominate their favorite grandma. Car accident lawyer? Start a program highlighting amazing first responders.

Done right, Community Marketing campaigns give people permission to thank each other, and verbally and visually recognize the greatness in humanity.

A grinning young man riding a bicycle, despite being blind

As anyone who utilizes social media knows, powerful, meaningful imagery has the ability to swell the heart. Only a few are lucky enough to be there in person. What is the next best thing? It is experiencing that same joy through a photo, video, or live stream, along with captivating words to describe the essence of the joy that is occurring behind the lens.

When you highlight on social media your Community Marketing efforts, the joy becomes contagious. Shares, likes, engagement will follow and soon you will have a feed filled with gratitude, without speaking one word about yourself.

Community Marketing programs provide endless fodder for professionals' social media efforts. Photos, videos, and commentary give you something to discuss other than the often-dry industry discussion that the general public may not be able to relate to.

Here are just a few of the beautiful words written after Community Marketing social media posts:

"My heart is full. Congrats to Jalen Ballard, 15, who is top of his class at St. Francis de Sales School, despite being blind, and who works to help other blind kids by creating computer programs, Braille kids menus, beeping Easter egg hunts, and fishing derbies. I'm honored to be a part of a program that gave him a tandem bicycle, so he can feel the wind in his hair and have a little bit of hard-earned freedom. Ride on, my friend! Thank you to everyone who nominated and came out to Wersell's Bike Shop for the surprise, especially 13 ABC and all the administration from SFS. You are so appreciated!"

– The congratulatory Facebook post I wrote on one of my favorite bike giveaways that garnered 407 likes, 55 comments, and 29 shares in the small market of Toledo, Ohio

"When I nominated my granddaughter, Caydence, I never in my wildest dreams thought she would receive a bicycle let alone be the first recipient. Although Caydence was very camera shy, she truly enjoys her new bicycle and loves riding it. I cannot be more thankful for the phone call that changed my day on May 29, 2018. It was so awesome, and they even learned a little about our family that had nothing to do with receiving the bike. I would also like to give a big shout out to Wersell's bike shop and WTOL 11 CBS News for all being a part of this wonderful program. Caydence loves her bicycle and all the accessories that came with it. It's so funny to watch her ride with her sister in tow on her big wheel trying to keep up with her. I just wanted everyone who was involved in making this program happen how much of an impact it truly made on my family. Thank you all from the bottom of my heart for offering this to kids who make a difference in someone's life or in the community."

- Gail, bike giveaway nominator

"Let me start this extensive post with a little flashback from Brie, the mother of my son Isaiah's classmate, from June 4th: So, I chaperoned the field trip today, and I saw Isaiah with his class. Later in the day, both classes were playing on the playground. One of the kids, I think his name was Gavin, fell and hurt himself. Your son was there right away, helping his friend up, and stayed by him until he felt better. You are raising a really great kid, just thought you should know!'

Fast forward to this past Monday, when we received a message from Brie stating that she had entered Isaiah into a contest, which rewards children who have done something beyond the ordinary to help make a positive impact in someone's life with a new bicycle, and that he had won! Michelle and I were in awe of the fact that not only had Brie entered him into this contest, but that he had won. This afternoon, the family went to Wersell's Bike Shop on Central the bike shop to surprise Isaiah. We were met by Brie, as well as people from the business who sponsor the program. Needless to say, Isaiah and his brothers were very surprised. They had no idea what we were doing there, or what was about to happen. As I watched the whole thing unfold, I could not help but to be inspired by a few people.

First, I was inspired by Brie. She noticed that a young child had stopped what he was doing to go and help someone who was hurt. And then, she took it one step further and told his story to others. The fact that she recognized and shared this as a special act made me think of how often I see things like this, but just accept it as the norm. What I should be doing, and will try to do more frequently, is to recognize the positive actions of others.

Second, I was inspired by the program for rewarding those kids who step up to help others. I think too often in life, we as parents expect our kids to be the best people on the planet but are not quick to recognize the extraordinary in them. Instead, we focus on the negative, and try to make it a "learning experience". It was after we left the bike shop and were talking to the kids about what had happened and why, that I realized that a day like today could have an everlasting effect on the kids. But we were careful to not make it about the reward, but instead about the positive impact their actions could have. You never know how much even the smallest of gestures could mean to someone, or who is watching.

Third (and as is the case everyday), I was inspired by my wife Michelle. She is the driving force behind the way our boys live life, and how the treat others. I'd be foolish if I said it was the other way around. I'm proud to have her by my side, and more proud to see the way she is preparing the world for the 4 men we will release onto it in the near future. Without her, there is no way that I would be even a fraction of the Dad, or man, that I am today.

Finally, I was inspired by my son, Isaiah. The kid watched a boy from his school fall and get hurt and stopped what he was doing to help him. The fact that he was thoughtful enough to run over and help a boy that he wasn't even playing with says a lot about his character. To recognize at 7 years old that someone needed his help makes me confident that he will do great things in life. Too often I see opportunities to help someone, but never act on it. Hearing about Isaiah's actions has inspired me to try to do better by those people who I encounter every day.

I'd like to say Thank You to everyone involved in making this a special day for Isaiah. And also, if you see a child do something that you think has made a positive impact on someone's life, please share their story with others."

– A bike recipient's dad, Brad Wingate

————

Authenticity is Key

The most important aspect of Community Marketing is making sure that it is driven by a true passion to build relationships and show gratitude – both online and off. If you are not the type of professional who feels comfortable doing that type of hands-on, kindness-filled work, enlisting a member of your team can be the next best thing (and build morale at the same time!). But if the true authenticity is missing, it's pretty hard to fake it. The Community Marketing effort will come up flat and not genuine, not only defeating the purpose but quite possibly backfiring, so if your heart isn't fully in it, leave it be.

Giving without expecting anything in return will translate into amazing social media success when done right. And it will help you sleep easier at night, knowing you did your part to spread a little joy online and in your community.

When Anneke Godlewski started her legal marketing career over a decade ago, she never would have anticipated that it would morph into a movement of giving that has reached all over the country. Since 2006, Anneke's passion for people and for story-telling has led to the creation of programs that have garnered hundreds of media mentions, immeasurable brand awareness, stronger relationships with clients and the community, and of course, an increase in profits. Anneke now helps firms all over the U.S. identify how giving without expecting anything in return can boost morale and improve their bottom lines.

For more information on how developing your own custom Community Marketing program, call Anneke Godlewski at 419.283.5573, emailing her at anneke@themarketink.com, or visiting her website, themarketink.com.

CHAPTER 26

THE POWER OF NEWSJACKING: HOW TO GET NOTICED, BUILD RELATIONSHIPS, AND GROW YOUR BUSINESS

BY MITCH JACKSON

Newsjacking is one of the most powerful marketing and branding arrows in my business success quiver. Except for personal referrals from family, friends and other professionals around the world, nothing, and I mean nothing, has helped me more to build my top of mind awareness and influence than newsjacking. It's has helped me expand my brand from local to global, bring in million dollar cases, and get on stage before audiences of thousands.

Did I get your attention?

Good. Stick with me. I think you're going to find newsjacking very exciting!

The Master of Newsjacking

Marketing expert, David Meerman Scott (he wrote the foreword to my book), popularized the term "newsjacking" long ago. Over the years, it's grown to become such a powerful marketing tool that, in 2017, the Oxford Dictionary included newsjacking on the shortlist for Word of the Year. How cool is that!

So, what exactly is newsjacking? David defines the approach as follows:

> *"Newsjacking is the art and science of injecting your ideas into a breaking news story to generate tons of media coverage, get sales leads, and grow business."*

I believe and I know David agrees, that by adding social media into the newsjacking mix, you will amplify your newsjacking efforts and accelerate your results.

Regardless of who you are and what you do, there are many different ways to newsjack. Several stories that come to mind that I've newsjacked over the last several years include the following.

Examples

Bill Cosby: When Bill Cosby was arrested for allegedly putting drugs in drinks, I wrote a blog post, from the perspective of a father of a daughter at

UCLA and, a trial lawyer. I shared safety tips for college students to avoid something like this from happening to them. The post took off. Several other examples that come to mind include:

Paul Manafort indictment: "So You're Going To Be Indicted. What's Your Next Move?"

Philip Seymour Hoffman: "Can a Drug Dealer Be Held Civilly Liable and Criminally Responsible When His Actions Result in a Death?"

Amanda Knox: "What Will Happen Next in the Amanda Knox Murder Case?"

Justin Bieber: "Justin Bieber Arrested for DUI- What you should do if you're arrested."

Rebecca Sedwick: "How This California Law Firm Handles Bullying Cases"

New SCOTUS Law: "Why Today's SCOTUS Case Changed the Internet Forever."

Melania Trump: "What is Plagiarism? What are the legal ramifications?"

Ryan Lochte: "Why it's Important to Tell the Truth in Business and Life."

Oscar Pistorius "The Blade Runner" Murder Trial: This was a bit different. In real-time, I did an ongoing blog post sharing daily updates, from the perspective of a trial lawyer, about what was happening in the South Africa murder trial of Reeva Steenkamp.

Amanda Knox: I did the same thing in the Amanda Knox murder case that took place in Italy. I wanted to explain what was happening, what daily trial procedures meant, and how this trial in Italy was so different than how the case would have been tried in the United States.

New California Law on Sextortion: A year after writing a blog post on this new law (I believe the law was poorly written and needed some work), USA Today's Maria Punte was searching for an expert in California to discuss the topic when the Rob Kardashian/BlacChyna Instagram naked pictures story broke. She did a Google search, found my blog post from a year earlier, called me, and our interview was prominently displayed and shared with tens of thousands online.

Now I'm a lawyer so I usually, but not always, try to put a legal twist on my newsjacking efforts. Having said that, it doesn't matter who you are or what you do. There's almost always an effective way to newsjacking a breaking story that compliments your business or practice.

Tools

Some of these newsjacking efforts were done using tradition blog posts. Others started with a quick Periscope or Facebook live video. Most of my efforts, which were also repurposed on social media via tweets, videos, livestreams and podcasts (see my chapter on repurposing content to learn how to do this), resulted in interviews and my firm being mentioned and profiled across not only the country, but around the world too.

A related benefit to newsjacking is that when others share your posts or interview quotes, they usually link back to your original blog or social media posts. As such, you create valuable inbound links to your online properties. This is huge for brand recognition (we're all brands) and SEO purposes and over time and an excellent way to naturally increase your SEO relevancy with Google.

There's a bit more to doing all this correctly, so let's dive a bit deeper into the world of real-time marketing and newsjacking.

The Newsjacking Dance

When breaking news happens, reporters immediately go to work to discover the facts and report the news. It's usually easy for them to determine the basic facts behind an incident and the first paragraph in their story usually reports these facts.

What makes a story about a breaking news event interesting to others is the "why" behind the event. Often times, what separates one reporter's story from the others is that it shares a unique perspective, offered by an expert (you) as to why the breaking news story matters.

If you act quickly enough to breaking news by provide persuasive, interesting, and credible second-paragraph content, you may either be contacted by reporters for interviews or, your content on Twitter, LinkedIn, Facebook or your blog, may be shared in a viral nature around the globe. When this happens, your brand is elevated above other people in your industry and over time you can build top of mind awareness and perceived expertise.

Real time newsjacking can work for everyone. If you sell digital services, you can newsjack your unique take on the next update or new competitor (what's different, better or worse). If you're an exercise instructor, you can newsjack the latest working routine or add your unique spin to why a 75 year old marathon runner was able to run 26.2 miles (diet, training, new technology...). It doesn't matter if you're doing business B2B or B2C, a nonprofit, or professional like me. The opportunities to newsjack are endless.

Speed is Your Friend

You must learn to act quickly if you want success with newsjacking. When breaking news happens, reporters are looking for valuable input to their story right now. They need and want information immediately, not hours from now. You need to learn how to act quickly with your newsjacking efforts.

Here's I go about all this. Let's say I'm down at Strands Beach for a run. During a break I check my phone and see an alert about a breaking news story. If I can add value, in a positive and engaging fashion, I'll fire up Periscope of Facebook Live and immediately share my unique take or spin on the breaking news.

Because Periscope is connected to Twitter, in real time my live video is shared with tens of thousands of people. Because I've been doing this for a while, reporters monitor my Twitter feed and reach out for interviews. When I get in to the office, I usually have several phone messages, or a few emails or DMs on Twitter, requesting commentary on specific related issues or, for a general interview on the story I just newsjacked.

It's fast, pretty simple, and works very well.

In other instances, for example, the new Internet Sales Tax SCOTUS case I newsjacked a few months ago, I called the office and had my team reschedule my morning schedule. I knew this was an important case that would change online internet sales forever, and so I immediately reached out to a tax expert and scheduled a live video talk show to share our respective thoughts on the new law. This particular effort took a bit more time and energy than other newsjacking efforts but in the end, we had a live video show with thousands of live and recorded viewers (combined) who asked questions and shared out content. The entire morning was a big success! You can take a look here http://bit.ly/socialmediabook-tax

That's how I newsjack. It's a real-time dance. It happens fast. It connects you with the world. In one word, it's POWERFUL!

Be Thoughtful and Careful

Newsjacking can be a two-edged sword so be careful. I usually focus on high-profile local, national or international stories I can add my unique perspective to. Topics of interest to me are law, social media, business and tech.

I try to keep my newsjacking positive and always try to add value to the story. I don't use newsjacking to bash others and share a negative perspective to a breaking story. In my opinion, good newsjacking is all about adding value to a story.

In the legal arena, I avoid tragic traffic collisions and natural disasters. I shy away from these stories because no matter my good intent, the risk of looking like an ambulance chaser or late night (bad) lawyer advertisement is simply too great.

There are however, a few exceptions.

When Hurricanes Katrina and Matthew struck the US, I did write and share several blog posts, podcasts and live videos providing valuable information explaining what victims needed to know and do when dealing with insurance companies and handling property damage claims.

In these posts, I shared links to existing Bar Association publications such as, "Tricks of the Trade: How Insurance Companies Deny, Delay, Confuse and Refuse." At no time did I include the typical call to action such as, "call us if you've been harmed because of Hurricane Matthew." If fact, I went out of my way to let the reader know I don't practice law in their jurisdiction and simply wanted to make this good information available to them. Remember, you're trying to add value to the reader and not to immediately bringing in new business to your company or firm.

Here's a timesaving tip: Repurpose your prior newsjacking posts. Several years ago I newsjacked the Fyre Festival with a post and live video. If you recall, the Frye Festival was an exclusive festival and music event in the Bahamas using social and influencers. The entire event was a big scam and fraud. In fact, as I write the chapter, the promoter was recently sentenced to 6 years in prison and ordered to pay restitution of $26M.

My original newsjacking effort from a two years earlier was focused around a big live video show with 9 people concurrently on the screen at once. One of my guest was a lawyer who happened to be at the event. We had hundreds watch live and thousands watch the recorded show. The recorded version is here http://bit.ly/socialmediabook-fyrc

Fast forward to this week. I was watching Thursday Night Football when this story came across my phone: "Floyd Mayweather Jr. and DJ Khaled Charged with Cryptocurrency Fraud." The story was about these two celebrity influencers allegedly failing to disclose their relationships with brands that paid them to promote the cryptocurrency. Because I found this story interesting, I did the following.

During halftime, I pulled up my two-year old Fyre Festival blog post (which discussed influencer disclosure obligations) and used it to create a new post about the Mayweather and Khaled story. I spent about 20 minutes massaging the prior content into a unique new post and shared it on social. Within hours my newsjacking effort was picked up and shared by others around the world and my brand, as a lawyer familiar with influencer law, was highlighted just a bit more. The next day I had multiple interview requests when I got into the office.

Remember that the idea behind newsjacking is to add unique value to a story. My take on all of these stories wasn't about the basic facts of the original story. I shared a slightly "what if" or "Does this mean" type of next step thought, and opinion, relating to the story. Consumers and reporters like this. Do this, and everything else will fall into place.

Here's one final thought, or tip, I think you'll like: As you develop relationships with reporters, keep their email addresses in a list. I use MailChimp and also keep track of reporters in a private list on Twitter.

I build my list like this. After speaking with a reporter who I know I've helped, I'll ask the reporter if he or she would like me to reach out the next time I have thoughts on a related breaking story. Without exception they always say yes (they want all the help they can get).

When you do newsjack a breaking news story, immediately share the story or link with your list of reporters. I have my list tagged with a few different categories including business, technology, law, and sports. I make sure to only reach out to reporters who will benefit from my new take on a breaking story. I don't want to waste anyone's time and, I only want to add value to their efforts and eventual story.

How To Find Breaking News Stories

This is probably the question I get asked most often. The good news is that finding breaking stories to newsjack is, in my opinion, the easiest part of the entire process.

With television, radio, social media, and the Internet, we're constantly being exposed to breaking news stories. Almost every morning on my morning run down at the beach or drive into the office, I hear about a new story that I could newsjack if I had time.

What I've noticed is that over time, I've been able to develop a "newsjacking mindset" which gives me a heightened awareness as to what is a good newsjacking opportunity is. Give this a try and after a short period of time, the same thing will happen with you. I know because I've watch friends of mine pick up this technique and literally master newsjacking in a month or two.

Conclusion

The two most valuable assets we all have right now are time and attention. Newsjacking allows you to save journalists time by giving them access to a unique and valuable perspective that will help their story standout.

To learn more about the art of newsjacking, take advantage of the tools and resources offered by the master of newsjacking, David Meerman Scott, at https://DavidMeermanScott.com

CHAPTER 27

HOW TO USE VOICE MARKETING AND VOICE SEARCH

BY NANCY MYRLAND

What Is Voice Marketing?

Voice (devices and technology like Amazon Echo and Google Home) is experiencing a major surge in marketing and business development. The way your target audiences search for and learn about you is shifting rapidly. In this chapter, I will help you understand two significant trends in the voice arena.

The first, which I am talking about in this chapter, is the way you can begin using voice marketing to distinguish yourself from others while attracting more of the people you care about doing business with. You'll do this by using a relatively new medium that is finding its way into the lives of millions of homes and offices, and that is via the smart speaker.

The second, which is closely connected, but will not be covered in depth in this chapter, is the way all of us are shifting the way we search for data on the Internet. We are speaking longer-form verbal search queries into our devices when we are looking for information. We are using complete sentences, vs. typing a few words into our browser to conduct traditional searches. It is having a profound impact on how your clients and prospects find the information they need when they conduct a search on a specific topic.

I want you to spend some time learning about how to modify your website to respond to this change as you need to make some changes to be found by those who are conducting voice searches.

The Rise Of The Smart Speaker

Back to the first trend I mentioned. This trend that enables you to use voice marketing to attract clients is the rise of the smart speaker. These are hands-free, voice-controlled devices with built-in microphones and speakers that operate via voice recognition technology. They listen for your commands and act accordingly. They become smarter as they learn your habits and what you want and need to find. For flexibility, they can be connected to external speakers or headphones via Bluetooth or a standard 3.5 mm audio cable that will then deliver stereo sound.

These speakers hold tremendous opportunity for you to connect with those you care about. In a study by OC&C Strategy Consultants in December 2017, the top 4 uses for these smart speakers were to play music (97% US), ask about the weather and news (94% US), ask general questions (90% US), and set timers, alarms, and reminders (87% US). News and general questions are the areas where the opportunities lie for professionals like you to demonstrate your knowledge and expertise.

In the same study, OC&C Strategy Consultants estimated that 13% of US households and 10% of UK households had a smart speaker in December 2017, with an estimated 6 million homeowners ordering products through these devices in 2017, accounting for $2 billion in retail sales.

OC&C Strategy Consultants predicts that voice-based eCommerce will be the next major disruptive force in retail, estimating $40 billion will be spent through voice commerce by 2022 (in the US) and $5 billion (in the UK), representing 6% (US) and 3% (UK) of all online spend.

Not surprisingly, in the same study, OC&C found that 70% of voice-shopping purchases were made by buyers who knew precisely what they wanted to purchase, vs. browsing in a traditional online and offline world. They found that groceries and known items such as electronics and household goods were the most common categories purchased using voice commerce.

It appears we are beginning to look to these AI-driven devices to help automate our homes, as well as our personal and professional lives. They allow us to set timers, turn on TVs, book flights, find out when our next appointment is, turn on lights, start coffee makers, play music from Amazon, SiriusXM, iHeartRadio, Spotify, Pandora, and others, check our weather, listen to audiobooks, radio, and podcasts, listen to news and education via Flash Briefings (more on that in just a moment), text your brother, call your best friend, teach manners to your children, order groceries, preheat the oven, find out what time it is in Dubai, help visually-impaired people "see" what is in front of them, order office supplies, create a shopping list, order food from your favorite restaurant, reorder your pet food, track your calories, find your telephone, find out when your child has arrived home safely, and so much more.

Business or Consumer?

My description thus far might make voice assistants appear to be mostly consumer products-oriented, causing you to think that their functionality and use in professional services marketing is worlds away from becoming a reality. This couldn't be farther from the truth.

PSFK, a research and strategy firm, recently noted that 65% of people age 25 to 49 interact with a smart speaker at least once a day. eMarketer tells us that the number of adult smart speaker users will surpass that of wearable (think smart watches) users for the first time this year.

Knowing that news delivery, as well as answers to general questions, were among the top uses of smart devices, we only need to let our creative professional minds wander for a few minutes to realize that we have an opportunity in front of us. More importantly, we have an opportunity to be in front of our clients and prospects in a manner unheard of just a few years ago. We are in the early stages of adoption and use, which means an opportunity for you if you choose to hop on board with others who are doing the same.

What Do We Call These Devices?

As with any product or service in its early days, a variety of names are surfacing. What I will refer to as a smart speaker in this chapter, others might call screen-free devices, AI-assistants, voice-first devices, voice-assisted speakers, Alexa-enabled devices, voice-activated home devices, voice-search enabled digital assistants, and personal assistants.

The devices are being produced under the brand names Amazon Echo, Spot, Dot, and Show, Google Home, Mini, and Max, Apple HomePod, the new Facebook Portal, and via apps on Android and iOS that connect to and perform the same functions as the device you own. By the time you read this, that landscape will certainly have changed.

The voice assistants you interact with on these devices are Alexa from Amazon, Assistant from Google, Siri from Apple, Cortana from Microsoft, and Bixby from Samsung.

Enter The Flash Briefing

In this busy, technology-driven world, where human beings have a need for efficiency and life-long learning, we have met and brought devices into our homes and offices that allow us to be entertained and informed at a moment's notice. They even allow us to have conversations.

These conversational platforms are having a significant impact on how we communicate with each other. Gartner's Top 10 Strategic Technology Trends for 2018 predicts that conversational platforms will drive the next big paradigm shift in how humans interact with the digital world.

I use voice search daily on mobile via the Google Assistant but have found Amazon's Alexa a contender in my education and marketing toolbox lately.

Earlier today I asked Alexa to play my Flash Briefing, which is a series of short audio broadcasts that deliver news and information I have chosen to subscribe to via the Amazon Alexa app on my phone. I was able to listen to the latest social media updates, become more educated in SEO and other marketing topics, learn what is in the news in Indianapolis and around the world, listen to a brief bible verse, and more, including re-listening to the latest episode of my own Legal Marketing Minutes broadcast just to make sure I sounded okay.

This is the opportunity I want you to take advantage of. Similar to a podcast, where you are invited into a private, coveted space, the ears of your potential clients, delivering content via audio and smart speakers helps to establish a close, trusted relationship with them.

I don't know if your prospects are currently searching for your specific type of services via their smart speaker. What I do know is that they are looking to their AI devices more and more for news and information. This is where the marketing opportunity lies. Why can't you be one of their sources of news? Even if this is merely a gateway to your knowledge and services, it could serve as a powerful contender in your marketing toolbox.

Imagine delivering your knowledge, observations, concerns, and general advice to anyone searching for your topic at a moment's notice even when you aren't physically present. This is the strength of most social and digital media marketing and content that has been strategically created. It is doing your job for you even when you aren't there. It takes the sales out of prospecting, rainmaking, advertising, and promotion because it is there when the client or prospect is ready. You don't have to be present, at least not physically.

How To Start Your Flash Briefing

Spend a few minutes thinking of topics you might like to discuss with your clients and prospects that would be interesting and educational to them. Don't spend too much time on it, and don't expect it to be New York Times Best Seller quality because you will never get started. You've heard of analysis paralysis? Don't be guilty of that because you will miss this opportunity.

Think of a name you might want to call your Flash briefing. Make sure it speaks to your target audience. Mine is called Legal Marketing Minutes. My tagline is Because Your Time Is Valuable.

Once you have the topics and title, you can either go directly to Amazon to register as an Amazon Developer, or you can use the service I use that acts as the host and delivery mechanism to perform this function for me, thus saving me time on an ongoing basis. The service is called SoundUp Now. Their website will walk you through the process of creating your developer's account with Alexa and will also be your one-stop shop for uploading your Flash Briefing. It is currently $14.99 a month (or $99/year), which I find well worth it to help save time and resources. I invite you to use my code: https://soundupnow.com/ref/NancyMyrland/.

Once you have your topics and your account established, you need to record your Flash Briefings. Your episodes can be up to 10 minutes, although I would suggest making them much shorter than that. If you are reporting on news in your practice area, you might consider 2-4 minutes. If you are going into more detail about a particular topic that you think will be interesting and that needs a little deeper dive to explain, you can add a few minutes. There is no one right way to do this at this point.

As I've written about and advised many clients over the years, once you create content you have to "market your marketing." You have to let people know what you've created, where you've created it, and why they might want to listen to it.

I also know that these are early days for Alexa Flash Briefings, meaning the listener numbers still need to catch up with my enthusiasm for creating them, so I repurpose by audio recordings by converting them into waveform videos that I then share on my YouTube channel, LinkedIn, IGTV (Instagram TV), my Facebook Page, in my social media for professionals group on Facebook, on Twitter, and shorter versions on Instagram. Always remember that we need to meet people where they are, not where we wish they were. It is our job to let people know what we do. To create these waveform videos, I use Headliner, which can be found at https://make.headliner.app. It is a great app that will also close caption your videos, but I do find I have to clean them up quite a bit. I can also download that closed caption transcript to turn it into a blog post, quotes, or any written content I'd like. Headliner is free for now, so I recommend you try it soon.

Bottom Line

It is our responsibility to provide the services our clients need to improve their lives and their businesses in a manner they appreciate and find useful.

These smart speakers are changing how we do business, both as consumers of goods and services and as service providers. It is wise to stay aware and on top of this trend to be prepared for the marketing and cultural shifts that are taking place.

I recommend taking advantage of this opportunity to use voice marketing to make a lasting impression on our clients and prospects as soon as possible as all signs point to voice continuing to grow as a way to accelerate the know, like, and trust factors they need, want and deserve.

Nancy Myrland is a Marketing, Business Development, Content, Social and Digital Media Speaker, Trainer and Advisor to lawyers, legal marketers and law firms, specializing in helping you grow your firm and your practice through the understanding, creation, and integration of marketing and strategic plans with content, social and digital media. You can connect with Nancy here http://www.myrlandmarketing.com

CHAPTER 28

USING SEO TO BUILD YOUR BUSINESS

BY SETH PRICE

Search Engine Optimization (SEO) is a mystery to many looking to build their brand and business online. SEO is an attempt to work within the Google algorithm to have your site shown, or rank, above other sites on a user's Search Engine Results Page (SERP). Google, at its core, attempts to give searchers the best user experience. In doing so, it wants to fill a user's SERP with the most relevant answers to questions that are asked.

SEO is the art of creating webpages that Google recognizes as the authoritative answer to the questions users are asking. Once Google views a site as authoritative, it will show that site as a top result, which will lead to increased visibility in search results and more clicks, calls, and revenue. Just like there is often a pecking order of lawyers in an industry in the world, Google is trying to figure out in its digital world who holds the most authority in an industry and, therefore, whose site should appear first.

Historically practices such as keyword stuffing and link spamming would result in highly ranked pages. Google has become more sophisticated and the ability to trick or game the system is drastically reduced. Today, law firms need to utilize strategies to build their authority online and show Google they are an authoritative player in the digital sphere.

SEO's Four Fundamentals

The art of SEO has become much more difficult and harder to accomplish over the years for two main reasons. First, the Google algorithm is becoming increasingly sophisticated and penalizes anyone who takes SEO shortcuts. Second, Google – in its hunt to raise revenue and help ensure higher stock prices – shows more ads before organic results than ever before.

In local search, the organic search results can generally be seen after the ads in two distinct areas. The first area is what is called the "three-pack." This is the section following the map showing the top three local results and their office locations. Because the paid search results at the top pushes everything down including the map, it is necessary and more important than ever before to have a business's site show in the three-pack or directly beneath in the top organic search results.

If a website is not showing on the first page of a SERP, there are four fundamental areas that, if effectively utilized, can move the needle and push a site to the top – content, links, technical, and local.

Content

As a lawyer and business owner, it is imperative to be able to demonstrate to Google your authority through the written word. Google is extremely sophisticated in its ability to decipher the difference between high- and low-quality content. Publicly available information on the Google algorithm and its patents make it abundantly clear that Google has focused on understanding semantics and how language is written to determine the level of sophistication in writing. For example, Google's algorithm can decipher international or non-native language from native language in a given location. It can determine the grade level of writing.

A good content strategy focuses on creating webpages that include informative answers to questions users are searching for based on a lawyer or business owner's practice. That content must also include an appropriate level of keywords that does not spam the page but tells Google the webpage's focus. A keyword can either be what is known as short-tail or long-tail, and in local search would typically include the location a business is targeting plus its practice area.

For example, a short-tail keyword could be "Maryland car accident lawyer" and a long-tail keyword could be "filing a car accident claim in Maryland." Each of these key terms would be the focus of their own webpage with that keyword and variants mentioned a few times and high-quality relevant content written throughout. While traditionally short-tail keywords were more likely searched, now with the serge of voice search, users are searching in Google with sentences and questions, raising the importance of optimizing and ranking for long-tail key terms as well.

It is good SEO practice to continuously add new content to a site based on different practice areas and locations within which a business operates. It is important to note, however, that Google recognizes when the same exact content is duplicated – or used across various webpages – and penalizes a site for this. Unique, informative, and sophisticated content that appropriately utilizes key terms is crucial when building webpages.

Knowing the importance that Google places on content, a business can and should leverage its own experts and focus on high-quality, substantive written webpages that utilize specific keywords to demonstrate to Google that it is an authority on the matter and answers the questions Google's users are asking.

Links

Links are an important contributing factor to a webpage's ranking. Links indicate to Google a site's trustworthiness, sophistication of content, and ability to best answer a user's search query. When authoritative sites endorse another website via a backlink, Google understands that the webpage being linked to is trusted as a reliable source from an expert in the industry. As the number of sites endorsing a website via backlinks increases, Google attributes greater authority to the site resulting in higher rankings and greater visibility on the SERP.

If Google had its druthers, it would not have to rely upon links at all as links can be easily manipulated and used to game the system. Over the years, Google has cracked down on methods that trick the system by penalizing those who use shortcuts, and instead encourages and enforces the use of white-hat techniques. These techniques allow Google to see votes in the form of link equity to determine which site is the leading authority for a given search query.

Through demonstrating offline gravitas online with inbound links, a law firm is able to show Google that its site deserves to be placed higher up in the search rankings leading to greater traffic, conversions, and ultimately increased revenue.

Technical

Just as Google wants to show sites that provide the best answer to a user's search query, Google also places value on sites that are coded properly. Proper coding matters to Google as it creates a better user experience. For example, a site that loads quickly and works across all digital platforms – computers, phones, and tablets of all kinds – is important. Given that over 50% of Google searches come from mobile users, a lawyer who only creates a desktop version of their site is missing out on over half of their potential customer base.

Google also rewards websites that signal exactly what the pages provide – for example, title tags and meta descriptions. Title tags and metas are nothing new, but those fundamentals should not be ignored and should be leveraged to a business's advantage. The law firm that uses a title tag to list its firm or company name is squandering an invaluable piece of digital real estate. Instead of a firm name, which Google already knows by crawling the site, a title tag should show Google specific information it needs to know about a given webpage. With this, a lawyer can help the Google bots identify precisely what information is on a page, which Google will then match to the relevant questions being searched.

Moreover, by using schema markup, a site can give important data to Google through the code including locations, reviews, and other identifying information. This data is useful to Google and further helps search results.

Finally, proper coding together with high-quality content can lead to rich snippets. Rich snippets are the information Google provides in a boxed outline within the SERP that directly answers a searcher's question. Google prefers to provide rich snippets as it gives the user an answer without the person needing to leave the page. As Google moves more into the arena of wanting people to stay on its pages, marking a site and having web content shown within a rich snippet as the authoritative answer on Google's SERP is, right now, as good as it gets.

Local

The Google My Business interface as we know it has morphed several times over the years. Today, the algorithm combines the Google My Business listing with local search factors including map consistency, local links, and local content. These factors, when appropriately done, demonstrate to Google that a webpage has the best answer for somebody in the location they are searching.

Local search results allow a growing smaller-scale law firm to compete even in a highly competitive market within their immediate area. Google is giving smaller players an opportunity by opting to show their website high on the SERP when their location is closer to a searcher than perhaps a larger more authoritative player.

Within the local Google My Business arena — name, address, and phone number otherwise known as a citation or NAP – consistency is extremely important. In addition, reviews, while currently not impacting rankings, also allow users to assess a law firm's trustworthiness when considering options in the three-pack.

Paid Search

While not a part of the four fundamentals, Google AdWords and Pay Per Click should not be ignored. Paid ads are the first search results on a Google SERP and are extremely powerful. For a lawyer, Pay Per Click should be viewed as a spigot that could be turned off and on, allowing the opportunity to expand or contract advertising at a moment's notice.

Google AdWords has its advantages and disadvantages. It can be an expensive option, where prices continue to soar as more players enter the market. The flip-side to this, however, is that a budget can be capped and a law firm can run ads to determine if users in a specific area are looking for specific lawyers or businesses.

As AdWords produce revenue for Google, they will likely continue to merge with organic search results. For example, ads now sometimes appear in the three-pack. For certain industries such as locksmiths or home improvement, Google has turned those areas in some markets completely pay-to-play. Whether this will happen in the legal sector remains to be seen and given some of the ethical differentiators in the legal space, it is unlikely. Even so, paid search can and should be tested by a business to determine whether a return on investment is possible.

There is another positive to paid search. Search Engine Optimization is an arduous process that can take time. When a site is first launched, it is essentially placed in Google's sandbox and generally will not be listed as a featured search until Google indexes the site and determines it is providing quality content and a good user experience. This waiting period can be frustrating, and Pay Per Click can be used to show a site on the SERP before Google does so organically.

With paid search taking up room at the top, there is simply less and less real estate for organic search results and more distractions in ads that very often look like organic results themselves. However, given that Google AdWords constantly increases in price, until Google eliminates organic search results, obtaining high rankings organically remains not just enviable but potentially more lucrative, allowing for a better long-term return on investment.

SEO is an Art

The true art of SEO takes place when the four elements – content, links, technical, and local — are tied together and utilized effectively. When a law firm participates in that process by helping to produce content and by giving back to the community – in turn allowing for link building, that is when magic happens.

The Google algorithm is always changing and will continue to evolve. What is a homerun one day can fail the next. Google's goal, however, has remained the same from the start: To provide a searcher with the best possible answer to their question. Lawyers have an opportunity to provide Google with that information, in turn, building their businesses' online presence. By creating a technically sound site with carefully cultivated content, generating authoritative inbound links, and building a local presence, a business is practicing the highest form of SEO which can yield tremendous returns on investment.

———

Seth Price, Managing Partner and co-founder of Price Benowitz LLP, is an accomplished attorney and transformational leader. Mr. Price links authoritative insights in law and business to strategic growth planning, resulting in the acquisition of highly talented and driven attorneys who are committed to the firm's client-centered philosophy and providing the best possible customer service. Mr. Price is also the founder and CEO of BluShark Digital, LLC, a marketing agency that provides digital marketing solutions to law firms. BluShark Digital helps law firms build a healthy web presence with a multi-pronged strategy tailored to the size and needs of the firm. More here https://blusharkdigital.com

CHAPTER 29

USER GENERATED CONTENT (UGC)
FOR BUSINESS OWNERS

BY TYLER ANDERSON

As a proud father of three beautiful children (ages, 8, 7, and 5) we are smack dab in the middle of school activities, performances, and many memorable events. As an entrepreneur, I'm blessed to be present for many of these moments. As a social media professional, of course, I want to capture as many of these magical moments as possible on camera.

One of these special moments was last winter right before Christmas break. My youngest son, Crosby, who was in pre-school had his winter performance. This event is the kind of performance where a bunch of 4-year-olds sing songs, play cute instruments and do simple choreographed dances. You know, all the adorable things you'd expect from 4-year-olds.

I always arrive early to these types of events so I can get a front row spot to capture the best photos and videos. For this particular event, I got there really early; I'm talking about an hour early. To the point where nobody else was even there. So what did I do? I did what every other social media marketer would do. I entertained myself on Instagram.

I was doing my usual Instagram check, a quick swipe up as I scroll through my news feed, liking and commenting on various items. Then I jumped back to the top of the feed to check out my friends' Instagram Stories.

One of the people I follow on Instagram is a guy named Field Yates. I follow Field because he and I share a love for fantasy football. Field also just so happens to work at ESPN as a football analyst.

On this particular morning, Field posted an Instagram Story where he was talking about working out of ESPN headquarters that day and carrying his laptop and other gear around in his new Nomatic backpack. His story was a simple single-frame story that featured a picture of the backpack. Field also tagged the brand Nomatic in this particular post.

At that moment, I had never heard of Nomatic backpacks. However, going through my head was something along the lines of, "Hmm. What's this? Field's a trendy and fashionable guy. This backpack must be cool."

So I did the natural next action. I clicked on the brand name that Field tagged in his post, and that took me over to Nomatic's own Instagram profile. I browsed around some of their recent Instagram posts, most of which featured this awesome backpack. It had modern compartments for almost anything an entrepreneur would carry. Individual spaces for your laptop, iPad, smartphone, portable chargers, keyboard, cables, keys, wallet, sunglasses, and more. You name it, it had it.

My curiosity, of course, led me to their website where they had a brief video explaining what the backpack was in detail and how it was one of the most popular Kickstarter campaigns. So that morning, right from my smartphone, I purchased myself an early Christmas present, I bought a $200 Nomatic backpack. Literally, in a total span of less than 7-minutes on my smartphone, I went from being first introduced to the Nomatic brand from Field's Instagram Story to purchasing their product. This story, my friends, is the perfect example of the impact of user-generated content.

What Is User-Generated Content (UGC)?

User-generated content is content created about your product or service by other people. These people could be your customers, potential customers, or even your employees. As for the content, it could be photos they share on Facebook or Instagram. It could be online reviews they share to sites like Google, Yelp, or Facebook. It could be videos they upload to platforms like YouTube. It could even be posts they share on their personal blog or third-party websites.

The type of content created is endless and will only continue to evolve. Just a few years ago, the Stories format wasn't even a thing. In 2019, Facebook is expecting people to share more content on platforms like Facebook and Instagram Stories than in traditional News Feed sharing. So we can only expect to see more UGC about brands and businesses in the Stories format.

Why Should You Care About UGC?

While there are many reasons UGC is impactful, I'm going to provide you with three reasons why getting your customers to create UGC should be a priority for your business.

1.   Influence - According to a survey by Wyng in 2016, 85% of web users find visual UGC more influential than brand content. Let's think back to my story about Nomatic backpacks. Would I have been influenced by their Instagram Story to make that purchase? First of all, I would never have been served a story unless they did so via an advertisement since I was completely unaware of the brand. It was my friend Field who influenced me. I have a perception that Field knows his stuff when it comes to cool products and services, so when he talked about Nomatic backpacks, he had my attention.

2.   Trust - UGC is more trustworthy than brand content. Be honest, when you go to a dentist's website, and they have some claim along the lines of "Rated #1

Dentist in [insert any city in the world]," do you believe it? If you do, you're in the minority. Only 16% of Americans trust information on a company website according to a Kelton Research survey. However, when someone else talks about a product or service we tend to take their experience as a credible resource. We trust it. Think about your last purchase on Amazon? I'm willing to bet the product had many reviews and probably had no fewer than 4-stars. That's what crazy; it's not just our friends and family we trust, we trust UGC from complete strangers too.

3.   Affects purchasing decisions - Many will argue that it's only millennials that are impacted by UGC across social media because they've grown up with it. That is true according to the Kelton Research survey, UGC influences 84% of millennials in purchasing decisions. But it's not just millennials, that same survey found that UGC influences 70% of baby boomers in buying decisions too. It's relatively simple, UGC impacts purchasing decisions because it's more trustworthy and influential than the brand content.

How To Get Your Customers To Create UGC

Newsflash, there is no secret sauce or magic potion here. You need to ask for it. You must be creative and think of ways you can get your customers or clients to share content about your business. Remember, when they share content across their social media, those are subtle recommendations for your product or service. Recently, I came across two different professional service type businesses that subtly had calls-to-action to get their customers to create UGC.

4S Pediatric Dentistry - This pediatric dentist had a sign at the front desk encouraging people to "check-in" and share their experience on Facebook. If you did, you'd receive a special prize. What kid doesn't want a special prize? Of course, I was curious, so I checked in. That special prize was a stainless steel water bottle (talk about a cool prize). The water bottle was branded 4S Pediatric Dentistry, so now they have me being a walking billboard for their business too.

This example provided three instances where I created UGC on behalf of the brand. First, my actual check-in on Facebook. That went out on my personal Facebook Newsfeed. Second, after I checked in, Facebook asked me to write a review of the pediatric dentist. Third, I'm now a walking billboard carrying around this 4S Pediatric Dentistry water bottle at the children's soccer fields every weekend. I should mention, there are plenty of other parents with kids on those soccer fields. Me carrying around a water bottle with their branding, well, that's just more social proof for them.

Cabrillo Pet Clinic - This is a pet hospital/boarding facility. Recently my family was going out of town on an 8-day vacation. At the last minute, our dog sitter had to cancel on us. We had no other option than to drop our beloved yellow Labrador retriever off at our veterinarian/boarding facility. This crushed me. However, when I checked her in, I was going through the waiver, you know, the one where I sign my dog's life away and protects the boarding facility from any wrongdoing. The last question on their waiver was a release for me to approve taking pictures/videos of my dog and sharing them on Facebook and Instagram. They also had their social media handles so I could follow and see what my dog was up to while I was away on vacation. Of course, I agreed to this. But it didn't stop there. What was I doing while on vacation? I was sharing the photos of my dog that the boarding facility was posting on their social media. Again, this is me subtly recommending to my family, friends, and followers that, "hey, if you need a boarding facility in San Diego for your beloved pet, I use this one." Again, it's more trustworthy, and it has influence. The boarding facility created original content prompting me to create UGC for them.

I cannot reiterate enough that you must ask your customers/clients to create UGC. Here are some other idea starters:

- Email newsletters
- Social media updates
- Contests/promotions
- Window clings
- Paper "tents" or table tops
- Signage on shelves
- Packaging
- Receipts
- Menus of products/services
- Posters/flyers
- Stationary
- Display screens
- Chalkboards
- USE YOUR CREATIVITY

Power Your Marketing With UGC

Getting your customers/clients to share UGC is already a win in itself. However, there is one additional topic we should discuss before we wrap up: the power of leveraging UGC to amplify your marketing efforts.

Benefits of leveraging UGC

1.   Expands your marketing - If you're a small business, odds are the employee or associate managing your social media also has a bunch of other responsibilities. With a proper UGC strategy in place, you get a team creating content on your behalf and distributing it in their news feeds, in stories, via reviews and more. Just think about the benefit of Facebook alone. It's widely publicized that brands are seeing their organic reach on Facebook dwindle. Well, individual profiles are not impacted as negatively as businesses when it comes to organic reach. If you can get others creating UGC on behalf of your business, you can help drive marketing initiatives without hiring additional staff.

2.   Solves the content problem - Some of these people creating content on your

behalf are excellent content creators. If you identify them, you can reach out to them and ask to repurpose their content and share it on your channels. Sharing their content frees up the time from your small team as they don't have to spend as much time to on creating content. Additionally, the content created by your customers is more authentic and trustworthy. Just be sure you get legal permission if you're going to use someone else's photo as your own. Merely giving them attribution is not enough. Of course, you should always give credit to recognize the creator, encourage more UGC, and identify the content as UGC and not branded content (which may be perceived as less trustworthy). Plus, when you use UGC on your business profiles, it generally gets higher engagement than brand content. There are some tools out there that can help streamline the process to obtain UGC legally. In full transparency, I'm the co-founder of one of them, Tack. You can find it at foundontack.com.

Where To Repurpose UGC?

Throughout your marketing and sales initiatives, there are many opportunities to incorporate UGC. However, I cannot reiterate enough, you must get legal permission. Do not just steal your customers content and use it as your own. Here are some idea starters:

- Social Media posts
- Social ads
- Website
- Digital displays
- Blog posts
- Email newsletters
- Sales presentations
- Offline marketing materials
- Menus
- Printed collateral
- Packaging
- USE YOUR CREATIVITY

It's Your Turn

I hope you've seen the benefits and impact that a UGC strategy can have for your professional services business. If you take one thing away from this chapter, please remember the importance of finding creative ways to get your customers and clients to share the positive experiences they have in doing business with you. People trust people more than they do businesses. If you have a solid UGC strategy in place, it can bring the marketing of your business to a whole new level.

Tyler Anderson is the Founder/CEO at Casual Fridays (Social Media Agency) and Tack (Social Media SaaS). He's the Executive Producer of Social Media Day San Diego and hosts the Social Media Social Hour, a top ranked social media marketing podcast. Connect with Tyler at https://CasualFridays.com

CHAPTER 30

13 WAYS PROFESSIONALS AND BUSINESS OWNERS CAN SAVE TIME BY REPURPOSING CONTENT ON SOCIAL MEDIA

BY MITCH JACKSON

Social media is all about sharing good content, helping others and building relationships. Results like building a well-known brand resulting in new clients and income, come from engaging, caring and providing value.

My general rule is that only 20% of my posts on the various platforms are about my firm or me. The other 80% are focused on sharing valuable tips, helping others, and curating good third party content that I believe will be useful to my audience.

Regardless of what kind of posts I'm publishing, I always try to share part or all of my content on as many relevant platforms as possible. This allows me to get the most amount of exposure in the least amount of time. If you're like me, protecting my valuable time is always an important goal.

Several Initial Thoughts

Before we get started, remember that in today's digital world, we're all media companies. Having a digital presence is critically important. Producing, sharing useful content, and engaging with others is mandatory to build your brand and long-term success.

It's also important to understand and appreciate the fact that while content is king, context and personality are everything. Each platform is different (some more than others), so care must be taken to post and share the right way to each platform.

Use the approaches shared in this book to help you create helpful and engaging content. Feel free to duplicate the process I share below to save time and expand your sphere of influence by repurposing quality content.

Step #1: Website and Blog

Share personal and professional news and updates in a properly written blog post. Use effective headings and appropriate keywords. Use a story format and write in your own voice. Try to avoid professional and industry-specific jargon if possible. Make the post interesting and easy to read. Increase interaction by always including a picture, graphic or video.

If you're writing your blog posts like all the other professionals out there, then you're probably doing things wrong. Be yourself and unique. Share your art. Use the communication tips in this book to stand out, make your point, and get people to take action.

If you don't have a website or blog, then get this done. This needs to be a high priority. Everyone is going mobile (smartphones and tablets) so make sure your site is mobile responsive (no exceptions). For more tips and details, see Thomas Wallin's chapter on websites and chapters by Chris Brogan and Nick Rishwain on blogging.

Step #2: Twitter

Share the catchy caption or heading of your blog post, together with a short descriptive sentence on Twitter. Include a link back to your original blog post. Use one or more relevant hashtags.

Pictures attract attention and create more engagement. As such, add the image you used in your blog post to your tweet. If you don't have a picture, use one of the free or paid online services to grab an image that relates to your story (I like Fotolia/Adobe).

One of my favorite ways to create a picture or video with my tweet is to capture a picture or clip of a video from my blog post using my computer shortcut (Shift-Command-4) or QuickTimePlayer on a Mac, use "Jing" or SnagIt by TechSmith. When using these techniques, always respect copyright law.

While you're thinking about Twitter, take your blog post and break it down into 5 to 10 240 word "teasers" highlighting key points and topics contained within your blog. Each snapshot or tweet is worded in its own unique and eye-catching way. I use Word or a Google Doc and keep a list of these mini-snapshot tweets for future use.

Sit down at night or early in the morning and use AgoraPulse, Hootsuite or Buffer (I prefer AgoraPulse because it offers more options and, I'm also a brand ambassador for the company) to schedule these additional tweets once or twice a day, over the next 5-30 days. If you're short on time, you can use the "auto-schedule or queue" function to let the service scheduled tweets. Link each tweet back to your original blog post. If you want to use AgoraPulse like I do, my link is http://bit.ly/socialmediabook-agora

Instead of doing written tweets, you can shoot a quick video about your blog post using the Twitter app (Twitter Live). In most cases, a combination of the above is the best way to get your message heard by the largest audience possible.

Twitter Live (also see Periscope below)

This live video component of Twitter allows you to hop on a live video and share (talk about) your original website blog post with your Twitter followers. Make sure to engage with your audience in the comments and share how your post will help them or solve a problem. Consistency is vital with live video, and over time you'll build an audience who will share your livestreams with their audience on Twitter. See Nancy Myrland's chapter on Twitter and Jennifer Quinn's chapter on live video to help you use these platforms the right way.

Step #3: Linkedin

Take one or more of the short content teasers that you have listed in your Word document and share them on Linkedin, linking back to your blog post. I usually do this in the above step by telling AgoraPulse to send out the tweets I schedule to both Twitter and Linkedin. AgoraPulse allows you to do this and is a great time saver.

In a fashion similar to Twitter Live, Linkedin video is another good way to share your blog post and stir interest on the LinkedIn platform. Jump on over to Chris Hargreaves' chapter on Linkedin to learn more.

Step #4: Facebook

Again, I take one or more of the tweets about my blog post listed in my Word or Google document and re-purpose the language for Facebook. Unlike Twitter, Facebook posts can be longer, so I usually add a bit more information in Word before posting on Facebook with the link back to my original blog post.

Images are powerful, attention-grabbing magnets on Facebook and will result in more interaction, shares, and comments. Because of this, and using the same approach that you did with Twitter, make sure to include an image with your post.

I have a personal and several business Facebook profiles, pages and groups, and depending on the nature of the content; I post to each once or twice a day. The key is to always think about how you can repurpose content more than once. Experts Stephanie Liu Azriel Ratz share outstanding Facebook use and advertising tips in the book.

Facebook Live– Jump on Facebook live and share your new post. Talk about some aspect of the content that you may not have shared in the post (your story and motivation behind why you wrote the post). Let viewers know they can click the link to your website to read the entire post. Again, use the live video and communication techniques shared in other chapters in this book to make the most of your livestreaming efforts.

Step #5: Pinterest

Take a look at Pinterest and see if there's a way you can embrace this platform when repurposing content. Try uploading the picture or screenshot relating to your blog post and add it to one or more of your Pinterest Boards.

After using the content in your Word document to complete the description in Pinterest, make sure to add 3-4 relevant hashtags at the end and, also include your blog post link in the source link box. This way, when someone clicks on the picture, he or she will be taken to your blog post or website. Learn more by taking a close look at Anna Bennett's chapter on Pinterest in the book.

Step #6: YouTube

If your original content included video, upload the video to YouTube and shared part of your description with a link back to your original blog post. If your original material didn't include video, think about creating a short video about your post and upload to YouTube linking back to the original content. Roberto Blake shares good YouTube tips in the chapter he was kind enough to contribute to this book.

Use the Youtube transcription service, or a third-party service like Rev, to create a written transcript of your video. Use the transcript to create a blog post, increase your SEO, and also comply with ADA needs (see Haben Girma's chapter).

Using almost any video editing software, it's easy to rip (separate) the audio from the video. When you do this, you can then create an audio post or podcast from your original video.

Youtube Live– Using the same approach as you might use with Twitter or Facebook Live or Periscope, jump on Youtube Live and create related content. Take advantage of this video feature and re-purpose content from other platforms.

Step #7: SlideShare

This often overlooked platform is well respected and used successfully by marking pros around the globe. I neglected this service for far too long.

Once I decided to get active on SlideShare, I repurposed a traditional PowerPoint on negotiation. Within the first 24 hours, it had more than 900 views and trended on Twitter and SlideShare. The response was so good that this presentation was then profiled on the SlideShare homepage. Two days later, we're over 2,000 views. Today this repurposed content is up to 38,000 views.

You can and should do the same thing. Take the blog post we've been talking about and break it down to a 10-15 slide presentation. Upload it to SlideShare and then include links back to your original blog post.

Step #8: Podcasts

Podcasts are very popular because mobile technology now allows us to easily listen to podcasts anytime and anyplace. Expert Nicole Abboud shared a great podcast chapter in the book that will get you up and running in no time.

Take your blog post and turn the content into a short 10-20 minute podcast. Start with a snappy and attention grabbing intro and then share your information using your own voice. Use your post as an outline and just share your message from your heart. Close with a call to action referring your website or blog.

Note, once my podcasts are completed and uploaded, I use the exact same techniques I'm sharing in this chapter to distribute the podcast to all of my other platforms. The heading and short description are slightly modified to better fit the platform I'm repurposing on. My podcast links are also shared on the original blog post or website page, just in case, a visitor would rather listen to the audio version instead of reading the blog post.

Step #9: BlueJeans, BeLive, and Similar Live Video Services

These and many other traditional and live video platforms allow you to share videos and even have your own social media television show. For me, live video platforms like BlueJeans have connected me with interesting and well-known people from all around the world. Using live video, I've been on shows with Katie Couric, Anderson Cooper, and one episode even ended up on TMZ. How cool is that!

When it comes to repurposing content, I'll sometimes use these services to pre and post promote and discuss the original blog post. I bring on guests related to the original topic and interview them. These services allow your audience from around the world to engage in live chat, ask questions, and even join you via live video to meet your guest and ask questions. See Jennifer Quinn's chapter on live video to get the best results possible with live video.

Step #10: Instagram and Snapchat

Take the screenshot image of the blog post and share it on Instagram with a reference back to your website or blog. I usually edit my Instagram profile and share the updated link there. Because you can't post a live hyperlink in the Instagram stream, simply share the link in your profile and let viewers know they can find it there.

If you're feely sassy, hop on over to Twitter and then share a tweet letting everyone know you've just posted a new Snapchat or Instagram. Include your handle or direct link to make it easy for people following you on Twitter to click over to your Instagram or Snapchat account.

Instagram offers different options (Instagram live, Instagram Stories, IGTV) so feel free repurpose your original post on one or more of these Instagram platforms for maximum effect and exposure. See Sue B. Zimmerman's chapter on Instagram for ideas.

Step #11: Periscope

Just like Facebook Live, Periscope allows you to livestream to the world. It's owned by Twitter, and your live video will appear in your Twitter feed.

When I have new content to share, I like to jump on Periscope, from wherever I am using my smartphone, and share the news with my audience. I usually share a backstory as to why I wrote the post, and I always make sure to let my viewers know where they can find the full post.

I've also found Periscope to be a fun and powerful engagement tool at community events and while flying my drone over the Pacific (yes, I live stream on both Periscope and Facebook Live while flying and engage in real-time conversation). The only limit to using Periscope, and most of the other platforms, is your imagination so always be ready to pull your smartphone out and "go live" whenever you can. If I were you, I'd take a look at Alex Pettitt's chapter on Periscope to see how professionals like him use the platform.

Step #11: Medium

This blogging platform is a great tool to reach an entirely different audience than who may be following your website or blog. I repurpose important or popular posts from other platforms on Medium and am amazed at the additional traction I get when I do so. Often I'll spend quality time re-writing the post before sharing on Medium. As with everything else, include pictures and embed videos when you can.

Step #13: Everyday Conversation

Too many people don't do this. When you have a conversation with someone about a topic, issue, or problem, you've blogged about or, shared on social, let them know and share the link with them. I do this all the time and it's one of the best and easiest ways to share content.

If you do interviews or speak from the stage, always try to incorporate your social media content into your efforts. There's no need to reinvent the wheel so when you talk about a topic or issue you've covered in the past on social, help people by letting them know about your earlier post. I always share screenshots, video clips, and links in my presentations.

Pro Tip: I keep a list of all my favorite posts and links (articles, podcasts, videos, live videos) addressing the most common 30 questions or issues that people ask me about. Then, when I'm online or offline, and the topic or question comes up, I let the other person know I'll send the answer over when I get back to the office. Sometimes I just send over a quick text from my phone (I keep a list of the posts and related links in the notes app on my phone).

Because links to blog posts and social media posts can be long, I use the link shortening service bit.ly to shorten all the links. This makes it easy for me to share a resource and link with someone else.

This is a great way to add value easily and quickly. Not only is the other person happy that you were able to help them with their question, but when he shares your social media post with his or her audience, and often times he will, that's where the magic happens. Always make it easy (keep the links short) for others to share your content.

Final Thoughts

The above approach of repurposing content works very well. A single blog post can be shared using the above method over several days, weeks and even months. Services like AgoraPulse make repurposing easy. Whatever works for you is fine. Just make sure to take action and get started. Use repurposing to share more content and save time.

Without a doubt, the best increase in influence and engagement I've experienced on the digital platforms have come from my efforts relating to my non-business interests that directly or indirectly complement my practice. When I blog about a legal theory or explain new statutes or case law, all I usually hear are digital crickets. But when I share a blog post or social media post about my passions, family, youth sports, or family trips, the engagement is strong. That's where the connections are made, and frankly, that's where the referrals and business come from.

Using this approach, I build trust and rapport with my tribe. When this amazing group of people has a legal question, or someone needs a lawyer, who do you think they reach out or refer to?

Conclusion

Today, smart business owners, professionals, and entrepreneurs use social media to inspire, inform, educate, add value, and build new relationships. Hopefully, you will use some, or all of these repurposing ideas, to do the same thing. I encourage you to use the different approaches in this chapter and start incorporating social media into your daily activity to expand your sphere of influence and create top of mind awareness.

CHAPTER 31

HOW TO USE AUGMENTED REALITY TO MARKET AND BRAND YOUR BUSINESS AND PRACTICE

BY CATHY HACKL

More than 752 million downloads; $1.2 billion in revenue; a cultural wildfire that spans all demographics, with particular popularity in the 18-to-34 age group. Statistics like these would get the attention of any marketer.

What exactly was this global phenomenon? Pokémon Go, a game launched in 2016.

The game's reach telegraphs what is to come. Marketing, along with sales and communications, is on the verge of a seismic transformation, as augmented reality (AR) moves from smartphones and games to headsets and daily life. Tomorrow's professionals will face new opportunities, as well as unforeseen challenges.

Marketers are just starting to embrace the power of AR. I believe savvy professionals should too!

AR is creating real-life invitations for clients and customers to engage directly with brands, services and yes, professionals. It's changing the way we view the world and enhancing our surroundings or helping focus on something specific.

It's also giving power to clients to go where they want, forcing marketers and professionals to create content that is meaningful and captivating. The customer and client-shopping experience have been flipped on its head. However, is it all going in the right direction?

According to Digi-Capital, the mobile AR market could hit over a billion users and $60 billion in revenue globally by 2021. There's also a clear shift in content beyond the 2D to content that is 3D, 360 and sometimes holographic making way for people to explore new things. AR will be a part of our everyday living.

It's no longer about how many people see your marketing efforts; it's about how many are engaging with them. Once that connection is made, professionals can receive feedback and continue to personalize their marketing to target audiences. With AR as a tool, professionals facilitate the sales and relationship building experiences while making clients brand advocates by allowing them to share their experiences through social channels.

For several months and even years, many marketers have stayed on the sidelines of the business case for augmented reality. Even fewer professionals have dipped their toes into the digital AR sandbox. But, with the possibility of having millions of mobile phone and users across the globe starting to embrace AR, their passivity is about to change.

The reason? Because augmented reality will contextualize a client's reality. AR will bring utility and context to clients. These new assets will forever change marketing, sales and, relationships. It will also change the way social media marketing and content marketing are done as well too.

We see most of AR technology being used on smartphones and other mobile devices. Many tech companies agree that AR will transition into headsets and smart glasses. Glasses will increase the usability of AR as your environment wouldn't be limited to just what is on your phone screen. You will be able to survey everything around you with AR as a guide.

Some have said that Google Glasses was ahead of its time, but I believe the market is now ready to receive AR into their world. Current AR headset options are expensive, tethered or provide a limited field of view, but as more clients start using AR on their phones, they will eventually want to move away from looking at a screen to looking through smart glasses.

There's a reason why Snapchat's dancing hot dog went viral. It's because consumers enjoy altering their physical environment and seeing the inanimate come to life. They'll eventually want AR to contextualize their reality, and it'll start with their mobile phones and move on to headsets/glasses.

According to Digi-Capital, the mobile AR market could hit over a billion users and $60 billion in revenue globally by 2021; this will probably be further accelerated if Magic Leap succeeds and if Apple enters the market with an AR headset.

There is a clear shift in content beyond the 2D to content that is 3D, 360 and sometimes holographic make way for your clients to explore new things. AR will be a part of our everyday living. AR will also need to provide utility and further contextualize client's realities to become fully adopted into the mainstream. Whether this will happen will be solely in the form of wearables or on display surfaces (or a combination of both) is still being debated.

According to Adweek the AR content a brand puts out must have a reason and purpose to stand out. It has to be part of the story and part of the reason why clients are going to engage with your practice. AR will be an interactive, personalized extension of a professional's practice and has to add value to your client's experience. Not accomplishing these will result in what Adweek calls using a fork to eat soup. Professionals and other consumer service providers will need to be quick to adopt the new technology and implement it correctly or fall behind.

AR is a new trillion-dollar industry and growing rapidly, according to AdAge. Hubspot identifies the primary purpose of experiential marketing to experience a brand in a tangible, offline way, but still wanting an online dialogue around it.

A study by the Ericsson ConsumerLab showed that shopping was one of the top reasons worldwide smartphone users were interested in immersive technologies and that is why brands are taking steps to get their hands on VR and AR. Professionals need to start thinking this way too.

Instead of clients visualizing in their minds what your product may look like, VR and AR give a clearer image of what they should expect from your products and features. Professionals can then offer personalized experiences to their clients. The "Impact of Augmented Reality in Retail' study by Interactions, an experiential marketing agency, indicated that "61 percent of shoppers prefer to shop at stores that offer AR, over ones that don't." I believe the same trend is going to happen to most professions. Professionals who successfully implement AR in their marketing and relationship building efforts will see an increase in client engagement and brand awareness.

The Swedish furniture store IKEA has developed a catalog app that allows customers to place and view their ready-to-assemble furniture right in their home. The digital item can be rotated, repositioned and manipulated to the customer's liking.

Using AR like this creates a culture of decisive purchasing amongst customers. Because they were able to view and adjust the product in their own home, a customer has made up his or her mind to purchase either the item they originally wanted, another product because the original didn't work out, or add-on items complimentary to what they are buying. Instead of hauling your kids to IKEA or walking around with a non-interested shopper to make a decision, you can save time, money and reduce the stress of shopping because of AR.

When people think about VR and AR, the first thing that comes to mind is gaming. Tabletop AR is just playing video and board games on a flat surface using augmented reality.

Some of my favorite examples are as simple as what Le Petit Chef has done for fine dining by using 3D projection mapping on dinners tables to bring food to life. According to Wired, " The 90-minute show, Le Petit Chef – In the Footsteps of Marco Polo, takes diners on a Silk Road-inspired culinary tour with the tabletop chef as their guide. His journey is beamed onto the table using high-definition projectors hidden in lampshades above." I had a chance to experience this culinary journey at AWE's Augmented Reality Playground in 2017.

Another favorite is the way that LEGO is using AR to augment its packaging so consumers can see a real-time model of the set and they can also play AR games triggered by the set. Their demo at the Apple's WWDC in 2018 was fantastic!

Tabletop AR is worth investing in because it provides customers with fun gaming options that can also lead to potential sales. There is role-playing, real-time strategizing and a goal to achieve. With tabletop AR, you immediately engage the user. It is also accessible. You don't have to wait for the user to find a specific location, they can whip out their phones and engage anywhere.

Vntana is a social augmented reality company that is tapping into the new era of experiential marketing. Vntana created a V-3 hologram system where they wanted to take advantage of hologram technology, specifically to empower artists, celebrities, and brands to reach and engage fans and customers in a whole new way, according to Tech.Co.

They have showcased hologram "photo booths of the future" and let customers interact with celebrity holograms at events. Brands need to use AR to create an engaging buying experience for the consumer. Even though customers are not physically in the store, they still need assistance, and the best customer service and Vntana understands this.

Holographic concierges and customer service attendants will also part of the future of retail, powered by AI, of course. Vntana believes that these attendants will help brands respond to customers' real-time wants and needs while driving revenue for the brand. It will allow the hologram to react and respond to consumers' questions without the need for wearables, collect data and deliver personalized advertisements. Be on the lookout for Vntana; they are doing some interesting things in this field.

Very much aligned to holograms is the subject of CGI influencers like Lil Miquela, who have taken the social media world by storm with 1+million followers on Instagram and deals with brands like Louis Vuitton and Diesel. I for one, am interested in looking at the creation of virtual humans and how brands will embrace these virtual influencers in the future to promote their products or even to personify their own brand in the future. Maybe there's a virtual human in your future to help promote your firm or practice?

Kino-mo, an award-winning British company developing hi-tech visual solutions based in London, is also doing big things in experiential marketing. New Atlas describes Kino-Mo's hardware as low-profile until they turn on what looks like a propeller or windmill mounted on walls and plugged into standard outlets. Its lightweight projection unit was designed to be easily used within businesses to reinforce the impact they are having with their customers. They can even be used remotely at different locations through a wireless connection. Kino-Mo's Hypervsn™ are "screen-less" displays that are easy to install and operate, cost-effective, and scalable for small- to medium-sized applications.

Kino-Mo is also bringing its technology to retail through its LED projection. They reel in customers into stores with their technology. Kino-mo also gives consumers the option to customize the product and its features, helping them make a more accurate purchase of what they want. According to Augment, "The primary drawback to online shopping is that many of the sensory elements that customers use to make their purchasing decisions are often lost. When shopping online, a customer cannot touch or feel an item, see how it works, or know how it will fit in their home. The loss of this interactivity and presence in the shopping experience leads to uncertain buyers and more abandoned carts." That is why retail is becoming the next AR frontier. Augmented reality is already changing the way we shop and spend money and shows how using AR can make retail more fun, more exciting, and more of an "experience" you can't get at home.

Niantic Inc., the creators of Pokémon Go, is getting ready to launch a new venture in 2018. The announcement of Niantic's Harry Potter AR game, I believe, sends a huge signal to retail spaces on how powerful AR can be. We all got a taste of it with Pokemon Go, but that was just the tip of the iceberg. This company is all about pushing the limits of technology to invent the future of augmented reality. They are creating an opportunity for Harry Potter fans to finally become real-life "wizards" in a Muggle world.

Another great example of this change is IZEA's introduction of Augmented Sponsorship. IZEA is an influencer marketing platform that helps brands connect with influencers that can share branded content on their network. According to IZEA, this is the first-of-its-kind Augmented Reality Influencer Marketing service that gives IZEA clients a whole new way for Influencers to engage with brands & produce compelling sponsored visual content. Dynamically target & deliver 3D assets to individual influencers who place and manipulate virtual objects and include them in their content creation process.

As Snapchat, Facebook and Instagram continue to use AR in the form of lenses, frames, 3D assets and holograms. I wager we'll see more of these types of branded posts in the evolution in influencer marketing. Watch the video http://bit.ly/socialmediabook-ar

Marketing tactics are already evolving with augmented reality leading the way and ushering in the future of marketing. Here are three things professionals just like you need to know:

1. Client service is changing.

Clients will expect faster customer service, and they won't always wait for a human representative to attend to their needs. Chatbots are already becoming a commonality of customer service online, and with AI getting faster and smarter we will start to see more AR attendants or holographic concierges emerge to fill the needs of customers and help with pain points. AR will also make it easier for clients to find products and services along with all the options.

2. AR needs to become cool - the Ray-Ban moment

I think most of us can agree that Google Glass was not a sexy product. Current AR headsets are not too attractive either. I love wearing a Hololens, but after 30-40 minutes I've reached my limit of wearing an all-in-one AR HMD on my head. If AR can get to that Ray Ban moment when wearing AR is viewed as cool and fashionable this can only help with mass adoption, especially as younger generations assimilate AR into their daily lives. If Snap, Inc., the parent company for Snapchat, had added AR to their Spectacles glasses and hadn't fumbled that marketing campaign we would be further ahead in making AR even more appealing to consumers and brands.

3.   AR marketing needs to have best practices and ethical standards

With data being collected left and right on how consumers act and engage with brands, it's critical for the marketing profession to become aware of the potential pitfalls of oversaturation of ads and marketing in an AR world. I'm pretty utopic about the future rather than dystopic, but Keiichi Matsuda's 2016 Hyperreality short shows what can happen if there are no best practices or ethical standards in place to protect consumers. Watch the video http://bit.ly/socialmediabook-ar-2

After reading this chapter, one of the things I hope you'll take with you is that marketing, branding, and building relationships, in all its forms (content, social, shopper, etc.) is facing a major shift. We're moving away from content that is 2D/flat to content that is 3D, 360-degrees and sometimes holographic. The way we share content and the way we communicate with the world is also changing, and the professionals that embrace this change will become the leaders of a future.

———————

Cathy Hackl is one of the most sought-after keynote technology speakers in the world. Considered one of the top women in augmented reality and virtual reality by media like NBC and VentureBeat, Cathy works at the intersection of future technology and storytelling bringing augmented reality, virtual reality and mixed reality to audiences across the globe and across industries. You can connect with Cathy at http://cathyhackl.com

CHAPTER 32

IF YOU DON'T HAVE A QUALITY WEBSITE, YOU'RE LOSING MONEY

BY THOMAS WALLIN

Websites are the first impression many of your potential customers have of your business. Without online visibility, your target audience is inevitably going to a competitor.

Social media is a tool you can use to bring people back to your business real estate also known as your website. In this chapter, I'm going to focus on the website aspect of marketing your business and building your digital brand.

Why Websites are Critically Important

Consider your professional website as your foundation online. It is your office and your informational hub for potential customers. They want to see what others are saying about your business and learn about what makes your brand unique.

Having a website is vital to growing your online visibility. Having a compelling website is essential to increasing your bottom line. If you are still on the fence about whether you need a professional website for your business, consider this - your customers expect it. You need a site for Google Search Results. A website provides a resource center for prospective and current clients. It allows you to showcase your products and services, and best yet: you own and control the narrative.

The Basics

Every professional website should have the following pages:

Home Page
About Us
Case Studies/Results*
Blog
FAQ Page - (Pro Tip: FAQ pages are a great place to include video)

*Before posting any case results or studies, professionals should always check with their governing body for ethical considerations and guidelines.

You should also have a web page or pages dedicated to legalese such as disclaimers, privacy policy information, terms, and conditions. Your website should link to all of your social media accounts and your blog (if it is separate from your actual site). You should include multiple content rich pages that describe different areas of your services or products. These are known as "sell pages" and should have quality content, images, and videos throughout your site.

Mobile First

In 2019 and beyond, your website should adapt to every device available with quick load speed. The first priority should be to mobile devices.

Check your website for loading speed on different devices. How does your website look and function on your phone and all other mobile devices? Is it navigable? Do images show up without distortion? Are videos available? While it is essential that your professional site looks great on a desktop and laptop, mobile functionality is key to the future.

Speed

Your website must load fast on all devices. Prospective clients will not watch a video if it takes too long to load. Consider that 53% of mobile visitors will leave a website if it fails to load in three seconds. This means that if your website does not load quickly, your target audience will move on quickly.

Google announced in July 2018, page speed would be a ranking factor for mobile searches as well as desktop searches. You can test the speed of your website with free tools like Pingdom and GTmetrix. Google offers PageSpeed Insights that can give you a good indication of how quickly your website is performing.

Visual Impact - The Importance of Video and Images

Video is becoming the primary way to communicate with your audience. You should have video on your website that is optimized for all devices. You want to produce quality videos that are professional, well-lit and have good sound. Invest in professional equipment to shoot your video or hire a company to assist you in the production of it.

The New Kind of First Impression

There are nearly 4 billion internet users. In 2010 and beyond, prospective customers are not walking down the street and randomly stopping in a law office or at a dentist's office. They are searching businesses on Google to find out everything about the services you offer. It should be a one-stop shop for your target audience to see everything that you have to offer.

Nothing is worse than an outdated website, make sure it is regularly updated. No matter what kind of business you have, you will benefit from having a professional site.

According to Statista, the number of digital buyers will increase to over 2 billion by 2021. A new generation of potential customers is coming of age, buying products and using services. This is an age of digital immersion. You must adapt, and adaptation begins with building a great website. Unless you are a digital marketing guru or graphic designer, let a professional build your site. You want to make a sound, lasting impression that builds trust through great content and brand consistency.

QUALITY over Quantity

Digital marketing can be overwhelming. While this chapter won't get into the nitty-gritty of SEO, PPC, and how to build an effective marketing campaign, we will go over some of the essential factors that go into a quality website.

Content matters. When discussing websites, you often hear the adage that "Content is King." In 2019 and beyond, the new phrase should be "Quality Content is King." The information you put on your website matters. While you want a lot of information for your target audience to consume, if it is duplicate content or keyword stuffed, you will not rank for Search Engine purposes. Worse, you will be turning away potential clients.

You want a professional website with quality content that is visually appealing to a digitally overwhelmed audience. You want to establish a relationship with prospective clients before they even pick up the phone. Truth and honesty build trust. Establish a connection with your client through your website by adding videos and images.

Consider adding videos on frequently asked questions and pictures of staff from the office. This will help build trust with online visitors that was once reserved for in-person meetings only. You want a website that invites visitors to engage online and purchase your products or services.

Pro Tip: Stay away from stock photos. Use professional photos of you and your staff. Have the photographer take headshots and editorial images. Be sure to get photo releases from employees.

Your Most Important Online Owned Assets

A website allows you to provide information to potential customers 24 hours a day, 7 days a week. This is marketing at its finest. You can sit back and let your website do the talking for you. Visitors are introduced to your business without having to meet you at the office, saving you time and money.*

Pro Tip: Make sure you are writing for your client/customer and not just writing about how great you are. Produce content, video, and images that are appealing to your audience - not just things that boost your ego.

Blogging and updating your website regularly with useful content will help increase traffic on your site and keep current and prospective customers informed. Adding video is crucial, not only for search results but also for connecting with your audience.

The website platform or content management system you use should allow you to make changes and add content with ease. If you are feeling ambitious, consider upgrading your blog to a vlog. A website is a great way to push information without having to spend a ton of money. Once a website is created, it can save you money in the long term.

Pro Tip: It is a great idea to include a recent news/update page on your website that helps current clients stay informed, and potential customers see what you are doing in your business and throughout the community. Consumers today want to feel a connection with the people they do business with, they want to go on a journey and share an experience. Tap into that.

Pro Tip: If you don't like writing, consider vlogging instead, using a series of videos instead of blogs. Also, consider using a transcription company like Rev.com - you can convert audio or video to text for $1 per minute. This is great for SEO and giving different ways for viewers to consume content.

The Truth about Social Media

You do not own your Facebook business page, your Instagram account or your YouTube page. Since you don't own it - you can't CONTROL it.

Facebook and other social networks are continually changing things. You want to be sure that you have social share buttons on your website and for each article and video. What you produce for your site should be easy for your audience to consume and share. It should work well on other platforms but understand that you only have ultimate control over your website.

Building Credibility

A quality website also helps you build credibility. By providing not only information about your product or services but also testimonials, you are increasing the likelihood that a prospective customer will want to choose you over a competitor. People want social proof that what you are selling, whether it be a product or service, is worth buying. Building a website that helps your business gain credibility will take time.

This is not an overnight, DIY project. You want your website to display the quality of service that you offer to your customers. It should be mobile-friendly with intelligent design. You want to have a marketing partner that you trust and can build a long-term relationship with. You wouldn't use scotch tape to hold together your house, why would you put a quick fix on the foundation of your business?

If you are considering hiring a company to build your website, heed the following advice from the Internet Marketing Experts at Scorpion:

1. Select a Google Premier Partner
2. Look for Proven, Transparent Results
3. Go to a company with a long track record that understands your market whether you are in   the legal industry, insurance or medical field
4. Find Examples of their Work and Ask About Client Satisfaction

Trusting a company to convey your image online can be difficult. You want to have a close relationship with your Digital Marketing Agency so that you truly capture the heart of your company on your website. Set a marketing budget and work within that budget to create the best possible product for your potential customers. Ask for referrals you can speak with; take a look at other websites they have designed and see how they function on mobile devices.

The Bottom Line

A professional website should:

· Load Fast
· Be easy to Navigate
· Be Mobile-Friendly
· Have Quality Content
· Be Easy to Share
· Have great visual impact with videos and images

A website will allow you to reach more people, more of the time. It can introduce your product and services to a whole new audience and turn more people into paying customers. A great website will display your business in its best light. A professional, easy to navigate website is essential to a comprehensive marketing plan. Bottom line, without a quality website you are losing money.

Thomas Wallin is the owner of the Wallin Law Firm which helps injured people across the country get the maximum recovery for their case. Mr. Wallin also works as SVP of Legal Marketing at Scorpion, one of the most respected digital marketing companies in the nation. Scorpion has won Google's coveted AdWords Channel Sales Champion of Customer Satisfaction as well as the Innovator of the Year Award for its technology. Connect with Scorpion here http://bit.ly/mitch-scorpion

If you would like to know more about building, maintaining or marketing your professional website, please contact Thomas at info@thomaswallin.com or 888.400.1770.

CHAPTER 33

RECOMMENDED TOOLS FOR SOCIAL MEDIA SUCCESS

BY MIKE ALLTON

While there's something to be said for just hitting the button, going live, and creating engaging video content on the fly... the fact is, a successful social media presence requires time, planning, and continual work.

Which means there is a lot of opportunities to bring in tools to help.

Great tools can save us time, enhance the results of what we're doing, and even make the entire activity more enjoyable.

But there's more than just apps to manage social networks (social media management tools). There are tools available to help create graphics, help post videos and stories, help measure results, and help collaborate with teams and influencers.

While I'm going to give you very specific tool recommendations within this chapter, what I want you to take from this is a sense for the variety of tools available, and an appreciation for how they can help you.

Virtually every great tool has a price tag associated with it. While it's easy to allow an abundance of subscriptions to pile up, don't let that dissuade you from trying different tools and giving yourself time to sort out the ideal combination. The result will save you far more time and money than the combined cost of the tools.

Social Media Management

Of course, your primary social media tool is going to be a "social media management tool" - these are tools designed to facilitate the various things you want to do and accomplish with your selected social networks. Typically, that includes publishing, scheduling, monitoring, listening and reporting.

Publishing - ability to create text, image and/or video posts

Scheduling - ability to set posts for a specific date/time, as well as repeat or queue

Monitoring - ability to view & react to mentions, comments, replies, and messages

Listening - ability to see posts and content of interest

Reporting - ability to track progress and success

If you're just getting started on social media, my best advice is to use every platform natively and track your activity and progress in a spreadsheet. That 'in the weeds' approach will give you a greater understanding and appreciation for that network's nuance.

Using the advice offered in other chapters throughout this book, you can get to know each platform and gradually mature to the point where you're ready to get a tool involved.

The highest rated social media management tool and my personal recommendation is Agorapulse (www.Agorapulse.com). I've used every tool available, and even wrote the book on Hootsuite, but have been using Agorapulse ever since I was introduced to the app in 2016.

Agorapulse supports Twitter, Facebook Pages, LinkedIn Profiles, LinkedIn Pages, Google+ Pages, Instagram and YouTube. So most of the major networks are covered.

What Agorapulse does exceedingly well is make it easy for brands to listen for comments, mentions, messages, and conversations.

As a professional, you'll appreciate being able to use Agorapulse to schedule out social media activity well in advance, and have just one place to go to keep an eye on engagement from your community.

Now, depending on your business goals, target audience, and preferred social network, you will find one or more of the following additional tools invaluable.

Graphic Design

Whether you're focused on tweeting a dozen times or publishing YouTube videos regularly, you're likely going to need to have some graphics created.

PhotoShop and Illustrator from Adobe are definitely top of the class when it comes to graphic design - but they come with steep fees and even steeper learning curves.

Instead, for most businesses, I recommend getting to know Canva. (www.canva.com)

Canva is a web-based design tool that offers you predetermined size templates so that you can make sure you're selecting the right size graphic for a Facebook Post or Pinterest Pin. And if you're just getting started with graphic design, you can avail yourself of the content templates for ideas on what to actually make your graphics look like.

You can upload your own images or pull from the available stock images - and at just $1 per use, the stock images are incredibly affordable.

While Canva is extremely easy to use and will save you a lot of time, the real beauty of the solution is in the management and team collaboration capabilities.

For a low monthly fee, you can upload your brand fonts, store your brand colors, and share folders & designs among your collaborators. And of course, all of your designs and uploads are libraried for future use.

If you haven't used Canva, or really any graphic design program before, I highly recommend going through the free tutorials. They'll get you up and running with great social media graphics in no time.

Reporting

After you've been posting to social media for a couple of weeks, it's time to start reviewing and reporting on the impact and success those posts have had.

First, each social network provides businesses with built-in analytics so that you can easily review key performance indicators (KPI) like follower growth, engagement, and reach. If you're managing multiple social profiles, a tool like Agorapulse mentioned above will be of great help here.

But, while social media post performance is important, that doesn't necessarily reflect bottom-line business results. For that, you need a tool like Google Analytics. (analytics.google.com)

With Google Analytics monitoring all of the traffic and activity to and on your website, you will be able to gauge the actual effectiveness of your social media presence.

- How much traffic did each social network send?
- Which page(s) did those visitors view?
- Which goals and events did the visitors trigger?

Properly configured and informed, Google Analytics can know exactly what your preferred business outcomes are, whether that's to fill out a lead generation form, purchase a product, or sign up for something else.

And if Google Analytics knows your goals, that means those goals can be tracked, including how your visitors came to complete those goals.

Additionally, when sharing links to specific URLs to social networks, you can configure the links with "UTM Parameters" like 'campaign' or 'source' so that links and posts can be identified. This will give you the ability to measure exactly how specific posts or networks perform and help your business.

Advertising

While some have complained over the years about Facebook's stance toward businesses - making them pay for the ability to reach new audiences - there's a simple, undeniable fact:

Facebook Advertising is the most cost-effective advertising medium available to businesses today.

Any business that thinks spending a few hundred dollars a month to get their brand, content and message in front of tens of thousands of targeted prospects needs to re-evaluate their priorities.

That's why AdEspresso (www.adespresso.com) is my next recommended tool - not only does it facilitate Facebook ads, it makes the creation, monitoring, and learning from those ads a piece of cake.

You can create and copy campaigns, call up easy-to-understand reports, and even split test key elements like ad placement or audience or text/imagery.

Collaboration

Is it just you running your social media marketing, or do you have a team involved? If you have a team (even if it's for more than just social media marketing), let's make sure you have an easy way to plan, communicate and track your social media campaigns, content and calendaring.

Asana (www.asana.com) is a worthy candidate for the job.

Asana lets you organize everything among Campaigns and Tasks, assign them to team members, create deadlines, and see it all within calendar or dashboard views.

You can even track company goals and milestones.

If you're currently using email or spreadsheets (or nothing at all), this is the tool for you.

CRM / Social Selling

Once you've gotten your feet wet on the sunlit shores of social media, it's time to start selling.

But wait! We're not talking about posting over and over again about your latest sale or service. Your social audience is NOT browsing Facebook just to buy from you.

Social Media is about being social which means building an audience and relationships. It's a long game. Whether you're targeting individual purchasers or influencers for access to larger pools of potential customers, you're going to need help tracking the people you want and need to talk to.

Nimble (www.nimble.com) is the perfect tool for that.

Nimble integrates easily with all of the major social networks, and your email/calendar, giving you access to powerful synchronization. Every time you tweet or email a key individual, it'll be reflected on their Nimble contact record.

You can tag contacts in a variety of ways to help you monitor segments, create reports, and track progress through pre-determined pipelines.

Most important, Nimble can help you make sure you stay in touch with the people that matter most to your business.

Content Creation

Finally, when it comes to social media success, the only way to be successful is to create content.

Tweets, Facebook posts, videos, blog posts, graphics... it's all just different forms of content. We've mentioned a few tools already that can assist you with the creation and management of that content, but you're going to need something else.

Google Docs (docs.google.com) is about to become your best friend.

First and foremost, Google Docs is a great place to draft blog posts and landing pages and other forms of text, both short and long. It's easy to use a word processor that also includes automatic backup, cloud access, and team collaboration.

Being able to see comments and revisions from team members can prove incredibly valuable.

You can also use Google Docs to create long-term resources for your business and social media activity:

- Useful statistics
- Lists of URLs to share
- Saved replies
- Tweets and other social posts
- Ad headlines, copy, and audience determination
- Campaigns and documented activity

Google Slides and Google Sheets are also very useful, and all can be safely organized within shared, Team Drives for easy, remote access.

Put Word or text editors aside and start using Google Docs in your everyday business!

With these or similar tools in place, you will position you and your business to achieve success on social networks, while at the same time save yourself time and money.

————

Mike Allton is a Content Marketing Practitioner - a title he invented to represent his holistic approach to content marketing that leverages blogging, social media, email marketing and SEO to drive traffic, generate leads, and convert those leads into sales. He is an award-winning Blogger, Speaker, and Author at The Social Media Hat, and Brand Evangelist at Agorapulse. Mike joins three other marketing experts in leading a private mastermind group called 360 Marketing Squad where he answers questions daily and leads live video training. Connect with Mike here https://www.thesocialmediahat.com

PART III

SOCIAL MEDIA COMMUNICATION AND SUCCESS TIPS

CHAPTER 34

HOW PROFESSIONALS CAN GET KNOWN

BY MARK W. SCHAEFER

When it comes to selling professional services, building a personal brand and becoming "known" in your field is absolutely critical, and "content" is the fuel for that presence.

In my workshops with business professionals, the prospect of developing original content to drive a brand is often met with folded arms and icy stares. Who is going to come up with this content? Who has the time for it? Where would I even start?

But creating effective content can certainly be achievable for any business, so I want to use this space to calm you down and tell you that it will all be OK. We'll figure this out together. How does a business create meaningful content on a budget?

The content imperative

By now, you probably have some idea of how content drives power on the web, but let me provide a short personal example of how this works.

A few years ago, I was interested in an emerging field of influencer marketing and wrote one of the first blog posts on the subject. By this time, I had been blogging at least once a week for about five years, so Google recognized that I was providing a steady stream of helpful information. I had built up "authority" in the search engine's view.

Three weeks after I wrote this post, I was contacted by a reporter for The New York Times who had done a search on "influencer marketing" and wanted to interview me for her article. I was quoted in this piece four times, and the article was syndicated, meaning it appeared in newspapers all over the world.

At the time, I was a solo entrepreneur. I hadn't written a book or appeared on any national stage. Now I was in America's leading newspaper ... and beyond. Would this have ever happened if I had simply posted my views on Facebook or LinkedIn? No. To have an opportunity for vast exposure in the world today, you need something bigger and bolder. You need "rich content."

Your rich content

While the world of marketing and social media might seem overwhelming, it doesn't have to be. In fact, to get started, you only have four content choices:

- Written content like a blog
- Video content like what you might see on Facebook Live or YouTube
- Audio content like a podcast
- Visual content like Instagram or Pinterest

If you're a small business with limited resources, pick one and do it consistently – one post a week is a realistic goal – for at least two years to give it a chance to catch on.

You see, Facebook, Twitter, etc. are simply distribution channels. By focusing on one source of rich content, you now have focus and direction that can propel your brand. But one which is right for you?

Creating content for the sake of creating content will almost certainly be a recipe for disappointment and disillusionment. Spend a little time thinking through a content form that is right for you by considering:

1.   Where are your competitors today? Is there a content gap in the marketplace you could fill? For example, if local competitors have saturated the web with blog posts, maybe your route to success is video or a podcast.

2.   Are there unmet or under-served customer information needs in your marketplace? Can you specialize in a theme or topical area that will help you rise to the top?

3.   What brings you joy? If you love to write, then write! If you want to try video because it might be fun, then do that. Personal choice is important because if creating content is a burden, this will be apparent to everyone, including your customers.

All things being equal, I would normally give blogging a priority over other content forms because it is so flexible and discoverable by the search engines. In any event, don't try to do too much. Pick one form and stick with it for at least a year or two to master it.

If you want to explore more about this topic and find exercises to help you build a powerful brand through content, I recommend the book "KNOWN," which I wrote to help guide you through this process.

Creating content that is RITE

Today, simply creating content is not enough. You also have to rise above the noise. This is nothing new. It's a media pattern that has been repeated over time.

In the early days of television, almost all of the content was created by local talent. In the 1950s, the community airwaves were filled with variety shows, cooking shows, and craft shows featuring the locals. As the channel grew in popularity, the quality of the content had to rise to remain relevant.

Today, a television show like Game of Thrones is as good as any movie you can see. That's what it takes to stand out in a world with so much content. I'm not saying you have to be Game of Thrones. No business can do that. But you do have to be the superior content in your niche or community. If you're not superior, you'll be replaced.

There is no marketing "easy button" anymore. To rise above the noise, you'll have to create content that stands out. To do that, follow the path of **RITE: Relevant, Interesting, Timely and Entertaining.**

Relevant: If you're creating content about the law, it will confuse readers for you to start discussing Scottish history and then your favorite barbecue recipe. Pick a relevant theme and stick to it.

Interesting: Never take a customer's time for granted. Deliver value every time they hear from you. Don't "sell." Help them.

Timely: What's going on in your industry or community right now that your customers need to know about? Have you come across some interesting data or research you can cite?

Entertaining: Think about the kind of content that you enjoy and share. Chances are it has some entertainment value. Your customers expect the same quality from businesses.

Being original means being you

Marketing has always been about making some meaningful connection between your business and your customer. To do that, you need to be original, and to be original, you have no choice but to add your own story to your content.

What I mean by that is that your customers don't need you to be a "reporter." They need you to be a friend. People are more likely to buy from friends and providing helpful content that connects with them in a personal way is an excellent way to do that.

Here are some ideas to make your content more human:

- Make a point by relating it back to a personal experience.

- Express an opinion. Do you agree or disagree with something going on in your field?

- Use your content to celebrate your customers and people in the community making a difference.

- Use humor to connect with your audience.

- Cite a piece of content in your field and comment on it.

- Talk a little about how and why you started your business and what it means to you.

Creating content for a business can provide so many benefits today, and you might even learn that it can be fun!

———

Mark Schaefer is a consultant, college educator, and the author of seven marketing books including "KNOWN: The Handbook for Building and Unleashing Your Personal Brand in the Digital Age." Please connect with Mark at https://businessesgrow.com

CHAPTER 35

THE 3 UNBREAKABLE LAWS OF COMMUNICATING ON SOCIAL MEDIA

BY CARMINE GALLO

Social media is simply a new tool to get our ideas to spread. Keep in mind, however, that the human brain hasn't changed since our ancestors began carving pictures into cave walls. Your understanding of the ancient brain will give you a competitive advantage in today's world.

The tools of communication have changed, but how people process information has not. Content in all of its forms that is meant to be persuasive or to change hearts and minds must obey three fundamental laws of persuasion. Your social media content must be: emotional, novel and memorable.

Emotional

Great communicators reach your head and your heart. Most people forget the "heart" part. More than 2,000 years ago, Aristotle wrote that persuasion cannot occur in the absence of pathos and emotion. And the best vehicle we have to convey emotion is through the power of story.

I learned a lot about the persuasive nature of story when I spoke to human rights attorney, Bryan Stevenson, whose TED talk generated the longest standing ovation in TED talk history. Stevenson successfully argues cases in front of the U.S. Supreme Court. He knows how to persuade.

I analyzed his now famous TED talk titled, "We need to talk about an injustice." Stories made up 65% of his presentation. In 18 minutes, he inspired his audience to donate a combined $1 million to his nonprofit—without asking!

Stevenson tells three stories in his TED talk. The first involves his grandmother. When Stevenson was just eleven years old, his grandmother pulled him aside and said, "Bryan, you're special." She asked him to make a promise—never to drink alcohol in his life. He was just a kid, so he accepted. Here's how Stevenson concludes the story.

"When I was about 14 or 15, one day my brother came home and he had this six-pack of beer -- I don't know where he got it -- and he grabbed me and my sister and we went out in the woods. And we were kind of just out there doing the stuff we crazily did. And he had a sip of this beer and he gave some to my sister and she had some, and they offered it to me. I said, 'No, no, no. That's okay. You all

go ahead. I'm not going to have any beer.' My brother...looked at me real hard and he said, 'Oh, I hope you're not still hung up on that conversation Mama had with you. Mama tells all the grandkids that they're special.' 'm going to admit something to you. I'm 52 years old, and I'm going to admit to you that I've never had a drop of alcohol. I don't say that because I think that's virtuous; I say that because there is power in identity."

In that story, the audience laughed, they were touched, moved and inspired to listen to more. "Narrative is hugely powerful in effective communication," Stevenson told me in an interview after that TED talk.

Stevenson chooses stories that are relevant to the topic, of course, but also repeats stories that are personal. By telling a story about his grandmother, he's breaking down walls between him and his audience. After all, everyone has a grandmother.

It's hard to tell a story in 140 characters, of course, but links to longer form content on blogs or websites, as well as short videos or articles, should contain stories. Stories don't have to be long. Stevenson's story about this grandmother can fit in an Instagram video of 60-seconds.

Novel

Neuroscientists who study communication say the brain cannot ignore novelty. We're always looking for something different. Neuromarketing researcher, Dr. A.K. Pradeep, once told me: "Novelty recognition is a hard-wired survival tool all humans share. Our brains are trained to look for something brilliant and new, something that stands out, something that looks delicious."

I call this the "Jaw-dropping moment," the one moment in a presentation that's shocking, surprising, or delightful. It grabs the attention of the audience is remembered long after the presentation is over. Steve Jobs was a master of the jaw-dropping moment.

In 2007, Steve Jobs introduced the iPhone. Remember, the jaw-dropping moment must include the element of surprise. Steve Jobs did just that. He told the audience that Apple would introduce three new products. "The first one is a wide-screen iPod with touch controls. The second is a revolutionary mobile phone. And the third is a breakthrough Internet communications device." Jobs repeated the three products again, and again. Finally, he revealed the twist. "Are you getting it? These are not three separate devices. This is one device. And we are calling it iPhone!" The audience erupted with laughter, cheers, and applause.

A surprise twist is irresistible. So is show-and-tell. In 2008 Steve Jobs introduced a thin, light, notebook computer called the MacBook Air. When Jobs introduced the "world's thinnest notebook," he walked to the side of the stage, pulled out a manila envelope tucked behind the podium and said, "It's so thin it even fits inside one of those envelopes you see floating around the office." With a beaming smile, he slowly pulled it out of the envelope for all to see. Most presenters would have shown photographs of the product. Jobs took it one step further. He knew the shtick would grab people's attention. It did. Most of the blogs, magazine and newspapers that covered the launch ran a photograph of Steve Jobs pulling the notebook out of its envelope.

None of these moments happened spontaneously during the Steve Jobs era, and they don't happen spontaneously today. Apple executive speakers, designers, and marketers spend months obsessing over every detail of a major product presentation. Every line, every slide, every demo is created to surprise and delight.

Find creative, interesting and unusual ways to convey your ideas on social media. You have to do something just a little different to get people's attention. For example, I enjoy following Bill Gates' blog because he's a student of communication. Gates has a challenge—how to get people motivated about helping people in other continents whom they've never met. He does it by doing shocking things that grab your attention.

You might have heard of Gates' TED talk when he released mosquitoes into the audience in a conversation about how malaria spread in under-developed countries. Well, he does something similar in other formats, too.

For a blog post about new technology that turns sewage water into drinking water, he included videos where he challenged people to take a sip from two bottles of water and decide which was the treated water and which was the real bottled water. On the Tonight Show with Jimmy Fallon, he tricked Jimmy and put the treated sewage water in both. It was humorous to watch Fallon absolutely convinced that one was better than the other. Once the laughter died down, Gates got serious. Surprise people to grab their attention.

Memorable

What good are your novel ideas if your audience cannot recall what you said or wrote? There's a reason why TED talks are not allowed to exceed 18 minutes in length. For a presentation, 18-minutes is an ideal amount of time to get a message across without putting people to sleep. You have a lot less time on social media, of course. How do make your ideas memorable in a blog, Tweet, or Facebook post? There are two exercises that can help: the headline and the rule of 3.

The headline is the one single overarching message that you want your audience to know about your topic, company, or product. I like to use Twitter as an exercise here. I often challenge my clients to describe their idea in 140 characters or less (not the expanded 280 characters). If you can't explain your big idea in 140 characters or less, keep working on your message.

Before becoming an author and a famous TED speaker, Daniel Pink spent his career as a speechwriter, thinking about words and crafting words for political leaders. Pink gave me this advice: Before a presentation, a speech or writing a social media post, ask yourself this question: What's the one thing I want people to take away? For example, the titles of all TED talks easily fall within 140 characters. The title is provocative to entice you to read, raise a puzzle in need of an answer, and are always short. Here are a few popular TED talk titles:

- Schools Kill Creativity (Ken Robinson)
- How Great Leaders Inspire Action (Simon Sinek)
- The Surprising Science of Happiness (Dan Gilbert)
- The Power of Introverts (Susan Cain)

Give me one reason and one reason only to read your content. And keep it within 140 characters.

The second exercise to make your content more memorable is the undeniable pull of the rule of three. Simply put, people cannot easily recall more than three chunks of information in short-term memory. Don't overwhelm your reader or viewer 18 pieces of information. Give them three, especially in a short Instagram video or post. Your content might contain: 3 features of a new product, 3 lessons you learned from a conference, 3 reasons to read a particular book, etc. Of course, you don't want to become predictable and always group your content into three. Anywhere from 3 to 7 pieces of information seems to be the sweet spot, according to cognitive psychologists. Above all, avoid overwhelming your audience with too much information.

If you can make your content emotional, novel and memorable, you'll stand out from the majority of social media content that is too long, too confusing or way too boring. Your ideas deserve to be heard.

———

Carmine Gallo is a keynote speaker, Harvard instructor, and author of bestselling books including: Talk Like TED and Five Stars: The Communication Secrets to Get from Good to Great. He can be found on LinkedIn, Instagram, Twitter and Facebook by visiting his website, carminegallo.com

CHAPTER 36

WANT YOUR CREATIVITY TO FLOW ON SOCIAL MEDIA? MAKE IT MORE LIKE SEX

BY COURTNEY SMITH KRAMER

O K. Before we start talking about how social media should be more like sex, let me preface this by saying creepers – get out. This is a book written by a lawyer, for God's sake! To me, social media should be fun. Sex should be fun. And people, in general, need to lighten up. <end rant>

Welcome to my chapter!

Sex can be fun to talk about. Most every adult has an experience with it in some way, so it's a very relatable shared experience that helps give context to just about any human emotion. Humor, anticipation, pleasure, joy, love, fear, anxiety, bliss, wonder... these are all feelings that we feel during sex that are in parallel to creativity.

But unlike sex, creativity is one of those things that many people feel they either have or don't have. We're trained from a very young age that we're either "right-brained" or left-brained" thinkers, causing us to self-select into one side or the other about whether we possess this coveted trait. To use sex as a metaphor to remind you that yes, you too are creative, even if you've never believed it yourself, is a very natural analogy to show you that your instinct to create should be listened to, and nurtured.

And being creative in your social media posts, ads and comments are no different. It's a forum to showcase your personality, to increase intimacy in your relationships with other people, and sometimes, to show your vulnerability. This means risking not being "perfect" (spoiler alert –> There is no such thing) to share something about your business' dream or desire.

Explaining yourself honestly can definitely feel like standing naked in a room full of ogling strangers. It requires vulnerability, rawness and an openness to reveal your flaws to the world. And this takes courage, which is defined as being afraid to do something but doing it anyway.

I remember early in my career when I was designing logos as a freelance graphic designer. My clients were solopreneurs or small business owners, and the logos they wanted were usually less about the business and more a visual reflection of themselves. The brand WAS them, and they always had very strong opinions about how they wanted to be perceived to build their reputation. This meant my job was to capture their emotions and package them up into an easy-to-understand visual. #Nopressure

The feeling of presenting to my clients the first round of logo designs was something I DREADED. It was akin to slicing my stomach open with a butter knife, laying my innards on the table, and asking everyone to assess my health while I sat there, trying to look objective and calm. #makeitstop

Doing something intimate, like sharing our own personal human stories on social media, puts us into a position of being judged by others. No one wants to feel inadequate or judged as a human, so sometimes, it's easier just not to share at all. But the unintended impact of this on others is that you're robbing potential partners, customers and friends of the opportunity to know the real you – the you they could maybe fall in love with and one day buy lots of things from – because at the end of the day, we all want to do business with people we like.

It feels great to support people we like, and it's high time that we free ourselves of the stigma that we should be ashamed about partaking in acts that give us pleasure. Did you know the word "erotic" is derived from the Greek word "erōtikós," which means "of love, caused by love, given to love"? When you share from your heart, that's your own brand of being creative, because no one else can do it like you do #thatswhatshesaid Giving of your love, caused by doing what you love, to give pleasure and purpose to yourself and others? Sign me up, please!

Just create

As a human, thinking that you lack the ability to create leaves you feeling like something is inexplicably missing, because, from the earliest sacred texts, we have been taught that "creating" is the most holy of actions. It is literally the first sentence in the Bible (religion aside, in reference to it being one of humanity's oldest sacred texts); Genesis 1: "In the beginning, God created the heavens and the earth." So at the deepest, most historic almost DNA level, our desire to understand creation drives us to want to create at all costs. When we feel like we can't do it, it literally sends us into dis-ease.

This dis-ease manifests itself into what people describe as feeling like they're in a "rut," or "being stuck." The feelings that come with it are as undesirable as you'd think; depression, anger, frustration, sadness. No one does their best, most positive problem solving (or sex, for that matter) in that state!

The truth is, everyone can do it, and use it to make the world a better place.

Some tips to inspire your creativity and maybe other fun things

It comes down to creating the right environment and circumstances to allow the neurons in your brain to make new neural connections. There are a few ways to do this (all also apply to sex, so pay attention):

Take a shower: You may have heard people say that their best ideas come to them in the shower. (This is true for me; the idea for the reasons why creativity is like sex happened in my own shower!) This happens because of what I call the "Double D's" – "Distraction" and "Dopamine." Dopamine is a neurotransmitter that serves as the "Pavlovian reward system" to things that make us feel good. Distraction refers to any environment where your brain isn't required to focus or fixate on any one input but instead is able to relinquish its functionality to a more passive state.

The shower is one of those places; producing both a warm, comfortable environment, as well as white noise, which helps our minds disengage and produce more interesting neural connections. This magic combination creates the right environment for your mind to wander, find new connections in your brain, and come up with some new, pattern-breaking ideas.

Do it with others: If you're someplace, that's not a shower (like at work), getting your ideas to flow can be tricky – especially in a group setting. There's the pressure of feeling judged if you share your thoughts, and if most people in the room feel like this, then the only ideas taken away from the meeting are from the loudest people in the room. A better way to group brainstorm is to engage in "brain writing," where individuals write ideas on a paper, then pass them along to each person in the group, who can add onto the ideas, creating new and interesting connections.

Tom Kelly, creativity expert and a founder of global design and innovation firm IDEO, created three techniques to get the ideas flowing: Mind Mapping, 30 Circles, and Empathy Maps. Each of these techniques offers a structure to help push divergent thinking, which helps generate creative ideas by exploring many possible solutions.

Make it a ritual: Carnegie Mellon recently conducted a study where they wanted to test whether frequency of sex determined a couple's happiness level. They asked 128 male/female partners to divide themselves into two groups: one, being asked to double the frequency of their weekly sex, and the other, with no directive other than to measure the frequency they naturally had sex. It turns out that after the study was complete, the group asked to double their weekly frequency reported being less happy than they were when they started. "It wasn't that actually having more sex led to decreased wanting and liking for sex. Instead, it seemed to be just the fact that they were asked to do it, rather than initiating on their own," observed Shilo Rea, a representative at Carnegie Mellon.

So I guess the takeaway from that is to not do it as part of a study? Just kidding. It's a lesson in approach. Certainly, doing things out of obligation, or habit, is seldom fun. A habit is something that is disconnected from the narrative of your day, is dutiful and task-driven, and relatively meaningless.

A ritual, on the other hand, is highly connected to your internal narrative, has meaning and purpose, and is performed as a positive action, aware of the outcome you envision. Steven Handel, Psychology journalist and self-improvement writer at TheEmotionMachine.com, described it like this. "Instead of feeling like every daily activity is something that 'just needs to get done,' it becomes an activity you feel serves a positive function in your life, and it becomes something you enjoy doing and look forward to.

Ultimately, the more meaning you can add to your daily activities, the more motivated you become to do them." For instance, getting dressed in the morning can go from an annoyance to an act of purpose if framed not as just getting dressed, but as something you are doing to contribute to your higher desire to be perceived as being confident and professional. It's about making a conscious effort to create the right environment and put your love and attention toward the act of doing it.

Imagine if you approached your own social media posts with the same ritualistic behavior? I'd be willing to bet that your consistency and connection to your stories will over time attract the right kind of people to you – and your business.

Make your social sexy

It's as simple as getting out of our own way, believing you can do it, taking an active role in creating the right conditions to do it, and making it a meaningful practice of your everyday life.

In short: Let people into your life – often and openly. You can do it, and yes, (yes, yes) don't ever stop! #ThatsWhatSheSaid

―――――

Courtney Smith Kramer Co-founder PureMatter and the H2HClub.com. She's a Forbes contributor and the author of "21 Reasons Creativity is Like Sex." You can connect with Courtney at https://CourtneySmithKramer.com

CHAPTER 37

TEN GREAT WAYS TO START YOUR NEXT BLOG POST, PODCAST, OR VIDEO

BY MITCH JACKSON

1 00 years ago the average attention span was 20 minutes. Today, some experts believe it's around 9 seconds, the same attention span as a goldfish.

Now I'm not too sure about attention spans getting shorter because I've watched people spend hours on things they enjoy doing, but what I do believe is that in today's world, there's simply a great deal more things to look at, listen to, watch and do. Because of this, people don't waste their limited time on things that they may have paid attention to 10-20 or even 100 years ago.

With this new dynamic in mind, one thing I think we can all agree on is that it's never been more important to immediately capture the attention of your audience so that they stick around and listen to what you have to say. One way to do this is to grab their attention right out of the gate when you share new content on social media.

To help make my point, let's say you're sharing a new post on social media revolving around the power of communication. To immediately grab the attention of your audience, start with one of these 10 approaches and then when done, circle back to the main content of your material.

Pro Tip: When I'm on stage speaking or, giving an opening statement or closing argument in a jury trial, I usually start with one of these 10 approaches. I take 60-90 seconds to develop the approach and usually try to do so in the form of a short story. If I've gone about things the right way, I can usually add a bit of interest or intrigue to the presentation and get everyone to sit at the edge of their seats wanting more.

As mentioned above, let's say the title to your blog post, podcast, video or live video is, "The Power of Communication." You may want to start with something like the following:

1. A quote: "The single biggest problem in communication is the illusion that it has taken place." – George Bernard Shaw

2. A statistic: "The next time you deliver a speech, keep in mind that 90% of what you're about to say will be forgotten within 60 minutes after everyone leaves."

3. A question: "Do you know what the biggest communication challenge is in today's noisy and crazy world? It's probably not what you think!"

4. A current news item: "Becoming an effective communicator got me on the evening news last night to discuss the Presidential election. During the show, you all saw what happened. I think it just might change the outcome of the election. Would you like to know what communication steps I took to connect with the producers and get invited on to the show?

5. A story that relates directly to your message: "I watched opposing counsel give his closing argument. He stumbled through the whole thing. It was a mess. Using four of the tips that I'll be sharing with you today, I stood, walked over to the jury, and gave a closing argument that resulted in a million dollar verdict. Would you like to know what those four steps were?"

6. A sincere thank you or acknowledgment: "Rotary International is truly one of the top community service organizations in the world. I'd like to thank Bob Smith for including me in the event and giving me the opportunity to share my communication tips with you."

7. Have your audience write something down: "There are five steps that exceptional communicators use, each and every time, to get people to take action on their message. Miss a step and it's game over. Do all five and getting people to buy your products and services is like shooting fish in a barrel. Would you like to know what those steps are? OK great, grab a pen and paper because you'll want to write each one down."

8. Humor: "The mind is a wonderful thing. It starts working the minute you are born and never stops until you get up to speak in public."

9. Make a prediction: "By the time we finish this presentation, I predict that you will increase your ability to persuade others by 25% to 50%.

10. A poem, rhyme or thoughtful statement: "Communication may be the KEY, but my hands are shaking as I start the ignition. How many of you feel this way when you stand to deliver a speech or presentation?"

There you go. Ten great ways to start your next social media post and immediately capture the attention of your audience.

CHAPTER 38

THE STORYTELLING FRAMEWORK THAT WORKS EVERYWHERE FOR EVERYONE

BY CHRIS LEMA

The Mistake We're All Making

If you were an inventor that created special shoes for people whose feet sweat a lot, you likely wouldn't put them online for sale with an ad that talked about how great they looked, right? You wouldn't pitch their fine and smooth leather, right?

No.

You would quickly get to the main selling dynamic, or the unique selling point (USP), which is that they're perfect for people who have sweaty feet.

We all know this. And yet tons of people create websites every day that can't, within a minute or two, articulate who they're for or what value they bring to the table.

This isn't because we all lack common sense. I think one of the biggest reasons we fail to communicate effectively - whether on websites or social media - is that we know that if we come across as prideful, we'll turn people off.

So we make the classic mistake that everyone does - we let our insecurities keep us quiet.

But what if there was a way to tell our story - whether we're a consultant, a lawyer, a marketer, or engineer, whether we're selling a product or a service - in a way that was compelling and that didn't make us feel icky?

What if there was a storytelling framework that could help us shape the narrative in a way that made it clear who we were trying to talk to, helped others, and highlighted our uniqueness? And what if it worked in every situation? And in every context (twitter, facebook, blog posts, youtube, etc.)?

The good news is that I think there is such a framework - and it's one I've been sharing with my coaching clients for years.

To introduce you to the framework, I need to tell you a story.

Getting Over the River

Imagine I woke up this morning and realized that tonight was the night of the costume ball that I had been invited to - and I still haven't purchased a costume. The first thing on my to-do list this morning would be that - getting to the store and picking something out that wasn't too crazy or expensive.

Luckily for me, I knew where the year-around discount Halloween store was. It was at the top of a hill that I could see from my front door. So that's where I was headed.

While there are certainly many ways to get there, the road right outside my house goes directly there, so I knew I just needed to walk out my door and start making my way up the hill.

After walking for a bit, the path I'm on abruptly stops at a river. So I do what any person in shorts and a t-shirt would do. I take off my shoes and start trying to walk across the river. However, just a few steps in I realize that it got deep fast, and I wouldn't be able to walk across. So I get back out.

I then put my wallet and phone in a plastic bag, stick it in my back pocket, and dive in to swim across the river. But just a few strokes in, I realize that the current is moving too quickly, and I'll never make it across. So I get back to the riverbank and sit there to dry off.

Then, even before I see it, I hear a motorboat. I'm thrilled to know that someone is heading upriver to help me. And then I see the boatman, and he asks if I've trying to get across. He tells me he can take me, for $10. So I grab the ten bucks from my wallet and hand it over. And that's when he takes off!

Now I'm wet, tired, and broke.

So I start walking up the river bank slowly, thinking of my situation. After about an hour, I see it.

A bridge!

I walk up to it and test it out. It holds. So I walk across it. And now I'm excited to walk back down the riverbank to the road.

When I get to the road, I'm about to continue on my journey when I notice there are people back on the other side of the river. Some look really mad - staring at open wallets. Others are wet and sitting, and a few others are just staring at the river.

I yell across, "Hey, I don't know if you're trying to get across the river, but if you are, be careful about walking across because it gets deep fast. Also, watch out for the current. And the guy who charges you $10 to boat you across is a thief.

"I don't know a bunch more than you, and I'm surely not better than you, but if you trust me, I'll tell you what I do know - about an hour up the river is a great bridge that I just used to get over the river.

"And if you're headed to the costume store, like me, I'm happy to wait here and then we can continue on this road together."

The Framework Explained

The story I just told you is easy to listen to, and even easier to remember. It consists of the following parts:

> The Objective / Destination - in this case, it's the costume store on the hill
> The Strategy / Route - in this case, the road that goes from the house to the store
> The Obstacle - in this case, the river
> The Failed Attempts - you'll recall we tried walking, swimming and paying someone
> The Discovery - We find the bridge late in the story
> The Offer - We shout to others, letting them know where the bridge is
> The Connection - We offer to wait so we can all go together

The problems we have with marketing today is that we pitch the offer way too soon.

> Without clarity of the destination, we're offering something that no one needs.
> Without clarity of the route, we're going to end up debating strategies.
> Without clarity of the obstacle, we haven't qualified our leads.
> Without clarity of our own failed attempts, we can't connect with others.
> Without the discovery, the pitch is inauthentic.
> Without the offer, we're not sharing the good news that we know where the bridge is.
> Without the connection, we offer a solution without a community.

Every part of the story is needed.

And when we get to the pitch, it's easy to be humble and say,

"Look, I'm not better or smarter than you. I just happen to have found the solution a couple of hours before you. Here is where it is, and if you want, I'm happy to wait, and we can continue together."

A Simple Example

You can potentially imagine that this framework works for a long landing page where I'm pitching something. But you'll recall that I said it can work for anyone, everyone, and in every context (like Twitter). So was I exaggerating, or can you really use this framework in a tweet (or chain of them)?

Let's wrap this up with a quick example to see how it works.

Let's assume you sell a service where people invite you to their wedding, and you paint their portrait, live, while the ceremony is going on.

I learned about a person doing this role just recently, and we used the framework to help them shape their message. So now we want to shape their message, and we're going to use a series of tweets to invite people to hire us.

Instead of starting with destination and strategy, we'll start at the river with the failed attempts.

Tweet One:

By a show of hands (or likes), how many of you spent hundreds or thousands of dollars on wedding photography on your special day and you haven't looked at them again in years?

Tweet Two:

Here's a follow-up - how many of you (by likes) paid for all those wedding photos and never ended up putting them on a wall to be reminded of that amazing and special day?

Tweet Three:

Last question on this - again by a show of likes, how many of you can quickly and easily find the CDs or photo albums of your wedding day photos? I'm specifically talking to the folks who were married before Facebook was a thing, so no, this isn't about digital copies.

Now let's make sure we get focused on our destination and route.

Tweet Four:

When we spend money, lots of it, on wedding photography (or videography for that matter), we're saying we want a keepsake. That's a lot of money to stick on CDs or in an album we never use. What if there was a better way to create a keepsake that we can cherish forever?

Now we'll introduce our bridge.

Tweet Five:

I just met a woman today who comes to your wedding and paints a picture of you, as a couple, during the ceremony. The painting is ready for your reception and can be hung on your wall as soon as you get back from your honeymoon - for all to see. If I were getting married again (which I'm not), I'd change my photography strategy for sure.

Now let's create an offer.

Tweet Six:

If this sounds interesting to you, or you know someone who might dig this, hit me up - I have 5 20% coupons that I can share, that would make this offer a ridiculously amazing deal. Check out: URL.

Lastly, we'll connect the community.

Tweet Seven:

Wondering if this is right for you? Let's hear from folks that have used ___(service name)____. You can also read testimonials here: URL. If you're like me, that's the first thing I did and wow - the quotes are amazing.

What you'll notice...

What you'll notice from these tweets is that they're not that special. Nothing amazing. No trickery. Simply the dedicated use of a framework to make sure you don't miss or skip key parts.

The same goes for landing page creation. Or sales page copy.

That's why I recommend it to everyone. Because it's a sound approach to people, who have already experienced the pain at the river standing in front of whatever they're trying to accomplish. Before we can transition to the gain, they need to know we connect with their pain.

I hope you'll try it and that you'll circle back and let me know how it goes. You can find me on twitter (@chrislema) writing all sorts of tweets, including those that are trying to help you cross the bridge.

———

Chris Lema is a product strategist, public speaker and blogger. He's a WordPress and WooCommerce evangelist and the creator of CaboPress. Chris is the VP of Product @liquidweb and you can connect with Chris at ChrisLema.com

CHAPTER 39

HOOKED! WHY METAPHORS SHOULD BE PART OF EVERY SOCIAL MEDIA STRATEGY

BY ANNE MILLER

Which whitepaper would you rather read?

- How to Save for Retirement
- Catnip or Caviar? Choose Your Retirement Carefully

Which LinkedIn description makes you want to know more about this person?

- Marketing Pro
- Marketing Sherpa

Which website title is more enticing?

- Your Daily News
- The Daily Beast

Which blog advice site would you visit?

- Blog Tips
- Blog Tyrant

Which service description is more compelling?

- We provide a full range of website design services
- If content is the body of a website, design is its soul. We provide the soul.

You likely chose the second entry in each group. Why? Because while the first choice is clinically correct, it is also sterile, colorless, and ordinary. In contrast, there is an image in each of the second choices that conjures up a picture in your mind that is evocative, emotional, and intriguing. All of these images are metaphors, figures of speech, that create word pictures and our brains are irresistibly drawn to pictures. (Just think about the explosion of videos and Instagram.)

You have heard of "eye candy." Metaphors are "brain candy." So, if you want to grab attention in your social media in our attention-deficit world, start using metaphors strategically.

Tell "Joe," But Sell to "Robin"

Everyone knows "a committee sell is a committee buy." When you are online, you are selling to a committee of two. Inside every reader's/viewer's brain is a two-person committee: the logical left brain which processes your information and the emotional right brain which "sees" and "feels" that information.

The left brain is like Joe Friday, the famous old-time TV detective, who was known for coming to a crime scene and saying to witnesses, "Just the facts, ma'am. Just the facts." The right brain, the home of metaphors, is like Robin Williams, spontaneous, visual, emotional, and imaginative. If you sell, persuade, influence, or motivate, you need to satisfy both "buyers." (Einstein said, "If I can't see it, I don't understand it.")

Moreover, we remember visually. When you walk down the street, and you run into someone you haven't seen in twenty years, what goes through your mind: words, numbers, or pictures? It's pictures. "I remember you! You had braids, and you sat behind me in third grade!"

Bottom-line, to seal the deal, tell the left, but, sell to the right. We tend to think facts and more facts will impress and be remembered. Facts are important, but facts driven home with visual language will guarantees greater impact and retention. Compare: "Joe is persistent, resilient, and hard-working," to "Joe is like Rocky. Knock him over, and he comes right back for more." Determination, persistence, and energy, captured memorably with a single image.

In a world where people are drowning in too much information, the metaphor is a communicator's lifesaver, and I submit that becoming a "Metaphorian," a master of metaphor, is the new essential skill set for communication success online and off.

Metaphor? Analogy?

A moment for definitions: Technically, a metaphor is a substitute of one thing for another where a common quality is shared by both. For example, "Jill is an angel" means Jill has the qualities of what we associate with an angel. A simile uses the words "like" or "as." "Jill is like an angel," slightly weaker than the metaphor, but the comparison is still there. An analogy is an extended metaphor. "Jill is an angel. She is always unselfishly helping others." The extension defines what we are to understand about the angel comparison.

No need to worry about these distinctions. I am using metaphor in its broadest sense to mean any comparison that creates an image in another person's mind to make a point.

That can also be an analogy, a story, a cartoon, a picture, a prop, or a saying used as a metaphor. For example, if you are expert in technology services, your site could say "Even if you're on the right track, if you just sit there, you are going to be hit and hit hard by a rapidly changing industry. We keep clients like you on track." Safety, movement, progress all embodied in one image.

Good News! You Don't Have to be Shakespeare

You already speak in metaphors. The reality is we use metaphors every day. In fact, it is rare to get through a conversation without using metaphoric language. (That movie just blew me away! The market took off like a rocket. I'm under the weather today, etc.) According to James Geary, deputy curator of the Nieman Foundation for Journalism at Harvard, it is estimated that you use some form of metaphorical language every twenty to twenty-five words.

The challenge is to go from our unconscious use of metaphors to an intentional use of metaphors to make a difference in your social media impact.

What are the Stakes & Challenges?

How much creativity you bring to your metaphor will depend on how high the stakes are for you and how challenging your situation is. The lower the stakes and the smaller the challenge, the less creative you can be.

What are the "stakes" for you?

- Getting followers?
- Getting likes?
- Increasing subscribers?
- Generating inquiries?
- Conversions?
- Other?

What are the challenges?

- You are in a commodity business?
- You are in a complex business?
- You are new to the market?
- You are rebranding yourself?
- Other?

Casual Metaphors: Low Stakes, Small Challenges

These are metaphors you use in everyday conversations without much pre-thought.

A client asks about your technology, and you say you tailor your services to their needs. A colleague wants to share a report with you. Stressed out, you reply, "Sorry, I just don't have the bandwidth to process that." After a successful meeting, you tell your teammate that she really nailed that presentation.

These metaphors tend to be clichés. There is nothing wrong with clichés as such, but they may not be strong enough or memorable enough for more important situations. Clichés are easy to create but usually, lack a real gut punch.

Higher Stakes, Sizable Challenges

Crafted and Creative metaphors require more deliberation than Casual metaphors.

Situations that benefit from more thoughtfully created metaphors can be when...

- You want a catchy title for your blog, site, tweet, video, post, or article
- You are presenting a new process or concept online in a podcast
- You are neutralizing a concern in the FAQ section of your site
- You are positioning your firm in the market
- Other?

When the stakes are considerable, and the challenges are substantial, use this five-step thought process to create your winner.

- Identify the point you want to make
- Think of the worlds your viewers/readers are likely familiar with (sports, the arts, transportation, history, science, families, travel, current events, weather, etc.)
- Ask, "What is this like in those worlds?"
- Aim for several metaphors/analogies until you hit the one that works the best
- Apply it in a way that is concise and appropriate in tone

The resulting image can be quite simple...

For example, suppose you have a home care service website, and you know that families panic and automatically assume it is Alzheimer's when they hear that a parent is diagnosed with dementia. A technical explanation by itself that all Alzheimer's disease is dementia, but not all dementia is Alzheimer's is not likely to register with relatives who are in shock when they hear the word dementia. Nor is it likely to result in a request for further information.

However, when you add that "It's like ice cream," everything changes. All chocolate ice cream is ice cream, but not all ice cream is chocolate," you are far more likely to have readers see their parents' dementia reframed in a less threatening light and have them reach out to you for assistance.

The resulting image can be truly unique...

When someone is starting out with a new concept and site, the stakes (being sustainable) are high, and the challenges are great (who are you again?). George Kao, now widely recognized social media guru initially needed an image guaranteed to hook neophytes to learn more about social media. He wrote online,

"The social networking space is way better than face-to-face networking because the size of the pool for potential contacts is so much greater. " It's like walking into a room with no walls and out onto the world stage, a kind of conference of the world which, by the way, is also open 24/7."

Wow! Who wouldn't want to be a part of that—and to sign up for his services!

When the stakes are high, and the challenges are great, metaphors are killer apps.

Strengthen Your Metaphor Muscle

Get the metaphor habit for maximum impact and resonance online. How?

- Always be thinking, "What is this like?"

- Read and watch media differently. Actively notice how strong communicators use metaphors from many different worlds. Read the business and sports sections of your newspaper. They are rich in metaphors. Check out Op-Ed articles which are studded with metaphors because they are designed to persuade you to a point of view. Listen to political commentators. They constantly use metaphors to characterize situations and to wrap up their points. Read theater and movie reviews. They can be both funny and scathing.

- Pay attention to good speakers and how they use metaphors to engage you.

Using Clichés online is better than nothing, but I encourage you to aim higher for a bigger payoff. Take the time to develop Crafted and Creative metaphors and watch how much easier, faster, and more profitable it becomes to get the results you want on social media.

Mark Twain said, "The difference between a word and the right word is the difference between a lightning bug and lightning."

Be the lightning.

———

For 25+ years, Anne Miller has been helping high profile firms, as well as small businesses in media, digital, financial, technology, and professional service industries, sell millions of dollars' worth of business. Presentation coach, seminar leader, and speaker, she is the author of "The Tall Lady with the Iceberg: the power of metaphors to sell, persuade & explain anything to anyone." Sign up for her monthly "Metaphor Minute" Newsletter and "Make What You Say Pay!" blog at http://www.annemiller.com Anne can be reached at amiller@annemiller.com

CHAPTER 40

FIVE STRATEGIES TO BUILD YOUR PERSONAL BRAND AND PROFESSIONAL NETWORK

BY JON FERRARA

Every day, the world is changing and evolving. This is also true for the world of business.

We're constantly barraged by emails, social media engagements; and virtual networking opportunities; all of these possibilities to connect with people in your industry can easily become overwhelming, even for the best of us. The buyer's journey is forever changing -- and it's our duty to change with it.

This is why I'm excited to share five strategies that have helped me build my own personal brand and to build global multi-million dollar technology companies -- without spending a dime on advertising. You can achieve your own passion, plan, and purpose in life by building your personal brand to attract people into your network who can mutually benefit from your collaboration and cultivate authentic relationships at scale.

Here are actionable tips you can immediately implement to network faster and more effectively with the right group of people using Nimble CRM, the simple, smart CRM for Office 365 and G Suite.

1. Be an interest magnet

Your network is your net worth; you should always be seeking out new opportunities to connect with prospects and nurture your existing relationships.

People have been using storytelling to stay top of mind with their customers, prospects, and community since the beginning of time. Staying top of mind requires you to become a trusted adviser to your prospective customers.

Rather than telling other people how great you or your products are, teach them how to be great, and the process, they'll figure out they need your product or service. If you give your knowledge away on a daily basis, you will build trust, intimacy, and influence with key people you need to grow your business. Inspire and educate your prospects and customers by sharing relevant, actionable content across your social channels that will help them build their own personal brand.

By building your personal and professional brand in and around the areas of your company's brand promise, people will turn to you when they need help solving problems your business can help them address.

I liken the process to dripping digital lures into the social river. If you sit in your office and you do nothing, no one is going to bite. Instead, if you drop digital fishing lures into the social business river with engaging content, you will see people respond. Attention is precious, so be prepared to respond quickly and take careful note of the type of content your audience responds well to.

Keep the conversation going, and you'll drive eyeballs to your site, gain a faithful following, and generate priceless word of mouth recommendations that will help grow your network.

The corollary is also true. If you don't respond to people who comment or share your content, you will lose momentum and miss out on many valuable opportunities.

2. Foster genuine relationships

Would you purchase anything from someone you didn't know, trust, or even like?

I didn't think so.

How do you get people to know who you are, or to trust you? The simple answer is: let your humanity shine through in all that you do. Reliability, relationships, and ethicality speak volumes in the business world. Never lose sight of these values in the rush to fill your pipeline with as many deals as possible.

At the end of the day, we buy from people — not companies. What makes us human is what makes people want to engage with us. Examine how your social body language translates to various social platforms or throughout your digital marketing strategy, and start to build your authentic personality into the ways you share.

I always say that people build relationships around "The Five F's of Life:" Family, Friends, Food, Fun, and Fellowship. Keep these relationship keystones in mind during every interaction in order to connect authentically with prospects or customers based on shared interests.

3. Listen First, Speak Second

Dale Carnegie knew it way back in the 1950s: get to know people and what they care about before you talk about yourself. I believe we're all here to learn and grow; and that the more you help others to grow, the more you grow yourself. Instead of steering your conversations into the sales territory, actively listen to the issues your customers or prospects need to address and solve.

The best way to drive the right conversation is to do your homework. Most business professionals have some kind of social presence or curate insightful content on their Linkedin or Twitter; use these platforms to take note of what motivates a given prospect and what they care about.

Pay attention to what people are talking about on social media; knowing what content they engage with, what excites them, or why they went into business in the first place can open doors to start a mutually beneficial conversation. When reaching out, make your approach all about the person and express genuine interest in them.

Once they invite you to reach out, don't be too shy to pick up the phone. While on a call with a customer or a prospect, you should aim to establish yourself as a listener and helper. Offer to make introductions, help to spread the word about the person's company and/or services, review their latest book, or leave a stellar review their product online. It can seem like a small gesture, but even the smallest acts of kindness can go a long way.

4. Cultivate a community of influencers

One of the easiest ways to build trust and open a dialogue with your prospective customers and buyers is by building trust with the people who influence them. Influencer Marketing has been around since long before social media and smartphones even existed. Over the lifespan of the Internet, it has gone from global to hyperlocal.

The key to running a successful social Influencer Marketing campaign is to identify the right influencers for your brand. Influencer Marketing looks and feels very different depending on the organization and the type of business, but typically involves content collaboration with self-syndicated opinion leaders your customers know and trust.

Ad tools like Facebook Audience Insights help you learn more about your potential influencers with information such as demographics, page likes, purchase behavior, and usage. Using Nimble, you can listen and identify the influencers within relevant communities that are genuinely driving interest and engagement and reach out to them on a meaningful level.

Additionally, tools like Little Bird and Buzzsumo can help you identify analysts, bloggers, prominent investors, and other thought leaders in your circle of interaction based on the number of industry insiders following them, their total number of Twitter followers, their centricity in the conversation, and their overall reach.

5. Effectively leverage social networking

There's no way I could have built a brand (personal or professional), a thriving network, or an engaged Nimble community without social networking.

When cultivating social connections into real relationships, be prepared to connect across multiple channels. I liken Twitter to working a crowd; LinkedIn to your storefront or reception area; and Facebook and Instagram to the collection of books, photos, and collections you have in your office. Each serves a different purpose when relationship-building.

As you build momentum across channels, look for opportunities to bring these relationships into the real world. Here's an example of how to leverage social networking effectively, from my recent experience:

TIffani Bova, a former Gartner analyst and current Global Customer Growth and Innovation Evangelist at Salesforce (who is also a friend of mine), once tweeted: "CRM isn't about managing 'command/control' – it's about empowering front-line resources to serve customers better and that there is a need for improving customer experience."

The head of CRM and Data at a top entertainment production company reacted to Tiffani's tweet by mentioning Nimble and me. He posted that he was impressed with Nimble, but was not sure if sales managers would loosen their grip.

Keen to learn more about this prospective customer, I used Nimble to "auto-magically" build a record about who he is, where he works, and what he does. I next used Nimble Prospector to find his contact information. After commenting on the Twitter stream, I decided to send him a follow-up email. He already knew who I was, what my passions are, and what my business was all about.

The success of the outreach was visible immediately as my prospect responded to me in a matter of seconds. We met the following Saturday for brunch, and he's since become a customer.

Closing Thoughts

In the old days, we developed intimacy and trust by going into somebody's office and looking at their walls, scanning the books they read, checking out schools they attended, and the knick-knacks they've collected along the way to identify areas of commonalities to share. We shared in those commonalities to break the ice and build the bonds that help kick-start relationships. Nowadays, we do it electronically by Googling people and looking them up on multiple social accounts, which isn't easy or straightforward.

When you take the time to actively listen to others, you will discover what's important to them and find ways to add value by addressing their needs to help them succeed. This is the way to not only build your own personal brand but to also nurture your network into mutually beneficial relationships that will stand the test of time.

Jon Ferrara is an American entrepreneur and the founder of Nimble. He is also best known as the co-founder of GoldMine Software Corp, one of the original contact management software companies. Connect with Jon at https://Nimble.com

CHAPTER 41

CREATING GLOBAL DIGITAL EMPIRES®

BY CHAD BARR

In working with, and observing some of the most successful global entrepreneurs, I have concluded that one of the key components of effective global thought leaders is their consistent and exhaustible ability to publish provocative and powerful content.

This content often manifests itself in various formats which includes posting tips and ideas on the various social media platforms, personal quotes, producing written articles on blogs, newsletters, print, and online publications. Increasingly, there are shared audio interviews and valuable episodes distributed through podcasts and webinars, published books, diagrams, and infographics known as my Transformation Visuals™, that craft a series of videos, and create live and online courses. Yet, many still struggle with getting their ideas out of their heads and wrestle with how to effectively manifest and leverage those thoughts, insights, and wisdom.

In order to resolve this challenge of developing great content and helping you in Creating Global Digital Empires®, I developed a simple framework, which has helped hundreds of my global clients. This framework can be used to construct a short article, podcast or video. It contains three parts:

1. Identifying one of the key challenges your clients are facing.
2. Defining three powerful insights to resolve this challenge.
3. Inviting them to contact you.

To clarify this concept, let me share an example with you. I want to create a short video that will engage and help my audience in finding where their key challenge is and how to create a successful web presence. The three insights or components I will discuss are strategy, content, and marketing. Here is a sample script using my framework:

"Over the past 30 years, I've been fortunate to work with some of the most successful global entrepreneurs and organizations. Yet one of the key challenges they all face is their inability to create a successful web presence that generates dramatic outcomes and results. So, if this is one of the challenges you or your organization are facing, there are three insights I would like to share with you to help resolve this challenge.

Number one is your strategy. You must first develop a powerful strategy by identifying your key buyers by age, gender, location, their preferences such as what they read, listen to and watch, and their challenges, hopes and aspirations.

Number two is crafting your amazing content, with tips on the various social media platforms, writing articles for your newsletters and other publications, creating podcasts, webinars and videos, publishing books, infographics, and online courses. For your content to be effective, engaging and remarkable, it should be pithy, powerful and provocative. The simple benchmark I use to determine the quality and provocativeness of the content is to analyze the immediate reaction to the content. Here are two possible responses:

1. "So, what?" meaning; I have heard this concept before, and it is mediocre at best.
2. "I've never thought about it this way" or, "wow, this is great stuff!"

Third, and lastly, are your marketing initiatives, of which I have identified thirty-four in my Marketing Blueprint transformation visual™ which are located on my website. Initiatives such as newsletters, special reports, social media involvement, assessments, eBooks, Workshops, Press releases, interviews and affiliate programs, to name a few.

Over the years I have observed that the most successful entrepreneurs and organizations are leveraging these three concepts to create an extraordinary web presence that generates dramatic success for their business.

So, let me ask you, are you leveraging these concepts to dramatically impact and increase your business? If this resonates with you and you would like to discuss how to transform your business, contact me to help you get started on making some dramatic changes that will make you not only a thought leader, but a business champion. Some of the best relationships I have created over the years have started with a simple conversation just like this one."

This is the essence of my framework. The key is to make sure the stated challenge is a pressing issue for your clients, and the shared insights are unique, powerful and generate interest.

All that is necessary is to record this video, present it with authority, passion, and enthusiasm, post online and let the inquiries come in.

Additionally, there is a hidden contextual treasure in developing content with numeric or bulleted lists. I could easily take any of the three points in my example above, and develop additional and detailed, unique content for each one of these points that could stand on its own.

Another question I am often asked is, Where Do Ideas Come From? Here are 21 Insights to Accelerate Your Creative Flow:

1. Books – Read great books and recap your key highlights.
2. Publications – Scan them to stay informed.

3. Curiosity – Ask questions to develop this sense.
4. Observe – Pay attention to your global surroundings.
5. Examine – Question your basic assumptions.
6. Travel – See the world and meet fascinating influencers.
7. Genius – Surround yourself with great thinkers who challenge you.
8. Brainstorm – Hold discussions with individuals you respect.
9. Self-Development – Invest in your continued education.
10. Summarize – Condense powerful insights and create trends.
11. Label – Give your findings unique names and invent new brands.
12. Provocative – Challenge the way people think.
13. Interviews – Conduct conversations with thought leaders.
14. Metaphors – Develop these to add interest and improved concept articulation.
15. Speak – Get on a stage and share your wisdom.
16. Teach – One of the greatest ways of mastering a new topic.
17. Content – Create and evolve your intellectual property.
18. Story – Share your fascinating messages to inspire others.
19. Instantiate – Make the complex, simple.
20. Models – Build and expand your processes.
21. Innovate – Push the envelope, Raise The Barr® and execute.

Since I am a strong believer in the power of visuals and that a picture is often worth a thousand words, I created this infographic to display the list above, which is also a great example of how to take a numeric list and showcase it visually.

So where does one start in creating content? I recommend you start with short insights that can be tweeted. Combine multiple tweets into a logical sequence and create a bulleted or numeric list. Take each of the points and further articulate their explanation using examples, experiences, and opinion. Add an opening and a concluding paragraph, and you now have your article or position paper. Organize multiple articles in a logical order, and you have now created an eBook or a book to publish. This book can then transform itself into a workshop or an online course where each chapter becomes a module.

You are now well on your way to create and strengthen your own intellectual property, digital empire and thought leadership.

Finally, as you consistently develop, publish and leverage your content, one additional concern is how to effectively get it to your clients. In addition to publishing in print and online, one of the concepts I created is called Targeted Value. The essence is to contact a selected individual(s), provide them with genuine value that addresses or resolves their issue(s) and suggest a follow-up. Here is an example:

"During our last conversation, you shared with me that your key challenge is how to grow your business and thrive rather than barely survive. Hoping it is of great value to you, I am attaching an article I just wrote that demonstrates the 9 secrets to significantly transform your business. I would love to get your feedback and also share with you two other ideas that I know will be of help to you. How about Thursday at 10AM?"

When this comes from a place of providing sincere and valuable help, the interest is significant.

So, let me ask you, "what is one of the key challenges your clients face and what are the three profound insights to resolve this challenge"?

Rome wasn't built in a day, and neither is your amazing content and digital empire. Begin creating and strengthening your content today and watch your business transform and your empire come to life.

———

Chad Barr is an Internet marketing strategist with over 30 years of experience growing businesses through technology innovation. He helps his global clients create their digital empires and leverage the power of the web to dramatically transform their business success. His firm, The Chad Barr Group, is recognized as one of the leading strategic Internet development organizations in the world. http://www.thechadbarrgroup.com

CHAPTER 42

THE 3-1-3® METHOD
IS THE FOUNDATION TO YOUR ONLINE SUCCESS

BY RYAN FOLAND

You have a website.

Your company spends tens of thousands on Google AdWords, but is it really driving the results you seek?

Chances are, you are completely missing out on an entire market. And that's because you aren't utilizing social media correctly.

Did you know that people constantly scour social media looking for experts like yourself, but aren't able to find them? And when they Google your services, they have so many sites to go through that they get analysis paralysis and give up on choosing a provider, which should end up being you.

There's a solution to this entire problem. And this solution will be able to drive a significant volume of new clients to your professional practice. What makes it possible is utilizing the **3-1-3® Method**, then combining it with a formula I call the **4 V's (Vision, Voice, Volume, and Validation).**

The key is knowing where to start before you start posting. This means discovering how to position yourself to differentiate yourself.

The biggest mistake I see professionals make when trying to "start" on social media is jumping right into publishing content without taking the time to think through and define their personal brand.

What is a personal brand? A personal brand is what you want to be known for.

But the reality is that people who don't know you make decisions about you based on the information that they can find. This is why you must discover what you want to be known for (Vision), then start communicating it with the world (Voice), where your target clients are looking for it (Volume), so that you become recognized as the thought leader you are (Validation).

Your personal brand is essentially the collective information you share about yourself on your website, online feedback, and social profiles. It includes content you create like blogs, images, videos, etc. It also includes the content that others produce about you, like features in publications, podcast interviews, and online reviews (both good and bad ones). When all of the bits of information about you are put together, it forms a representation of you. That "you" is your personal brand.

Everyone has a personal brand already, but not everyone is taking control of their own narrative. When you take control of it, the world opens up.

In your circle of associates, you are probably seen as the top dog, but when it comes to clients, how do they see you? Chances are they are shopping "you" against your colleagues. The reason for that is because they aren't sold on you.

They went to your site, they read your information, but they weren't drawn to you. Why? Because you aren't making a virtual connection with your prospective clients.

But how do you make that connection? Let me walk you through the 4 Vs.

4 V's (Vision, Voice, Volume, and Validation)

Vision: Position Yourself for Your Target Audience.

Working as a professional means you are a specialist. This gives you a competitive edge compared to others who find difficulty in defining what they do. Having this information also allows you to define the problem you want to solve and helps identify your target market.

The 3-1-3 Method allows you to go out and explain who you are in three sentences, down to one sentence, then onto three words. Whether you're talking to someone in person, online, or over the phone, this process will help you pique the interest of the people you're speaking with so they are more interested in learning more about you and what you do.

This is much better than the alternative: selling them on exactly what it is you do and giving them too much information up front.

Most people struggle with answering the question of "what do you specialize in?" Answers usually overload the audience with information that can leave them feeling confused.

The 3-1-3 Method helps people communicate in a more effective manner and will allow you to define your vision.

The 3-1-3 Method works like this:

Step 1: Explain what you do in three sentences.

In order to explain what you do in three sentences, you look at these three factors:

1.   The problem you solve

2. Your Solution
3. Your Target Market

In honor of Mitch, I will share a Mad Libs-esq example of how a lawyer might approach the 3-1-3.

1. The problem that you solve (P). Define the exact problem.

Example: The problem is that when people hire the wrong lawyer for _____ (criminal, divorce, etc.) cases, they end up_____ (in jail / losing children / etc.).

2. The solution to the problem (S). Define the exact solution.

Example: I specialize in _____ (criminal, family, etc.) law, keeping keep my clients out of _____ (trouble, jail, etc.).

3. The market that you cater to (M). Define the exact market.

Example: People between the ages of ____ to ____ years of age who find themselves in trouble with _____ and need the best _____ attorney they can _____ (find / afford).

Step 2: Explain what you do in one sentence.

When you complete step 1, you end up with three points: The market (M), the problem (P) and the solution (S). Now you can rearrange these into any order, which gives you six potential ways to explain what you do.

Example of three elements in one sentence in the order of Solution, Market, Problem (SMP)

(S) I create the strongest defense possible for (M) people who have gotten into a _____ (serious, expensive, heart wrenching) legal mess (P) and don't want to _____ (go to jail, get fined, lose everything, etc.)

All six formats:

PSM - The problem is this, and I solve it by doing this, for these people.
PMS - I solve this problem, for these people, and here is how I do it.
MPS - These people, have this problem, and this is how I solve it.
MSP - These people, need my solution of this, to solve this problem.
SMP - My solution is this, for these people, who have this problem.
SPM - My solution is this, which solves this problem, that these people have.

By the end, you will be able to create six different one-sentence explanations of what you do. As you can see, this keeps your brand message focused, while helping you communicate it in various ways. This will help you avoid sounding like a broken record in the content that you are creating and posting on social media.

Step 3. Explaining what you do in three words.

The final step of the 3-1-3 Method is to take two things that nearly everyone could relate to and combine them together, creating an analogy that people quickly grasp.

This is NOT a tagline.

It's designed so people can easily picture what you do in terms of other things that they understand. For example, many people understand what certain professions are, like blacksmiths and carpenters. They also know who famous people are, like Oprah, Kobe Bryant and Tony Robbins. And they know fictional characters like Rambo, Batman, and Wonder Woman. By taking two familiar elements and combining them together, people will naturally try to figure out the relationship in their head, and they will be intrigued to learn more about what you do.

Below are examples of descriptions for specific professional services using this metaphor method. Can you guess which one goes with which industry?

a. Oprah of Litigation	____ Mortgage Broker
b. The Blacksmith of Branding	__ Certified Public Accountant
c. Batman for Vegans	____ Banker
d. The Tony Robbins of Blogging	____Paralegal
e. Elon Musk of Accounting	Web Designer
f. Robin Hood of Real Estate	____ Insurance
g. Life Jacket for Houses	____ Professional Chef
h. Wonder Woman of Depositions	____ Marketing Manager
i. Uber of Finance	____Freelance Writer
j. Cardiologist of Websites	____ Lawyer
	____ Insurance Agent

The minimum amount of words to accomplish this is three: one element, a relational term and the second element. If the elements you are using are multiple words, then the three words could become four to five words total. The idea is to create a metaphor of what you do, leveraging what people already know.

When you think of related words and names to compare yourself to, you can take the credibility and thoughts a person has about something or someone else and incorporate those analogies into how they perceive what you do. This method helps you stand out and communicate more effectively.

It also piques interest, where normally people would just fluff over.

Benefits of the 3-1-3 Method:

Quickly communicating what you do. When communicating with someone for the first time, whether online or in person, you can spark interest with your three words metaphor of what you do. If they are interested in what you have to say, you can tell them what you do in three sentences, one at a time. If they are still interested, you can sum up what you do again in one sentence. If they are still interested in learning more, you can use this opportunity to potentially land new clients or client referrals.

The worst thing you can do is blend in. If you're a trial lawyer, you don't want to sound like every single other trial lawyer out there. If you're an accountant, you don't want to sound like every other accountant either. If you are a professional (insurance agent, banker, freelancer, dentist, doctor, accountant, etc.) you want to stand out from your competition.

Here are the exact steps to a 3-1-3 exercise.

> Step 1. Write out the problem that you are solving in one sentence.
> Step 2. Write out the solution in one sentence.
> Step 3. Write out who your market is in one sentence.
> Step 4. Combine these core elements into a single sentence.
> Step 5. Do step 5 three times in different orders.
> Step 6. Create metaphors using relational terms.

Voice: Create Content That Connects

Once you have clarity on your Vision using the 3-1-3, it is time to start sharing your Voice. This means creating content with your expertise through writing, videos, and/or imagery.

Want to know a secret about content creation?

Don't ask, "What do I want to promote?" Instead, ask, "What do people who require my services want or need to hear?"

Let's pretend that you are startup lawyer who specializes in corporate formation, and may be eager to produce social content on that topic.

Now put yourself in a prospective client's shoes. Perhaps they might be interested in learning about incorporating after seeing a friend start a company, or coming up with a new idea, but they may have no idea where to start. Why would they care about your content?

Consider what your clients want to hear and not just what you want to tell them. If you needed a startup attorney, what would your lifestyle be like? Would you be thinking when you wake up? Would you be overconfident in your ability to do it yourself? What type of questions would you be looking to have answered? Would you be embarrassed about how little you know? Would you be scared? If you were still working, and were ready to quit your nine to five job to pursue your startup, what would you tell your boss? (want a challenge? Try making a list of 10 questions that your target market would ask themselves.)

What an entrepreneur who is not yet incorporated wants to know goes way beyond how a company is formed or what tax benefits you get based on the different ways to incorporate.

What they really want to know is how to get their company set up right, at the right time, in the right way. They want to take the next steps from where they are at. They want to know that you care about their problem and that you can help them. They want to know that before they commit to a life-changing decision like starting a company that they know all of the options available. They want to know the risks and the real costs. They want your help in guiding them through more issues than just the incorporation itself.

In this example, when looking at a startup client through this lens, what do you think they would be more than likely to click on to read or watch:

- This Is How Incorporation Works
- These Are The Top 5 Fears Holding You Back From Incorporating Your Business (And How to Overcome Them)

When creating your content, keep what your client wants to hear in mind, not what you want to promote.

Volume: Amplify Your Content by Syndicating Your Content

With your Vision in position and your Voice taking the form in strategic content creation, it is time to turn up the Volume. Volume is all about the amplification of your content so more people see it. Most content creators feel so much frustration after they start putting their material on the internet. They feel like they spend so much time creating something, for only five people to see it. When you think of how much time it truly takes to create something of quality, you can feel the frustration that one experiences when very few people get to appreciate that content.

In order to counter that, what experienced marketers do is syndicate their content. That means taking content you've created and republishing it on multiple platforms.

Think of social media as an amplification tool. Create the core content that your audience wants to consume, then based on where they are likely to be, you can syndicate a single piece of content over many platforms.

Consider taking your content and sharing on platforms like:

Your Blog - helps to bring people back to your site

LinkedIn.com - a platform that allows for short and long form content.

Facebook.com - a platform that helps you hyper target ads based on target audiences

Medium.com - a popular blogging platform.

Quora.com - a popular question / answer site.

Instagram.com - an image and video based platform.

Twitter.com - a great place to share links of your content from other platforms.

No matter what type of content you create, it should be able to be repurposed into various formats that you can then share on various platforms to increase the volume of views. One trick I teach executives is to record the audio from presentations, then transcribe them and turn the content into multiple articles. Remember that a talk can become a blog, a blog can become a video, and it could also be turned into an answer to post on Quora. Then you could tweet about it!

For example, if you are writing, "These Are The Top 5 Fears Holding You Back From Incorporating Your Business (And How to Overcome Them)," you are answering the question that someone may have about what to do when they are in the early stages of thinking about starting a business.

Once you figure out what question you are answering, you can use Quora to find the most relevant question to answer.

You can copy and paste your content there, then clean up any formatting that may have been altered during the transfer. This answer, based on your article, can now reach others who are following that same question.

Now, you want to post that same content onto Medium and LinkedIn as well, through their publishing tools. This way, you have separate audiences that see your content and push it out to their networks.

If you're making a video, you can upload it to Facebook and Twitter, Instagram and LinkedIn. You can even add the video to a Quora answer too. When you do this, you have multiple ways to distribute your video where each platform will push your content out to their respective networks. This will get your content in front of a wider audience, especially before you've built a following.

Validation: Measuring Growth Through Analytics

Once you have built an online presence and you are creating content and syndicating it across multiple platforms, you will want to measure your results and measure the Validation. This will give you the opportunity to see what is and what isn't working. You will be able to see what people engage with and what they don't.

When you look at social media analytics from the surface, you may feel that no one is paying attention to your content. It's easy to feel that way. Content on social media platforms from professional services can be particularly tricky for building engagement because of people's self-consciousness about certain topics and privacy concerns.

If you are a doctor and you posted on whether or not a symptom is due to hemorrhoids or colon cancer, a lot of people would be too embarrassed to publicly click a "like" on the content. They would be even more embarrassed to publicly share the content with others. On the surface, it would look like you created a post with zero likes and zero shares. And as a content creator, it may feel like no one is looking at what you're creating.

But in actuality, would people read it?

Chances are, if they are experiencing the symptoms, they would. That's why it's so important to be able to look at the analytics in the back end of each platform, so you can see if what you are creating is actually being utilized and to make sure people are clicking through to get the information they need.

As a professional, you are helping people with their problems. And for many of these potential clients or patients, they don't want let others know about their problems. Someone deep in credit card debt and not able to make their mortgage payment will not share an article about filing for bankruptcy. Many people are out there searching the internet for information that they don't want others to know that they are searching for. But they are searching, and you have many of the answers to their questions.

But how can you measure engagement other than likes and shares?

Welcome to the world of analytics.

You can measure your growth in the analytic tools on each platform.

On Twitter, you can visit analytics.twitter.com and view dashboards that show you how each tweet performs.

On your business Facebook Page, you can click on the insights tab and see how many people see your posts, how many people click on them and what actions they take. To track Facebook ad results, you can click on the manage ads link next to the create ads link to see how well they are performing.

On LinkedIn, you can go to linkedin.com/notifications and there will be an indicator under each post that allows you to see analytics for each particular post. On Quora, you can visit quora.com/stats to see how many views, upvotes and shares your content is receiving.

On Medium, you can visit medium.com/me/stats to see how many views, reads and fans you receive on each of your articles on a weekly basis.

When people read, like, share, and engage with your content, it is Validation. Use your analytics as a guide to what content you need to create more of and what kind of content to stay away from.

Eventually, as you create and share more and more content, your name will start surfacing to the top when people search for the answer that they are looking for. You will become sought out for your professional expertise and the leads will start coming to you. Publications will begin asking for your input in articles, and news outlets will ask to for expert commentary. You might land a book deal or even get paid to speak at conferences.

These things are a direct result of building and growing your personal brand.

Will this happen overnight? No.

What I covered here is just the tip of the iceberg.

There are so many more components to the 4V's that will drive your practice to massive success. Mitch only gave me a chapter, not an entire book. But if this methodology is resonating with you and you would like to experience a full workshop for you and your partners, executives or employees, you can email me at ryan@ryanfoland.com to discuss which package best suits you.

———

Ryan Foland is an international keynote speaker and Managing Partner of InfluenceTree, where he and his business partner, Leonard Kim, help professionals harness the power of a personal brand. Learn more about Ryan's business at InfluenceTree.com, and more about him at https://ryanfoland.com

CHAPTER 43

THE 5 STEP PLAYBOOK FOR
HANDLING SOCIAL MEDIA COMPLAINTS

BY JAY BAER

Dealing with complainers and haters in social media can, of course, be tricky. What you need is a framework for how to do it right. This is that framework.

Caught in a maelstrom of customer questions and real-time uncertainty, the Indianapolis Motor Speedway could have used such a playbook.

Torrential rains washed out the first day of driver qualifying for the 2015 edition of the Indianapolis 500, the largest and most famous automobile race in the United States. When the cancellation was announced, after just a few cars had tried to qualify in a pre-torrent mist, many ticket-holders went to social media to ask about refunds.

Drew Hester asked on Twitter: "@IMS since qualifying is rained out can tickets purchased today be used as a rain check tomorrow?" The racetrack replied, but they did so with a startling lack of compassion and nuance:

"@drewhester12 Today's tickets will not be honored tomorrow."

The Speedway sent similar replies to many customers on Twitter, and posted fundamentally the same message on Facebook: no refunds. The outcry was swift, both about the lack of refunds for an event that had essentially not taken place and especially for the unsympathetic and abrupt social media replies from the track.

Eventually, the IMS yielded, and tickets were made valid for the following day's successful, rain-free qualifying.

Here's the playbook the IMS evidently didn't have; the formula for handling social media complaints. In social media, the key lessons to remember are **F-E-A-R-S:**

> **FIND** all mentions
> Display **EMPATHY**
> **ANSWER** Publicly
> **REPLY** Only Twice
> **SWITCH** Channels

You may notice that I didn't include "be fast" as a specific component. This is because it is axiomatic. Today, nearly 40% of all social media complainers who expect a response, expect that response to arrive within 60 minutes, according to the research I conducted for Hug Your Haters. Yet, the average length of time for businesses to actually respond is five hours.

Closing that gap is critical and should be a focus for any legitimate social media customer service program. I recently gave a presentation (in Indianapolis, ironically) and found an example of an accounting firm that habitually answers the phone on the first ring, and emails clients back within five minutes. They have MASTERED the "fast" part of customer service!

1. Find All Mentions

It's impossible to hug the haters you never see. In the legacy, offstage channels of phone and telephone, this isn't an issue. If someone calls your business, you know they called. The phone was either answered, or the caller left a message. The same is true for email; there's no detective work needed to find them, they just show up on your computer, phone, or tablet.

But it's harder with social media and other online customer complaints venues. At the basic level, all professionals should be using social media listening software. Buffer would be a terrific choice for small business.

Are you looking at your reviews on Yelp and other local discussion boards and forums where customers and clients may be discussing your work? You should be, and someone in your organization (maybe you) should be monitoring your reputation at least weekly.

2. Display Empathy

Though social media complainers and haters may not expect a reply, they definitely desire an audience. That's why they raise the stakes and take grievances to a public forum. They want onlookers to chime in with variations on the theme of "I'm appalled! How dare they treat you this way!" Their complaints are often filled with language that vacillates between colorful and outrageous. It creates the reaction they seek, from the audience and possibly from you. They are angry. They write something scathing and post it online. Now you're angry too.

When you read a highly negative comment about your business (or about yourself), you not only feel angry but experience a very real physical reaction. This is especially true for small business owners, as a customer complaint feels like someone is telling you your baby is ugly!

But engaging in a sequence of acrimonious accusations with customers in a public, online forum never works. The business is never the perceived victor, even if they were truly in the right. Back-and-forth "flame wars" are not rare. They happen a lot, and they happen because the person answering customer complaints is unable to put empathy for the customer ahead of their physiological desire to fight.

Inserting empathy into your interactions with social media haters doesn't mean that you give them all wet, sloppy kisses. It doesn't mean you bend over backwards. It doesn't mean the customer is always right. It does mean the customer is always heard, and you should acknowledge, instantly and often, that the person is having a problem that your business likely caused somehow. A short "I'm sorry" goes a long, long way.

3. Answer Publicly

Replying in public is an important part of the playbook for handling online complaints (and praise).

Remember, online customer service is a spectator sport. Sure, you want to make the hater happy, but the opinions of the onlookers are the bigger prize. Whether you're in apology mode or responding to a positive comment, if your client is choosing to interact with you in public, respond in the same way, at least at first. If you respond in private, you are squandering the trust capital gained by being open and transparent in how you handle customer feedback.

You might think, "Well, who cares if they leave us a Yelp review of our firm, and we reply back to them with a private message? At least we're replying!" The spectators on Yelp don't know you replied.

Even if they rant and rave and call you names, you'll answer coolly and publicly. It probably won't change the behavior or attitude of that one person, as it's almost impossible to turn a crazy lemon into lemonade; the fruit is already rotten. But by replying in public, you show your temperament, your values, and your belief that all customers deserve to be heard.

4. Reply Only Twice

This is the question I get most often about the hug your haters system:

"What if I respond to a hater, and he replies back with something even more negative?"

It happens all the time. Social media complainers see you respond and believe they have a foil, an opponent, a punching bag. But they do not. Because you and your customer service personnel know the key to effective onstage interactions: Jay Baer's Rule of Reply Twice.

My Rule of Reply Twice is simple and developed and proven across my 22 years as an online marketing and customer experience consultant. The rule is:

Online, never reply more than twice to any one person in any single conversation

Violating the Rule of Reply Twice can drag you down into a vortex of negativity and hostility, and it's also a waste of your time. Here's how it works in practice. We'll use a fictional hater called "Chad" (just a coincidence and not in any way related to the kid of the same name who tormented me in high school).

Chad: "You guys are the absolute worst. I can't believe you actually have the guts to accept American currency for your terrible tax preparation service!"

Business: "We seem to have fallen short in your eyes, Chad. Can you tell me more about what happened, and I'll do whatever I can to assist?"

Chad: "It won't matter. It's not like an idiot like you can fix all that's wrong with this ridiculous company."

Business: "I'm sorry you're unhappy and would like to help if possible. Please contact me via private message if you'd like me to give it a try."

At this point, if Chad continues to complain, just let him do so. You've made two legitimate attempts to solve his problem. He has acknowledged this to be true by replying back to you, and the spectators will see the same. Now it's time to let it go and walk away.

Nothing will be gained by replying again and again. You've done your part. You're on record. Move on.

The Rule of Two does not dictate that you always have to answer twice, just that you never answer more than twice.

5. Switch Channels

The truncated nature of many social communications means it may be impossible to fully address a complex complaint in only two interactions. For example, you may need the client's account number or other sensitive details to assist them, and you should not ask them to expose that information in full view of the digital spectators. So for nuanced customer interactions that require research to resolve, your goal should be to switch channels after your initial, public response.

More than 60 percent of businesses say they are not capable of handling customer issues in one contact in social media. Whenever you need to take a public, onstage customer interaction private, do so in the hidden chambers of the original contact channel. Fortunately, almost all onstage channels offer this functionality to businesses. Take advantage of it.

If a client reaches out to your business on Twitter and you need their account number to investigate, in your first reply apologize and ask them to send a direct message with their account number. Same thing with Facebook Messenger, Instagram, Linkedin and beyond.

So there you have it, the playbook for handling social media complaints. Just remember **F-E-A-R-S.**

———

Jay Baer is the author of , "Hug Your Haters: How to Embrace Complaints and Keep Your Customers." Jay shares a special bonus offer available at HugYourHaters.com. Find out why Guy Kawasaki calls the books "A transformational work in the history of customer service."
https://www.jaybaer.com

CHAPTER 44

HOW PROFESSIONALS CAN WIN
AT SOCIAL CLIENT CARE

BY DAN GINGISS

The advent of social media brought worlds of opportunity to professionals who are using social media to market their practices, but it also brought something new and somewhat frightening: Social is the only channel where clients, patients, and customers (together I'll be referring to as "clients") can talk back! This initially took professionals by surprise, and they weren't equipped to handle the deluge of client inquiries, complaints, and service needs that emerged simply because professionals decided to interrupt our otherwise pleasant Facebook and Twitter feeds with marketing messages and helpful "how to" content.

There is a simple formula for determining which client experience gets shared on social media. It is: Experience Expectations + Emotions = Willingness to Share. Clients begin with expectations about what their experience should be like with a professional. The vast majority of those expectations are perfectly reasonable – they want it to be fast, easy, friendly, reasonably priced, and so on. How a professional performs against those expectations has a strong influence on whether clients will share their experience on social media.

If a professional exceeds expectations, clients are happy, and their willingness to share their experience in social media is high. If a professional simply meets expectations, clients are neither happy nor sad ("meh," as the Millennials might say), and the willingness to share their experience is low. If a professional misses expectations, clients are unhappy (or even angry), and unfortunately, their willingness to share their experience is high.

Most experiences fall into the "meets" (or "barely meets") category and therefore are not shared on social media. That presents an enormous opportunity for professionals to be able to control some of the social media conversation – by ensuring that professional experiences consistently fall into the "exceeds" category.

But truth be told, most professionals are still seeing a majority of their inbound posts being questions or complaints about the experience.

Documenting a process for engaging with people in social media is an absolute must because there are so many scenarios to consider. And while the only constant in social media is change, a well-written process document can provide stability and a clear roadmap to new and existing employees, as well as managers, leadership, auditors, regulators, and anyone else interested in your social Customer Service program. It also helps provide a consistently high level of Client Service, which is key to retaining clients.

Here are some of the things you should consider as part of your formal process:

When to Take Discussions Off-Channel

It is always best to answer a question on the channel of the client's choice if possible. The client likely knows you have other Client Service channels, but has chosen to use social media instead. This may be because another channel has failed him/her, or it may be because social media is their first-choice channel. Serving the client in the channel of their choice is the best way to ensure their happiness and satisfaction, and the last thing someone who's been on hold for two hours wants to hear is, "Please call our 800 number for assistance"! Answering inquiries publicly also allows others in the social media community to see that your practice or company is responsive, that it cares for its clients, and that it provides great service. A further benefit may be to help others who have not even asked a question yet, potentially reducing future Client Service expenses.

Managing Personally Identifiable Information (PII)

There are situations which absolutely require moving a conversation out of the public spotlight. Inquiries (or their answers) that include Personally Identifiable Information (PII) or Protected Health Information (PHI) must be taken to a private space immediately due to privacy laws. PII is any information that can be used to identify a specific individual and is often separated into "sensitive" and "non-sensitive" information. You should check with your company's lawyers for their exact definition of sensitive PII, but examples include Social Security Number, Driver's License Number, birthdate, addresses and phone numbers, account numbers, and the like. Non-sensitive information is that which is releasable to the public, such as information on one's business card. Where it gets tricky is when the client includes sensitive PII in his or her social media post; while they are making their own sensitive information public, that doesn't necessarily give your practice the right to verify or repeat it. Again, check with your company's lawyers for exact details.

Escalation Procedures

Your process document should indicate who should be called and under which circumstances for as many scenarios as you can dream up. Think about the situations in which you should call management, Public Relations, Human Resources, or even the police.

• When to call management: Be sure to escalate issues where you think (or know) your practice has really screwed up. This could be a faulty product, an erroneous marketing campaign, a system outage, or a particular circumstance where a client was just not treated in the right way. These are generally issues that you won't be able to solve for the customer by yourself.

• When to call Public Relations (PR): All inquiries from the media should immediately be sent to the PR department. Any questions relating to your company's stock, earnings reports, or other investor/analyst questions should be sent to PR and/or your company's Investor Relations department. In addition, any scenario that has the potential to devolve into a scandal or crisis should be immediately directed to PR so they can prepare an official company response that includes social media.

• When to call Human Resources (HR): If you encounter an issue that involves any of your company's employees, it's time to engage the HR department. This can involve posts that reference specific employees, posts from disgruntled employees or ex-employees, any violations of your company's Social Media Policy, or general or specific threats against any employee.

• When to call the police: If you ever encounter a post which discusses or threatens criminal activity or harm to oneself or others, you should contact local authorities. This is best done through your PR or Security department. It can sometimes be difficult to distinguish innuendo ("If they don't answer my call in the next 5 minutes I'm going to kill myself!") vs. an actual threat, but it's better to be safe. Even if you're wrong, you can rest easier knowing that you showed compassion and tried to do the right thing for another human being.

Crisis Management

The most important things to do in a crisis situation are to remain calm and have a plan. Full-blown social media crises are actually pretty rare, but "mini-crises" may seem like they are happening every day. Having a plan that details procedures that anyone working Social Client Care that day can easily begin implementing will allow the company to respond confidently to almost any situation.

Empowering the Team: It is so important to empower your Client Service team to provide "surprise and delight" moments in special situations. A "surprise and delight" moment can be anything unexpected for the client; it should be genuine, show appreciation, and generally of nominal monetary value. Happy clients help your company in many ways. They tend to spend more with your company, have a longer tenure, are more resistant to competitors' temptations of sales and start-up promotions, have more patience when you mess up, and – perhaps most importantly – tell their friends about you, potentially bringing in even more happy clients. Happy Client Service agents also help your company; it feels good to make someone's day, and happy employees lead to happy clients. Be sure to give them explicit permission to "make someone's day" and the guidelines about what is and is not acceptable.

Responding to Compliments: Don't just respond to complaints! Many professionals don't bother responding to compliments on social media, which is a big mistake. When somebody takes time out of their day to tweet at a professional or post on their Facebook page something positive about their experience, the last thing you want to do is ignore them. Compliments are pretty foreign to most Client Service teams (how many times do you think someone has called a toll-free number just to say, "You guys are doing a great job!") so instructing them on how to handle compliments is very important. Always say thank you, engage back with the happy client, and "Like" or retweet their comment to make them feel extra special.

Dealing With Trolls: A troll can be defined as a person looking for attention (in the form of an audience) through incessantly negative banter about a brand. This can often be confusing for Social Client Care agents because they are used to people having problems that they try to solve. But trolls don't really want resolution; they want attention. Often their "complaint" is so amorphous that it isn't solvable anyway. The best way to deal with a troll is to respectfully answer the first post by offering to help. However, here's the interesting part: Because trolls generally aren't looking for resolution, they are often surprised that the professional has engaged them at all. Many times, this will cause them to shut up. If, however, the person remains persistently negative for no apparent reason after a couple of back-and-forths, it's OK to ignore and/or block the person from future communications.

Proactive Client Care: More and more sophisticated professionals are learning that proactive client care can create a great client experience, provide marketing benefits like brand awareness, and even save Client Service costs down the road. Proactive client care can take several forms, including indirect mentions (when someone tweets or posts about your brand, but does not directly "tag" the brand with a handle); proactive alerts (when a practice tells its clients that something is wrong before the clients have a chance to complain about it); industry mentions (when professionals use social listening to identify trends or pain points within their larger industry, rather than about the practice specifically); milestones (when brands reach out to people to celebrate an event or an accomplishment, like a birthday, wedding, new job, pet adoption, or birth of a child); and competitor mentions (when a practice steps in after someone complains about a competitor).

It has been said that "the best defense is a good offense," and this is true in social media. Professionals that are prepared for anything and empowered to make clients happy are the ones that are "Winning at Social Client and Patient Care."

Dan Gingiss is a consultant, speaker and author of "Winning at Social Customer Care: How Top Brands Create Engaging Experiences on Social Media." Connect with Dan at https://www.winningatsocial.com

CHAPTER 45

HOW PROFESSIONALS CAN USE SOCIAL MEDIA, AND TRADITIONAL MEDIA, TO BUILD THEIR BRAND

BY WAYNE POLLOCK

As you have seen so far throughout this book, social media can be a means to a number of ends. It can be a means to reaching current clients and customers. It can be a means to reaching prospective clients and customers. It can be a means to building your brand and creating awareness for you and your organization. And, of course, it can be a means to generating growth and business for you and your organization.

As you incorporate what you are learning from this book into building your social media following and strategies, I urge you to not ignore another kind of media: "The Media." You know— newspapers, television news programs, online media outlets, and the like. Before there was social media, there was the all-powerful The Media. Despite the world-changing impact of social media, there is still The Media. Moreover, while you have no doubt likely read an obituary or two about The Media, media outlets in all of their various forms remain potent ways for you to build your brand and grow your organization.

The kicker? Unlike social media, when you or your organization receives positive publicity, the people who are reading and consuming the news article you are featured in may not have previously (i) been familiar with you or your organization before reading that article or (ii) shown an interest in you or your organization before reading that article. If either of these two things had been true, those readers would likely already be your clients or at least perhaps following you on social media. In other words, by earning publicity for you and your organization, you can reach new audiences who may have had no idea that you or your organization existed.

The key to earning ongoing publicity for you and your organization is building and maintaining targeted relationships with reporters and media outlets. Specifically, you need to build relationships with specific reporters and media outlets who would be interested in hearing what you have to say based on the topics they normally cover. As you provide reporters and media outlets on an ongoing basis with information that is relevant to them regarding topics that fall within their "beats" (in other words, their areas of coverage), you are likely to be rewarded with their interest in reporting on—and thus published articles in credible media outlets regarding— (i) what you have to say about those topics, or

(ii) what you and your organization are doing in connection with those topics.

Let's talk targeting first

The first thing you should do when you are ready to ramp up your publicity-seeking efforts is to find reporters and media outlets whose beats overlap with what you and your organization do. This includes local and national media outlets as well as trade publications that either cover your organization's industry or cover industries that your organization serves.

When compiling this list of media (including reporters' email addresses and social media handles), you should be thinking about reporters and media outlets that might be interested in the knowledge you have and the work you do. Start with your local media outlets. But depending on the location and the outlet itself, there may not be reporters who cover a beat as narrow as you might prefer. For example, if you are a dentist, local media outlets do not have reporters focused solely on dentists. You will need to go one up one level to local health reporters. If you are in a community where there is no dedicated local health reporter, you should find a local business reporter. If you are still out of luck, your only choice might be a general news reporter.

Don't, however, just focus on local media outlets near where your organization is located. You should be thinking about publications that cover the business or industry that your organization is in, or that cover or target the kind of clients or customers your organization serves. In certain industries, you may find online media outlets and blogs that focus on one niche within a particular industry. If you or your organization fits within that niche, you have found a media outlet with which you should build a close-knit relationship.

Coming back to our dentist example, there are certainly healthcare and dental industry media outlets. If you are a dentist, you may want to target those media outlets because they would be receptive to hearing about the innovative things you are doing on the business side of your practice. However, your prospective patients may not be reading those publications because they don't care about the business side of your practice. They do care, however, about innovative products and services that might make their lives better. To reach them instead, you should be focusing on the kinds of media outlets where prospective patients would expect to read about new and exciting dental services and products: media outlets that focus on health or beauty, or national media outlets that have such reporters.

The number of reporters and media outlets you will target will vary from one organization to another based on the characteristics of that organization. Certain organizations like law firms or accounting firms may be able to build relationships with reporters from a number of different beats at the same publication depending on the various practice areas within those firms. Those same firms may be able to build relationships with reporters and media outlets from a number of different industries based on the industries those organizations serve.

Your list of targeted outlets is a living, breathing document. Reporters come and go. Their beats change. Publications come and go. You should expect turnover at these outlets on a regular basis. I recommend that your organization create a list that can be edited and updated by you and your colleagues to ensure that when they encounter a change at a media outlet, they can record that change and keep the list up to date in real time.

Building Relationships

Now that you have assembled (and will continue to refine) your list of targeted reporters and media outlets, it is time to begin building and maintaining relationships with those reporters and outlets.

First, begin building your relationships by introducing yourself. Email is the most suitable medium for this. Your email introduction should give reporters roughly a paragraph's worth of information about the kinds of topics you can comment on, and roughly a paragraph's worth of information establishing who you are and why you are credible.

Because reporters seem to prefer Twitter over any other social media channel, you should also follow your targeted reporters on Twitter. A short time after you have emailed the reporters, consider engaging them on Twitter by occasionally replying to or retweeting their tweets. Note that unless a reporter suggests that you do so, or you have an established relationship with a reporter, I do not recommend direct messaging reporters on Twitter or on other social media channels. I do not think "cold" direct messages are as welcome (or at least, tolerated) as cold emails.

After you have introduced yourself, the hard—but fun—work begins. You can and should build and maintain relationships with reporters by engaging them on a regular basis with information that is relevant to their beats and interests. The vast majority of the time, "a regular basis" is not daily. It probably isn't weekly either.

With the exception of breaking news that you or your organization can comment on (more about that in a moment), for most organizations, a once-monthly email to targeted reporters about something in the news or in the organization's industry that the reporters might have missed but that would be of interest to their readers should suffice. This will require you to be an active observer of your organization and your industry, as well as the larger, outside world. You should also become an active news consumer. Only after reading your targeted reporters' articles whenever they are published can you get a better feel for their views of the world, what their "angle" seems to be about topics in the news, and how to become part of their articles.

There are generally two kinds of articles you or your organization will be a part of. First, you may be part of articles about your organization, such as your organization launching an innovative service or product, opening a new location, its involvement in some kind of high-profile event or with a high-profile person, etc. In any "pitch" emails to reporters about your organization concerning these kinds of articles, you will increase the chances of a reporter writing about the development if you can explain why the development is important and why the reporter's audience should care.

Second, you might be part of an article about what is happening outside of your organization—often in the form of a breaking news story of local, regional, or national significance—but for which you are qualified to provide an "expert" opinion on the event or development at the center of that story. For example, the next time a big company is hacked and has a data breach, reporters might want to hear from information security professionals about why the hack should be of concern to the reporter's audience, what the audience could do to prevent a data breach, how the audience should respond to a data breach, etc. When you see a story in the news that you can comment on and that you think a reporter would be interested in covering, you should email the reporter as soon as possible after you read that news story and provide them with an explanation of why their audience should care and why you are qualified to comment. (This "expert resource" outreach regarding news events is the older cousin of "newsjacking." Whereas newsjacking helps draw media interest to you through social media or blog posts about breaking news, this expert resource outreach relies on you to contact reporters as soon as possible after news breaks).

Conclusion

If you follow the blueprint I've laid out for you in this chapter, you should start to see a funny thing happen after a while. Instead of you reaching out to reporters all the time, reporters will begin to proactively reach out to you.

They might contact you about your organization when they hear that your organization is doing something new or exciting. When they want to write about a topic in the news that they think you can comment on, they will see you as an "expert" who they will turn to for comment on that topic.

A reporter's proactive outreach to you is a sign that you have built a strong relationship with that reporter. With these strong relationships should come more and more publicity for you and your organization. With this increased publicity should come more awareness of you and your organization amongst your key audiences. With this increased awareness should come more growth for your organization and the ability for you to take your organization to new heights.

As you begin building and maintaining targeted relationships with reporters and media outlets, you need to know something about working with media outlets and reporters. They are notoriously unpredictable and fickle. There is a reason why publicity is known as "earned media": there is no guarantee that any single communication with a reporter or general strategy for dealing with the media will be successful.

You are not paying any money to secure a placement like you would with a typical advertisement or sponsored content. Every day, thousands and thousands of public relations and marketing professionals across the world send thousands and thousands of pitches to reporters across the world. There is only so much space in print and on media outlets' websites to devote to "news," and only so many people at these outlets to produce "news" content.

Even when you connect with a reporter and things are going well, there is still potential for things to go wrong. A reporter may be pulled off of your story to deal with breaking news. Or that reporter might go on vacation, only to return at a later date when your potential story idea is no longer timely and thus no longer newsworthy. Alternatively, a media outlet might eliminate a coverage area for which your possible story was a perfect fit. Or you might not hear from a reporter for a period of time and then magically, they want to run your article and interview you that same day—but you are out of the office and miss that opportunity. These things happen.

For these reasons, and because of the way reporters work and the inherent characteristics of the news business, it is rare that a one-off communication to a reporter will lead to news coverage for you or your organization. That's why you will need to engage in an ongoing (but not annoying) campaign during which you continue to build and maintain targeted relationships with reporters and media outlets. These relationships are the key to increasing your odds of securing publicity for you and your organization.

Now, get out there, get started building targeted relationships, and start using publicity to build your brand and grow your organization.

––––––––

Wayne Pollock is the founder and managing attorney of Copo Strategies (www.copostrategies.com), a national legal services and communications firm helping lawyers and their clients manage media interest and public interest in those clients' legal disputes. Copo Strategies also helps lawyers tell their stories to the media, prospective clients, and referral sources. Wayne can be reached via email at waynepollock@copostrategies.com, phone at 215-454-2180, or Twitter at @waynepollock_cs

CHAPTER 46

CUSTOMER AND COLLEAGUE COLLABORATIONS TO BUILD RELATIONSHIPS AND DRIVE ENGAGEMENT

BY NICK RISHWAIN, JD

What? What does that title mean? It seems like a lot doesn't it? Well, it is. There are many buzzwords in marketing. Sometimes they mean very little. The truth is, I'm talking about working collaboratively with friends, colleagues, and customers on different pieces of content, whether it be written, audio, or video. For this chapter, I'm going to focus on blogging, as that is where I've been spending a significant portion of my content creation time recently.

Why do this? Several reasons. Of utmost importance to me, collaborating with others makes the job of creating content far more fun and engaging. Another good reason is creating a piece of content with colleagues or customers reduces the workload for all participants. Further, when you have cooperated on a project, more individuals are willing to promote and amplify the message. Finally, if you involve customers or friends, it is beneficial for all parties. My job involves promoting those with specialized expertise. When I create content, I like to include others so I can better highlight their expertise.

As mentioned above, my most recent focus on content creation has, strangely enough, focused on blogging. It sounds bizarre to me because blogging has been around for about two decades and, in years past, I directed my efforts on live video and webinars. I still use live video, webinars, and other tools to create content. Why have I been spending my time blogging? There is still significant value. Add collaboration into the mix and the value skyrockets.

Who to involve in the collaborative process?

There are different pools of people you should look to involve. First, for business reasons, it's important to look to your customers. If you are looking to build rapport with your existing clientele, take a look at their business, practice, or specialty, and start thinking about how you might involve them in a blog project to help build the relationship.

For example, if you're a lawyer who recently helped your client Nicole, a mechanic, purchase her first auto shop. You may ask Nicole to co-author a blog post on automobile maintenance and safety issues. You could write your part of the blog about common car accident issues you have dealt with in your practice. Nicole can then provide some insights on tire pressure and rotation, brake pad replacement, windshield wipers, and brake lights. She can also talk about issues of regular maintenance.

The benefits of this combined effort are multi-dimensional. Asking your client to participate in writing something beneficial for your audience, and the public at large is going to make your client feel good. You didn't just help her in one aspect of her business; you're still thinking about her and wanting her business to succeed. Working on a piece together builds that bond. The next time she needs assistance, Nicole is more likely to reach out to you instead of another lawyer. You may luck out, Nicole may be a real go-getter, and her one-woman shop turns into five locations in just a matter of years, and you've helped her in every purchase.

Additionally, in the section to which your client contributed, you're going to include a link to the client's website and maybe additional contact information (i.e., "find Nicole's auto shop at the corner of Weber and Center"). Although there is some debate over the weight of "backlinks" for search engine optimization (SEO) purposes, you want your readers to visit your Nicole's website the next time they need a mechanic. If the backlink helps her SEO, it's all the better for all involved.

Further, once the blog post is completed and published, guess who is going to help you promote the post through social media, email and hard copy newsletters? That's right, Nicole is going to help you amplify your message by sharing the blog post with her friends, family, and customers across her social and digital channels. This increases readership of your blog and exposes your firm to other potential clients. The goodwill you have shown Nicole goes a long way with prospective clients.

Finally, your client may then ask you to participate in a similar publication on her website. This time she wants to write about a constant problem she sees with a particular type of automobile. Maybe the car has some defect, or it is really common for these cars to be "lemons." She asks you to provide some insights on auto recalls, warranties, or another legal issue altogether. You happily oblige because the relationship is important.

Why is the relationship important? You are helping each other build your businesses, amplify your messages, promote one another, and essentially become better friends and mutual referral sources. You think of Nicole any time a client has a car issue, and she thinks of you anytime a customer has a legal issue. Why? You decided to write a blog post together.

This same practice can be used across businesses. If you're a realtor dealing in single-family homes, you might want to use this practice with storage facilities, moving companies, insurance companies, and landscapers in your community or beyond.

If you have dozens of different customers and colleagues in your network, you can write on your blog regularly and involve others who will be willing to do the same. I recommend interacting with those who are "digitally competent." It is less beneficial for you to involve those unable or unwilling to share the message.

I should also mention, the insights of others will help your blog to be more authoritative. You're having someone write about a topic in which you have no specialization, but you're able to bring in a specialist to contribute.

Examples of those who have participated in my blog

My employer, Experts.com has a blog, Experts-Blog.com. I am the primary writer for the blog and, as such, I am responsible for the content. In many ways, I am blessed to write this blog because we have so many customers with so many elaborate types of expertise. You see, we are an online marketing platform for expert witnesses and consultants. We market our experts to the legal community, hence my above example.

Our website maintains profiles for experts in over 1,300 areas of specialization. With all those fields of expertise, I have extensive topics to choose from and a massive database of customers to involve in the writing process.

In the last year, our blog has become hugely successful. We have thousands of readers in a niche area (expert witness marketing). We have been able to write on a wide range of topics outside the usual expert witness marketing topics.

When writing a post, I generally involve one or more of the following sets of individuals: customers (experts), lawyers, and friends/colleagues. I do this to build relationships, backlinks, amplification, reciprocity, and authority.

Here are a handful of the topics I've been able to write about: the Opioid Crisis; traumatic brain injuries; a fist fight on a Carnival cruise; school violence and safety; the death of a former Russian spy; securities fraud; a fatal bridge collapse; dating apps; self-driving cars; robots; North Korea; social media; the Golden State Killer; 3D printing; Salmonella; trade secrets; and wildfires.

In writing about these topics, I've been able to involve the following people: forensic engineers, safety experts, medical doctors, security professionals, law enforcement professionals, patent lawyers, copyright lawyers, personal injury lawyers, defense attorneys, accident reconstruction specialists, computer scientists, aviation specialists, image analysts, serologists, psychiatrists, audio analysts, injury attorneys, food safety professionals, accountants, and property restoration experts.

These are just a few of the contributors I've involved, many of whom have been customers. Others are lawyers and friends with whom I regularly interact through

Mitch Jackson's LegalMinds Mastermind Group.

Conclusion

My position affords me a certain level of creativity on a wide variety of topics. Many will read this and say, I don't have that type of variety at my fingertips. My point is you are only limited by your mindset and your network.

Reach out to your customers, colleagues, and friends. Ask them to participate. Explain the bencfit to them (greater exposure). Ask them to provide their insights (people like to talk about the things they know). Hit publish. Ask your contributor to share the final product. Don't be afraid to ask them to participate again in the future. Keep building that relationship through jointly published projects.

Most importantly, have fun! Several of those I've collaborated with have expressed joy in the collaboration process. We had fun helping each other and our businesses.

———

Nick Rishwain is the Vice President of Business Development at https://Experts.com. He is the co-creator and co-host of LegalTechLIVE, an online video show highlighting legal technology startups.

CHAPTER 47

THE POWER OF CRM: MANAGING GROWTH, AUTOMATION AND YOUR SOCIAL MEDIA SUCCESS

BY DAVID BITTON

Building a brand and marketing your professional practice on social media is going to result in more people contacting you for professional help. With the new clients, patients, and customers, it's going to be a challenge staying organized and on top of things. But hey, that's the kind of problem you want in your practice, right?

To help you deal with this problem- you know, the kind of business problem every business owner would like to have, Mitch reached out and asked me to share the solutions I describe in detail below.

But before I do, writing this chapter reminded me about when I opened my first business. Well, it actually wasn't much of a company: I was just stringing tennis rackets for a living, and I was only 13 years old at the time.

How did I keep track of my clients? It was a very archaic system that consisted of a notepad and pen. The funny thing is, fast forward a few decades and many professionals are still using this same system, even though technology has greatly evolved.

As I moved onto other businesses, I became a little more advanced and started using Excel spreadsheets. I then moved to the cloud, using Google Contacts and Google Sheets to keep track of my clients and how much everyone owed me. I kept track of meetings, appointments, tasks, and deadlines using just Google Calendar.

I will admit that, for years, I thought I was the greatest and most organized businessman in the world. The catch was, the company was no bigger than just me and a few subcontractors.

When the company started growing, and we made our first two hires, I quickly realized that this system was not going to work if I ever wanted to scale and build the company. Sure, things were working fine, but I knew it would be impossible to grow beyond just 10 employees while still maintaining some form of order and organization.

And don't even get me started on taxes. My accounting was a joke comprised of Excel spreadsheets and the free version of mint.com to track my expenses across multiple credit cards and bank accounts. I still feel the pain of spending weeks trying to organize everything and properly categorizing each expense for taxes every year. Looking back, I probably could have saved thousands of dollars on potential deductions had I done things right from the beginning. The problem is, no one teaches you how to do these things; you try new methods yourself and learn the hard way. Hopefully, this chapter can save you a ton of headaches and problems that I already went through myself.

To be honest, I only realized that there was a better way when I took one of my first real jobs with another company. This was over 10 years ago, and they were using SalesForce to track everything humanly possible. When that company rapidly expanded, there were no issues. We were extremely efficient collaborators because every single phone call, email, note, task, meeting, file, and more were all centrally located in one place. Salesforce opened my eyes more than any other person or book could. It was a real-world example of how this company was crushing their competition and growing exponentially, with many thanks due to the organization and efficiency that SalesForce brought them.

With that being said, I usually don't recommend SalesForce to others unless they have a full-time in-house developer who is an expert in setting it up and maintaining it. It's challenging, if not impossible, for the average person to do themselves. Luckily, there are hundreds of alternatives that are significantly more user-friendly to set up yourself.

I eventually became so obsessed with CRM software that I partnered up with a successful programmer, along with our wives (both attorneys), and built our own CRM and practice management software for law firms. The goal was to have the feature set of SalesForce, with the ease of use of your iPhone. If it weren't for using the CRM system ourselves, we would never have been able to grow to tens of thousands of customers worldwide, with over 50 employees.

No matter which system you use, the benefits are usually all the same:

1. Organization
2. Increased collaboration
3. No more missed deadlines
4. Transparency
5. Automation

They may sound like generic benefits, but let me elaborate further on each one.

When your business is growing, it becomes increasingly difficult to stay organized. You forget to answer emails, get back to customers, or follow up with potential leads, and you barely have any time to focus on growing the business. You're too busy doing busy work. It becomes tough to take a step back and look at the big picture.

When you have a system and process in place, it's actually quite rare for things to slip through the cracks and not get done. A lot of these mundane tasks can even be automated, but that's an entirely separate chapter that I could talk about for days on end.

In the case of our current law practice management software, PracticePanther, social media played a pivotal role in our exponential growth. We grew a lot more quickly than we ever imagined, and word spread faster than I thought. If you have the right product or service, and you're honest and trustworthy, referrals and word of mouth are among the best ways to generate new business. And the best part? It's all FREE! That's the beauty of social media - unless you're sponsoring or boosting posts, it's all 100% free!

Here are some of the ways we generated a following, buzz, and new clients through social media that you can apply too:

1.   Posted consistently every single day on Instagram to stay top of mind. Our target audience was here, but none of our competitors were capitalizing on it. We connected Instagram using IFTTT.com, so every time we made a new post, it automatically posted to Facebook, Twitter, and LinkedIn too.

2.   Posted funny content (i.e., jokes and memes). Once again, our competition wasn't doing this, so we took a gamble, and it paid off. The typical boring business posts received around 20 likes. The funny meme received over 200. It was obvious what content we had to keep producing. See what content your audience engages with and double down on it.

3.   Posted personal stories and a behind the scenes look at our company, office, and team. People want to see who they're doing business with, so we showed them!

4.   Reached out to potential clients by following them, liking their posts, commenting, sending direct messages, and engaging.

5.   Created contests and competitions. For example, we made a post on which the first person to reply won 6 free months of our software. Think about how you can apply this same strategy to your business. What can you give away for free? Maybe a free consultation, white paper, etc... One of our first and best customers till today came from one of these giveaways, and they have referred over 20 new clients already!

6.   Used Facebook Live for any significant announcements. This always generated thousands of views and comments from friends, family, and existing clients. When everyone sees your content every week, they automatically assume you're doing well and refer you the more they see you online. If you follow Mitch Jackson, just think how much you see him online on a weekly basis!

7.   Donated to a charity with the help of our fans. We told everyone on Facebook that we would donate $1 for every like, $2 for every comment, and $3 for every

share we got on a post. The result: over $500 donated, hundreds of people engaged, and even another business that matched our donation! When Facebook or any other platform sees someone engaging with your content, they show them more of it. Without even realizing it at the time, this was an easy way to get our audience to interact with us, stay top of mind, donate to a good cause, and get a tax deduction all at the same time.

With our social media strategy in place and a ton of new business, we knew we needed a better way to track and organize all our new clients.

What I recommend doing is exactly what we did at this stage of our company (ideally, even before you get to this stage). Create a simple step by step procedure that everyone in your company can use.

Once you get a CRM software, the process looks something like this:

What to do when you receive a new lead:

1. Add them to your CRM software.

2. Add them to your email marketing drip campaign (if you don't have this yet, I highly recommend it).

3. Send the lead an email, quote, or anything else needed.

4. Schedule the next call or action item to continue the sale.

5. Create a task to follow up with them in a certain number of days if they don't get back to you.

That's it. Very simple! Just remember to actually check on and execute all of your tasks each day.

If you happen to be a personal injury attorney, look up and contact Brent Sibley from Sibley Law. He has mastered the art of processes and procedures and is always more than happy to help or even teach, consult, and share his processes and success.

Right now, we have over 150 pages of procedures written out. I'm not saying you should have the same, but once you get started with the mentality of systemizing everything, you will eventually build a great database of processes that anyone can follow.

The next topic is collaboration. This is broken down into two sections: collaboration with your team, and transparency and collaboration with your clients.

I want you to think for a moment of how you currently collaborate with your team. If you need to see where something stands, you have to ask them. If you're out of the office, you have to call them. If you're on vacation, you have to email them. No matter what, it usually always involves everyone having to waste each other's time when there is a much more efficient way to collaborate on clients and matters.

The easiest way is to simply take notes on every interaction, phone call, email, or task with a client. Imagine the day when anyone in your business can look at the client's profile and instantly know everything that's happening without ever having to pick up the phone or email you. Imagine the amount of time saved for everyone in your business by not having to ask so many questions. Have you ever gone to a dentist who seems to remember everything about you, including the names of your kids and pets? They do this by taking detailed notes and looking at their CRM software before your appointment. It's the same concept- just applied to your business. Documenting every client interaction is also extremely important to ensure that no one ever forgets any piece of data, important task, deadline, or price quote.

Transparency and collaboration with your clients. Probably the most critical topic in this entire chapter. Without transparency, it's hard to build trust with your client. When clients don't feel as though you have their best interest at heart, it's hard to win them over. When they're uncomfortable with how much you're going to charge them, they're going to look elsewhere.

Have you ever gone to an attorney and worried how much the bill would be at the end? How about renovating your house and always wondering if one of the contractors would rip you off? You need to put your clients at total ease to win the sale. One of the easiest ways this can be accomplished is with clear, straightforward pricing, and a client portal to keep them updated with your progress. With a client portal, you can tell your clients that you are a transparent and modern business, allowing them to log in to their portal from your website.

In the portal, they can send you secure, encrypted messages and share files, as well as see all their invoices and payments, and see how much money is left in the trust account (if they're working with an attorney). They can also make payments, view incomplete tasks assigned to them, see upcoming meetings or deadlines, and much more.

With all this transparency, and the fact that barely any of your competition is most likely doing this, the client should feel at ease giving you the business. This may sound complicated to set up, but it actually only takes a few minutes.

With the right CRM software, anytime you add a new client, you just check a box which automatically sends their login and password to their email. With one line of HTML code, you can place a link or button on your website directing clients to your client portal. It can even be completely white-labeled with your own logo and colors, so there is no mention of your CRM provider. The best part is, most CRM providers should be able to set everything up for you completely free. That's the best part of software as a service - you also get the tools and support to make your business better.

Have you ever had a doctor or dentist appointment scheduled, and received a text message and email reminder before the appointment? Or have you ever walked into any practice and they handed you an iPad to check in or fill out a digital form?

Do you remember the feeling you had when you received all of this high tech service? I'm guessing you felt very impressed, and it reinforced your decision to do business with them or come back. You actually have the same tools at your disposal when using the client portal or intake forms. Instead of collecting data from your customers through paper forms, you can email them a form online or even give them an iPad to fill out from your office. Once information is completed, it can automatically go into your CRM software, send you an email, and even automatically add your client to a MailChimp email campaign list (or a similar list on any other email software). That's the beauty and power of automation. The goal is to get more done in less time and show your clients how fast you work and how professional you are.

To get started, you want to search Google for "CRM software with client portal and intake forms." Usually, once you sign up, there should be someone to help train you and set everything up with you. Within two hours, you should be ready to go.

Two of the most significant issues business owners face are following up with clients on time and missing deadlines. Most of the time, the company that calls back first, follows up consistently, and replies to messages right away will receive the business. You are only as good as your weakest point.

And if your weakest point is your follow up, you may need a good task management system that can help remind you when to reach back out. Two of my personal favorite tools for this are Streak and Rebump.

If you use Gmail, you can install the Streak extension for Google Chrome for free. You can also use the new version of Gmail, which is called Google Inbox. Both allow you to snooze a message for the future. I use it to snooze any emails I need to follow up within a few days, weeks, or months. When the time comes, the email will return to the top of the inbox reminding me. It's a great little feature that I've been using for years now.

Rebump, on the other hand, automates my email follow-ups. All I have to do is send an email to a client and BCC Rebump. Rebump will know if that person replied back or not. If they did not respond back, it will automatically send them an email in the same thread as my prior email asking, "Hey, did you receive my last email?" If they don't reply to that, it will send up to four more automated follow-ups every few days for me. The best part is, I can set it up to send the emails whenever I want - for example, every three days -and I can also customize what the emails will say. You have no idea how many times this automatic method has saved me in the past. The websites you should visit to learn more are http://rebump.cc and http://streak.com.

I recently wrote a book along with 15 other legal industry experts called "The Secrets to Marketing and Automating your Law Firm," featuring Mitch Jackson in one of the most popular chapters. The book applies to any business and can be found on Amazon.com. The main topic was automation. I don't have enough room to reveal all the tips, but I'll leave you with a few of my favorites that help automate your business so you can get more done in less time.

The first question to ask yourself is, how much is your time worth? An easy way to calculate this is to take your annual income and divide it by 2,080 hours. With 52 weeks in a year and 5 business days in most weeks, you get to 260 working days. Multiply that by 8 hours, or however many hours you work daily, and this brings you to around 2,080. If you work more or less days (like weekends), or more extended hours, then change the equation. Assuming you make $100,000/year, divide that by 2,080 and you get $48/hour - that is how much your time is worth today. If you're in a career where you charge $250/hour for your services, you could also use that as another metric to how much your time is worth. There are many ways to look at it, but come to a number and think about how valuable your time is.

Now that you have your number think about how many mundane administrative tasks you do throughout the day that can be automated, outsourced, or delegated. Here are some typical examples, along with suggestions of how they can be taken care of faster:

1.   Generating your own invoices - Instead of spending 8 or more hours every month, use a CRM or practice management software to generate all of them in 1 click.

2.   Mailing your own invoices - You can email them to all your clients in 1 click.

3.   Following up with clients about payments, or anything else - A good CRM system should automate your follow-ups by sending automated emails, or use an email marketing platform like MailChimp or InfusionSoft if you really want to get advanced.

4.   Creating documents or contracts - Look for a software that has "document assembly, generation, or automation" that can do it for you.

5.   Working on your website - Outsource this to a freelancer on UpWork.com (an entirely different chapter if you've never used UpWork before- it will change your life!)

6.   Taking client information over the phone or in person with a paper form - Send them an intake form online, put it on your website, or hand them an iPad in

person to fill out, reducing data entry and human error from mistakes reading poor handwriting.

7.   Creating tasks and reminders for every client - Look for software with "task and event workflows." This allows you to create a list of tasks and events that you can copy to any client, like a template. So, if you're an attorney that practices in multiple areas, anytime you get a family law client, you simply copy the tasks, events, meetings, deadlines, and calendar rules for a typical family law case. You can even auto-assign them to anyone in your company. That's what I call the power of automation and delegation working perfectly together!

8.   Scheduling your own appointments - Look into a website called http://x.ai, which uses artificial intelligence to schedule appointments for you. Or use a service like http://acuity.com or http://calendly.com to send clients a link where they can select a time on your calendar to schedule a meeting.

9.   Adding the same information into multiple programs - This one is a bit more advanced, but you can use a website like http://Zapier.com to add information into multiple programs at once. For example, every time you get a new lead, you add them into one location like your CRM software, and Zapier can automatically add them into all your other programs too, like MailChimp, your Google Contacts, etc... This reduces the amount of time spent adding the same details numerous times.

10.   Sending email newsletters - I know I've mentioned this many times before because it's so important, but this can easily be automated using an email marketing program like MailChimp or InfusionSoft. You set up a series of emails and have them automatically send to your clients every few days, keeping you top of mind. Pro tip: make them personal, text-based emails without any fancy graphics or links. This makes it feel like it's actually coming from you instead of an automated program. In our experience and testing, these get the most engagement and replies.

Now think about the time and money savings. The average client of ours saves over 8 hours a week! If you save 32, or even only 8 hours a month, how much is that worth to you?

Explain to your clients that because you automate so much in your business, and have great systems and processes in place, you're able to work faster than your competitors. This allows you to pass the time and money savings onto them.

I hope I've been able to open your eyes to the world of CRM and automation and the many benefits available today. I encourage you to use these approaches and tools to allow your social media success to be a manageable and profit generating asset in your practice.

If there's ever anything I can personally help with or any questions you have, please don't hesitate to reach out at dbitton@practicepanther.com. In Mitch

Jackson's words, you have to give back as much as possible. So I'm giving back by giving you our free book on the secrets to marketing and automating your business. Just shoot me an email, and I'll be more than happy to send it your way.

Enjoy!

———

David Bitton is the co-founder of PracticePanther, a simple, easy to use, and secure law practice management software. Thousands of solo practitioners, virtual, small, and mid-sized firms worldwide use PracticePanther to save time, work faster, and grow their firms. Learn more at https://PracticePanther.com

CHAPTER 48

THE AMERICANS WITH DISABILITIES ACT. WHAT BUSINES OWNERS NEED TO KNOW WHEN CONNECTING ON SOCIAL MEDIA

BY HABEN GIRMA

Producing Positive Disability Stories: A Brief Guide

How we describe disability experiences on social media can help or hurt the disability community and your professional brand. Positive portrayals promote inclusion, increasing opportunities for education, employment, and social integration.

People with disabilities represent the largest minority group, numbering one billion worldwide. Reaching an audience of this scale benefits media producers. Those who choose to produce positive disability stories also move us towards a more inclusive society. While we can't change our past, we can influence our future through the messages we send.

Positive Messages To Send

•   We respect and admire disabled leaders, just as we respect and admire our non-disabled leaders.

•   We can always find alternative techniques to reach goals and accomplish tasks. These creative solutions are equal in value to mainstream solutions.

•   We're all interdependent and go further when we support each other.

Harmful Messages To Avoid

•   Non-disabled people should feel grateful they don't have disabilities. This perpetuates hierarchies of us versus them, continuing the marginalization of people with disabilities.

•   Successful people with disabilities overcame their disabilities. When the media portrays the problem as the disability, society is not encouraged to change. The biggest barriers exist not in the person, but in the physical, social, and digital environment. People with disabilities and their communities, succeed when the community decides to dismantle digital, attitudinal, and physical barriers.

•   Flat, one-dimensional portrayals of people with disabilities. Stories that reduce a person to just a disabled person encourages potential employers, teachers, and other community members to similarly reduce the person to just a disability. We are all diverse and participate in multiple communities, and flat stories make it harder to participate in many communities.

• Avoid victimizing language when describing medical conditions and other aspects of the disability experience. E.g., "She is blind" is neutral, but, "She suffers from blindness" encourages pity.

• Avoid using the phrases "special needs," "differently abled," and person-first language like, "person with a visual impairment." These linguistic gymnastics perpetuate stigma. We plainly state other human characteristics. We write, "She is a girl," rather than, "She has a special gender." The words we use to discuss disability should similarly be straightforward. Tiptoeing around our differences is also cumbersome.

E.g., "He uses a wheelchair," compared to, "He is a person who uses a wheelchair." Keep it simple and just say "disability" or the specific disability. The word disability has some great connotations: civil rights, Stevie Wonder, Stephen Hawking, innovation, and more. Society will move away from the stigma associated with the word if we promote more positive disability stories.

Storytelling Practices

• Spotlight the voices of people with disabilities. Stories about disability have a disturbing pattern of marginalizing disabled voices in favor of the voices of the non-disabled parent, teacher, friend, etc. Practice focusing the story's attention on the perspective of the person with a disability rather than the perspective of the non-disabled person.

• Avoid assumptions and ask questions. Many disability myths are so deeply entrenched in our culture that people assume them to be true. Should you use blind, partially sighted, low vision, hard of sight, or legally blind? Ask the person being described rather than making assumptions.

• Challenge yourself to create a disability story without using the word inspiration. The overuse of the word, especially for the most trivial things, has dulled its meaning. People sometimes even use the word as a disguise for pity.

For example, "You inspire me to stop complaining about my problems because I should feel grateful I don't have yours." Messages that perpetuate us versus them hierarchies contribute to marginalization. Engage audiences by moving beyond the inspiration cliché.

Make Your Stories Accessible

Creating accessible stories allows people who use assistive technology to access your content. Blind individuals use software called screen readers that allow the content of websites, apps, and documents to be read aloud or displayed in Braille on a connected Braille device. Captioning on videos provides Deaf viewers access to audio content.

Guidelines exist to help you make your information accessible. The Web Content Accessibility Guidelines 2.0 is a set of technical standards for making websites accessible to people with disabilities. To design accessible mobile apps, refer to the iOS and Android accessibility guidelines for developers. The tips below will help you with the social media accessibility basics.

Videos

• Provide captions so that Deaf individuals can access the audio content. You can learn how to create captions on YouTube, and upload captions to Facebook videos.

• Provide audio descriptions so that blind individuals can access the visual content. Audio descriptions are spoken narrations of key visual information that is inserted during pauses in the dialog.

• Provide a transcript that also includes key visual descriptions. This is particularly helpful for Deafblind viewers.

• Here's an in-depth guide for making accessible videos: University of Washington: Creating Accessible Videos. https://www.washington.edu/accessibility/videos/

Podcasts/Radio

Provide a transcript to ensure access for Deaf viewers.

Images

Provide an image description near the image. The image description should communicate key visual information. On Facebook and Instagram, type the image description in the Status/Caption field. For images on Twitter, follow Twitter's guide for inserting image descriptions.

Articles

Please make sure the text in your social media posts and articles are machine-readable. Machine-readable text can be read by software used by blind viewers to convert the text to speech or digital braille. Most text on the web is machine-readable, so your text is probably accessible. One way to check is by selecting, copying, and pasting a sentence into a new document. If the sentence copied correctly, then it's machine-readable.

———

Haben Girma is the first deafblind person to graduate from Harvard Law School. She is a lawyer, speaker, consultant and advocate for equal opportunities for people with disabilities. Haben has received many acknowledgments and awards including President Obama naming Haben a White House Champion of Change. Haben also received the Helen Keller Achievement Award and a spot on Forbes 30 Under 30. You can connect with Haben at HabenGirma.com

CHAPTER 49

COST OF ONLINE BULLYING AND CYBER-SHAME TO YOUR BUSINESS AND CAREER

BY SUE SCHEFF

There's an old saying, you never get a second chance to make a first impression, and in today's digital world, we're all just a click away from digital disgrace. The fact is the average person, your potential client or customer, doesn't take the time to decipher cyber-fact from cyber-fiction. They will simply move on to the next lawyer, doctor, landscaper, plumber or whatever they are searching for.

Is Google God? No -- the Internet is a machine, however, today 85 percent of people will believe online reviews as much as personal recommendations.

It only takes one disgruntled client or customer —maybe an angry employee or former worker, and beware the jealous competitor — armed with a keypad, and your career or business can crumble. Consumers are not the only ones influenced by harmful content about you. A CareerBuilder survey revealed that 71 percent of job applicants won't apply to companies with negative online publicity.

We're living in a participatory culture, from the moment we wake up until the time we doze-off, people are checking into to social media -- engaging, embracing and interacting on their favorite platforms. There has never been a better time for businesses and professionals to be part of the digital landscape, but it also means you must be prepared for the ugly side too.

"I can't believe they posted that!"

Being a target of Internet defamation and cyber-shame myself, I learned firsthand how your online reputation dictates your future. In 2003 I became aware of my digital Scarlet Letter after a psychologist (they refer clients to me) called to ask me if I was aware of what Google was saying about me.

The first three pages of Google were a smear campaign created by a vindictive woman, that gained momentum with the help of a mob of anonymous trolls. They had a mission -- to destroy my career, which they very nearly did.

This was only a fraction of what the worldwide-web was reading about me:

"Sue Scheff is the biggest fraud there ever was..."

"Cons like Sue need to be exposed..."

"She places kids in risky programs…"

".. Scheff and her associates are crooks…plain and simple…"

But in September 2006 I won a landmark case in Broward County, Florida. A jury awarded me an $11.3M verdict for Internet defamation and invasion of privacy, compensating me for damages done to my organization and my reputation. Although Lady Justice cleared my name, I quickly realized that Google is not nearly as forgiving.

Fortunately for me, the very first online reputation management (ORM) opened their doors that summer, and I was one of their first clients. Today I tell people it was my lawyer who vindicated me; however it was ORM that gave me my life back - both emotionally and financially. That's the importance of your digital real estate and your online behavior.

Digital wisdom is digital survival

The best defense, as they say, is a good offense. According to PEW Research, 41 percent of adults have been harassed online, and 67 percent of young people (18 to 29) have been a target of digital abuse. In a YouGov survey, over a quarter of Americans (28 percent) admitted to engaging in malicious comments to people they didn't know, while 1 in 5 people will leave false reviews on products or services they've never used.

Cyberbullying and online cruelty is human behavior. Unfortunately, this is something we can't control in others, but we can control how we respond to it. There will probably never be a shortage of trolls or people who will leave distasteful reviews or comments, but if you are prepared, you can lessen the sting tremendously.

Most people don't believe an online attack would ever happen to them, or they underestimate how bad the damage can be. Because of my experience with Internet defamation, I'm not only passionate about monitoring my online reputation, I'm also being proactive in engaging on social media.

Being cyber-savvy

Your online reputation is everything today. We're facing a crisis where people from all walks of life are in jeopardy of losing their jobs, teens are sacrificing college scholarships (or even acceptances), and relationships are breaking down due to careless tweets, reckless posts, or misconstrued text messages.

Today you must be self-aware of your online presence as well proactive in building your digital footprint. It's not only about what you share online, but how you share it that builds your brand.

For businesses and professionals, being cyber-savvy starts with understanding that you will never please everyone and trolls will always be part of the online landscape. It's how we handle them that will help define us.

Once you've surrounded your online persona with positive information, one small negative comment, say, a blog post by a spiteful ex-employee, won't be able to drown out the good.

Dealing with negative online reviews can be challenging but can also be opportunities to educate readers on your services:

- Respond cordially and promptly to online reviews.
- If possible, don't just respond to the issue but resolve it too.
- Stay positive. Use the negative as a chance to share your strengths.
- Take disputes off-line as quickly as possible. Be pragmatic with refunds and other ways to "make it right" for the customer, even if they're wrong.

A tweet can get you hired! Your positive cyber-image.

No matter what line of what work you are in, being a part of today's social media scene is where the majority of businesses and professionals are finding future customers and clients. A post or tweet has the ability to drive your sales up or in some cases, put you on red alert.

If a disgruntled customer started posting a smear campaign about you, would you be ready? If your answer is no, then you must get busy building and maintaining your digital space.

5 Takeaways to build a strong online presence:

1. Claim your social media profiles on social sites such as Facebook, Instagram, Twitter, LinkedIn and more. Be sure your website is set-up with a blog inside of it that you keep updated. Your blog and website is an extension of your business card. Statistics show 54 percent of people will visit a website of a company after reading positive reviews. Make yours stand-out.

2. Engage and educate your audience. Don't be one-sided. Have back and forth conversations. Create surveys about your business or profession. For example, if you're an estate planning attorney, ask a question on your Facebook page (or other platform), such as: Do you know the difference between a living trust and a will? Constantly interact with your readers, never hesitate to share your wisdom and educate them on your expertise in your field. The next time they need a lawyer, or a friend asks for a probate lawyer recommendation, they will remember your social feed.

3. Build positive relationships online with your followers. Not everyone will become a customer or client, but having a solid online support group can help you if you are ever digitally attacked. Being empathic and excited for others when they share their pain or happiness is part of being a team player online.

4. Encourage customers and clients for reviews. Did you know that 7 out of 10 people will leave a review or comment when they are asked? What's important to recognize is this is a constant since the majority of consumers will read an average of 7 reviews before trusting a company or person, and consider reviews over 3 months as no longer relevant.

5. Checking your digital results regularly. If you haven't set-up your Google alerts, do it. It's important to know where your name is being used and how. In addition to your alerts, you should Google yourself (and your company name) regularly. Be sure to go back to the third or even fourth pages. You will know if any negative results are coming your way.

There are no short-cuts in online reputation management, but the end result is priceless. Take this from someone who didn't have this wisdom over a decade ago and nearly lost everything due to a lethal, and legal, weapon: a bully armed with a keypad.

The Internet is a place where so many great things are available and possible, yet there will always be those few haters joined by their followers. Armed with a gang-like mentality of trolling, they just might try to destroy your digital success. But being forewarned is forearmed.

Let's face it, online is not any different from offline -- it's not all a daisies and buttercups, there are thorns that can poke you. But being prepared will save you when (if) a digital disaster strikes.

———

Sue Scheff is a Nationally Recognized Author, Parent Advocate, and Family Internet Safety Advocate. She founded Parents Universal Resources Experts, Inc. in 2001. She has three published books, Wit's End (HCI 2007), Google Bomb (HCI 2009) with a foreword by Michael Fertik and her latest, Shame Nation: The Global Epidemic of Online Hate (Sourcebooks 2017) with a foreword by Monica Lewinsky.

Sue Scheff is a contributor for the Psychology Today, HuffPost, NBC's Education Nation, Washington Post, Orlando Sentinel, Stop Medicine Abuse, Dr. Greene and more. She has been featured on ABC 20/20, CNN, CBS This Morning, Fox News, Anderson Cooper, Nightly News with Katie Couric, Rachael Ray Show, Dr. Phil, and more. Scheff has also been in USA Today, LA Times, NYT's, Washington Post, Wall Street Journal, AARP, just to name a few. You can connect with Sue here http://suescheff.com

CHAPTER 50

MASTERING THE ART OF BUSINESS REFERRALS

BY JOHN H. FISHER

I'm a business owner who happens to be a lawyer.

This is how the referral dance usually begins.

A highly motivated, young lawyer asks to pick my mind about a new legal malpractice case. The young lawyer is excited about handling the case and makes it clear that he does not intend to refer the case. I agree to lunch.

Over a 2-hour lunch, the young lawyer (almost without taking a breath) tells me everything about his case and his strategies for proving liability and damages. I spare no detail in giving the young gun my best advice.

As we walk out of the restaurant, the young lawyer stops dead in his tracks, seems deep in thought for a moment, and then blurts out, "Why don't you handle the case and we'll split the fee." I knew this was coming.

Why Referrals are Gold

This story illustrates one point: marketing is nothing more than relationship building. Specifically, building relationships with prominent, influential persons who can be a source of referrals. Once you've established strong, lasting relationships built on trust and backup up with results, the end result will be a pipeline of consistent referrals of high-quality clients and patients for many years to come.

Referral relationships are a valuable asset for all business owners. In this chapter, allow me to make my point by showing you how we do this in my law practice. Regardless of what kind of business owner you are, the same approach may work for you too.

Take these ideas and approaches and put them to use with your business or practice. When building them out, add a digital and social media component to the steps and approaches I talk about in this chapter. Amplify the tips I share below by building communities on social media and implementing effective communication techniques as shared with you in the other chapters in this book.

OK, let's get started:

Let me take you by the hand and back into my world. Let's talk referrals as they apply to my legal practice (remember, this same approach will work for almost any business, professional, or entrepreneur).

When it comes to building a law firm, most lawyers appreciate the fact that good referrals are gold. With lawyer referrals,

- referring lawyers (a/k/a your "referral partner") bring their best cases to you,

- cases are prescreened for merit before the client is referred to you,

- clients arrive at your doorstep with a stamp of approval from your referral partner, and

- you don't spend a penny on advertising.

Lawyer referrals are the source of your most valuable cases. But when you ask lawyers about their systems for acquiring lawyer referrals, they look at you with a blank stare, as if to say, "You mean I'm supposed to have a system for lawyer referrals?" Oh, yeah, it's kind of important--in fact, nothing is more important for the growth of your law firm.

A Marketing Strategy that is Radically Unique

Get started with a marketing strategy that is laser-beam focused on lawyer referrals. Our firm has a marketing strategy that is devoted entirely to acquiring lawyer referrals.

Acquire high-quality referral partners who can refer a consistent stream of referrals.

Our mission? To have 600 referral partners by October 19, 2020 (a referral partner is a lawyer, judge or paralegal who have referred at least one case in the last 5 years). Currently, we have 313 referral partners. And yes, picking a specific measurable goal with a deadline is crucial when creating your mission.

"Entrepreneurs must get their vision out of their heads and down onto paper. From there, they must share it with their organization so that everyone can see where the company is going and determine if they want to go there with you." - Gino Wickman, "Traction"

Next, share your marketing strategy with your team and celebrate when you acquire new referral partners. You might create an infographic that lists the 3-year mission and the annual goals (a/k/a "basecamps") and post the infographic in your lobby and conference room. This creates alignment around a common goal.

Your "Ideal Client" is Not Who You Think It Is

Your ideal client is not an injury victim—banish this thought forever. Your ideal client is a lawyer who will refer you a steady stream of new cases over the rest of your career, ideally every week. Every marketing campaign should be focused on acquiring and nurturing relationships with your ideal client.

What are the demographics for your ideal client? Write this down, with their age, geographic region, and practice area. For our medical malpractice firm in upstate New York, our ideal referral partner is:

• a relatively young (e.g., 30-50 years old) lawyer,

• partner in a high volume plaintiffs' personal injury law firm in New York State, and

• and does not practice in the area of medical malpractice.

Create a list of your top 20 prospective referral partners (your "Whales") and invite them to lunch. More often than not, your prospective referral partners will have lunch with you, and the simple act of breaking bread creates a personal bond. Weekly lunch dates with your current and prospective referral partners might be the best thing you do.

"Defining your target market is rewarding. The difference in my clients' attitude and awareness after doing so is like night and day." -Gino Wickman, "Traction"

Next, build "the list" of your prospective referral partners. You can get a list of your prospective referral sources from companies such as Exact Data (ExactData.com). For a fee, Exact Data will provide you with the name, address, and email address of the members of the American Association for Justice ("AAJ") in your state. With approval from AAJ, you can send an introductory welcome letter to your "list." Other industries and professions may have their own resources and lists.

The 5 Pillars of Referral Mastery

Most lawyers are sitting on their own diamond mines, e.g., relationships and friendships with lawyers who are willing to refer cases to you. Rather than nurturing those relationships, you search for the shiny new objects in marketing and devote a king's ransom to internet marketing and pay per click ads. Why? Because this is what every other lawyer is doing.

It's time to become radically unique with tactics that will transform your law practice into a referral-based machine. With these 5 referral tactics, you will be unlike any of your peers.

Referral Pillar #1: Why Every Lawyer Should Have a Book

A book gives you instant gravitas. You are perceived as an authority because you wrote the book. Books are sacrosanct in our culture; even though some will not read your book, they'll never throw it away, and it will sit on their coffee table for the next 15 years. A book is an asset that you'll have for the rest of your career.

Provide as much value as possible in your book to your ideal referral partners. I wrote my first book, The Power of a System, about marketing and management principles for plaintiffs' personal injury lawyers for one reason: this was the best way to deliver maximum value to our referral partners, e.g., plaintiffs' personal injury lawyers. Just one rule: GIVE VALUE and ask for nothing in return.

The Power of a System is on the curriculum of 3 law schools and has been cited as a reference at "judge's school" in New York. Our goal is to add The Power of a System to the curriculum of all of the 17 law schools in New York and get the book into the hands of every plaintiffs' lawyer in New York State.

How to Create New Referral Relationships with a FREE Book

Don't sell your book—give it away. Send an announcement to the prospective referral partners on your list that makes an irresistible offer. Here's a sample of our advertisement/sales letter to prospective referral partners:

Wouldn't you know it, my book publisher printed 79 extra copies of my new book, The Law Firm of Your Dreams (but I won't tell them if you don't). It took over 4 years to write this book, so I want to make sure you get a copy.

Just go to www.TheLawFirmofYourDreams.com, and let me know where I should mail your book. Within 24 hours, we'll be happy to send you a hard copy book at no cost (I'll even pay the shipping).

No catch or strings attached—just the best marketing and management advice I've learned in 25 years of practicing catastrophic injury law. Oh, and by the way, I'll even send you a hard copy of my first book, The Power of a System.

Sound too good to be true? I'll let you decide. But you have to act quick, once the 79 books are gone, you'll be flat out of luck.

When the prospective referral partner goes to your website to get your free book, you pre-qualify them with a series of questions to determine if they meet the criteria for your ideal referral partner. We pre-qualify leads with 3 questions on our one-page website:

- Is plaintiffs' personal injury at least 50% of your practice?

- Do you practice in New York State?

- Is medical malpractice a practice area for your law firm?

If the prospective referral partner answers "YES" to the first two questions and "NO" to the third question, they qualify as an ideal referral partner. Those who qualify will be sent a signed copy of our books and entered into the mailing list for our monthly print newsletter, Lawyer Alert.

If the prospective referral partner answers "NO" to the first or second questions or "YES" to the third question, they do not meet the criteria of our ideal referral partner. Those who do not qualify are sent a digital copy of our books (The Power of a System and The Law Firm of Your Dreams) via email and given the option of joining the list for our weekly email newsletter.

Either way, new lawyers are added to our list of prospective referral partners, and we nurture those leads with educational content that is delivered through a variety of multi-media touchpoints, including email newsletters, print newsletters, and invitations to parties and educational workshops, e.g., "The Jury Project."

Referral Pillar #2: Becoming a Rock Star through Public Speaking

Nothing beats public speaking. As a public speaker, you receive the endorsement of the organization hosting the event, and you are instantly viewed as an authority. Hell, you're practically a rock star before you step on the stage!

Why aren't more lawyers doing this? Simple, lawyers aren't trying to get speaking gigs. You can't sit back and expect organizations to seek you out as a speaker— you must have an outreach campaign that is consistent, systematic and unique.

First, make a video consisting of 10-second video clips from your speaking events that are funny and provide useful information. Send the video to the event's organizer with a copy of your book and an introduction letter/email. Your introduction letter should be brief and right to the point (anything else will be ignored).

Letter/Email to Trial Lawyer Organization Requesting Speaking Opportunity

Dear Ms. Jones [CLE organizer],

Thank you for your work on behalf of our profession.

I believe a speech about lawyer-to-lawyer referral based marketing would be one-of-a-kind and provide tremendous value for your members. I would be happy to give this speech at the AAJ Winter Convention in Miami Beach in February, 2019.

I've been a featured speaker about lawyer-to-lawyer referral based marketing for the National Trial Lawyers, PILMMA and Great Legal Marketing and I've written extensively about lawyer referrals in my books, The Power of a System and The Law Firm of Your Dreams. Additionally, I have been called,

- "a master of referral marketing" by Ben Glass, III, Esq. of Great Legal

Marketing,

• Selected as the national marketer of the year in 2013 by Great Legal Marketing, and

• Founded a national mastermind of elite plaintiffs' lawyers known as the "Mastermind Experience."

Click this link for a 90-second video from one of my recent speeches.

Please feel free to call me, 518-265-9131 or email (jfisherlawyer@fishermalpracticelaw.com), if you'd like to explore this opportunity for American Association for Justice.

John H. Fisher

Follow up with the CLE organizer about a week later after the initial pitch. Use www.FollowUpThen.com to remind you to follow up 5-7 days after your initial pitch. If the organizer does not respond, don't press the issue—follow up in a month or two (don't be a pest).

If you have a friend who has previously spoken for the organization, ask them to recommend you to the organizer. That is the surest way to get a speaking gig.

Referral Pillar #3: Staying Top of Mind With Your Referral Partners

Once you've built your network of referral partners, you can't ignore them. Newsletters—print and digital—are the best way to stay top of mind with your referral partners.

Provide massive value to your referral partners with a monthly print newsletter that delivers your best marketing and management tips and sprinkle in photos of your kids, spouse, and pet. Be funny and let your personality shine. A monthly print newsletter is the best thing I've ever done for my law practice.

Don't stop there—connect with your fans every week with an email newsletter that is delivered to their inbox on the same day and time. Your referral partners and fans will appreciate your updates on the law, tips about marketing and funny stories about your pooch. With 1k email subscribers, you'll have loyal followers who will buy your books and register for your seminars/workshops.

Referral Pillar #4: Networking That Will Build Your Tribe

Networking is seriously under-rated. You will not drum up new business at the local chamber of commerce meetings—that is a waste of time. You should network only with influential, prominent lawyers who will send you a steady stream of new cases.

Join a workshop of trial lawyers. I attend a monthly workshop of 50 trial lawyers who practice trial skills and cross-refer clients. Just about every lawyer in our workshop refers their medical malpractice cases to me, and I reciprocate with referrals of car wrecks and slip and falls. The workshops are fun, educational and produce a flow of referrals.

No workshops in your town? No problem, my friend. Create your own mastermind of 10-15 high achieving lawyers in your county. Meet monthly to challenge each other and share your best tips for growing a law practice. You'll develop a better practice, and the members will cross-refer cases to each other.

Referral Pillar #5: Building Referral Relationships with Random Acts of Kindness

Nothing beats a party with your current and prospective referral partners, e.g., Blues Cruise for Lawyers. Host a happy hour at the pub across from the courthouse and invite all of the lawyers in your county. Hold an educational "lunch and learn" about internet marketing and give the attendees a free lunch and copies of your book.

Always confirm referrals in writing on the first day you receive a new referral. Share an infographic describing your processes for evaluating a new case and create a website portal that gives unfettered access to the case file to your referral partners.

Spend time at least once a day updating a referral partner about the status of a referred case. With every update, you're building equity with your referral partners and virtually guaranteeing you'll get their next referral.

The Highest Return on Investment You Will Ever Make

Lawyer referrals provide the highest return on investment of any form of marketing. I think this is true for most business owners, professionals and entrepreneurs.

With this long-term referral marketing strategy, your marketing costs will be decreased, and the quality of your cases will improve. And with just a few of the right referral relationships, you will have a steady pipeline of new referrals, and you won't have to spend another dollar on traditional advertising, digital advertising or SEO.

———

John Fisher is a New York medical malpractice lawyer. His book, "The Power of a System: How to Build the Injury Law Practice of your Dreams," is available at his website, www.ultimateinjurylaw.com. You can connect with John at https://protectingpatientrights.com

CHAPTER 51

THINKING OUTSIDE YOUR PROFESSION TO BUILD YOUR BRAND ON SOCIAL MEDIA

BY MIKE BIRES

Social media is one of the most significant community policing tools ever developed. It allows the breaking down of barriers between various neighborhoods and cultures and their local police departments, offering valuable information, insights, and new communication opportunities. Today, the speed and skill of this communication can literally mean the difference between life or death.

My involvement with social media started way back in 2012 when my police chief asked me to build the department's website and look into something called, "social media." Having a background in web development and design, it seemed like a great assignment. However, the social media part was going to be a challenge, as the most I knew about it was people posting what they were eating or where they had "checked in" at for a function. I didn't get the concept or necessity for social media.

After getting some training on social media, completing the website development, and navigating through the political sphere of city management and local politicians, we finally had the green light to go live on January 1, 2014. Since then, everything has changed in a big way.

Two weeks later, I hosted a meeting a Wednesday morning meeting at our police department with local agencies to launch the San Gabriel Valley Law Enforcement Social Media Group. I believed forming a group with other local law enforcement agencies new to the waters of social media, would benefit us all. One of the topics was providing social media mutual aid in the event of large-scale emergencies or disasters. No one in the room could foresee what happened next.

Baptism By Fire

I woke up on Thursday morning and turned on the local news in Southern California. As I typed on my laptop in another room while listening to the TV in the den, I quickly learned a massive forest fire was burning directly above and dangerously close to the city of Glendora, which is the community immediately east of my city. When I looked at the TV, I saw the flames were quickly approaching Azusa.

I called my captain and asked him if he needed me to come in to handle social media. He told me they did, and he also requested I send out messages (alerts, tweets, and Facebook posts) advising people in our community that evacuations were mandatory.

As I drove to the police station, which was 20 miles away, I could see the columns of smoke. Since I needed to get to the station immediately, but also needed to get the messages out, I called my colleagues over at the Arcadia Police Department. One of my mentors, Sgt. Tom LeVeque, immediately stepped up and logged into our social media accounts, and began disseminating critical information to the community. It is very rare that a member of one police department will become involved in the distribution of information on behalf of another police department. In this instance, and using social media, we had broken an archaic way of thinking and were able to provide the community with real-time and possibly life-saving information.

For the next four days, I was creating and pushing out information on Facebook, Twitter, and YouTube. This was before the days of easy to use live-streaming options, or else I would have utilized those platforms too. Our content and consistency were so good that the local ABC affiliate, KABC7 placed our department's twitter feed at the bottom of their news program. I was indeed "baptized by fire" in the use of social media and later wrote a white paper under that same title.

Because of this experience, my mindset on the use of social media changed. I saw the extreme power of its use when done effectively. I also experienced something rarely heard or seen in law enforcement, and that was the community's appreciation for the job all the first responders had done with the fire. It felt terrific having people so appreciative, and our officers had in a way, became celebrities. People thanked them, waved at them, and hung banners up in their communities thanking them and the firefighters for a job well done.

This caused a massive shift in who I was as a police officer. For years, my mission was to go to calls for service, get them completed as quickly as possible, and move on to the next case. I didn't interact with people on these calls. I communicated with victims, witnesses, and suspects. It was a Joe Friday, "Just the facts, ma'am" way of how I handled my duties.

Throughout the months that followed the fire, I was frequently stopped by people on calls for service, while eating my lunch, or getting a cup of coffee. They would recognize me as the officer "on Facebook," and thanked me for the information I provided. I had become an evangelist for the department, without any intention. Suddenly, because of social media, I became the face of our department. I had no other option but to change who I was as a police officer. I was now thrust into the spotlight, and if I was going to be representing my department and the profession as a whole, I better change my way of thinking and performance on the job.

New Doors Open

Although I am a police officer by profession, my passion for social media opened doors for me that I proudly walked through. I was called on frequently by other law enforcement agencies to speak about skills, tactics, and techniques on using social media for government agencies.

I was fortunate enough to realize one significant thing; the business sector had mastered the art of social media branding and marketing, and they continued to evolve daily. I knew various law enforcement agencies were teaching social media skills or holding conferences, but they lacked the "social" side of social media, or they were scared to push the envelope with innovative approaches to getting their message out to the world.

The idea of creating a 30-second video with words flashing on the screen like a news release (we used to call them press releases, but that isn't correct anymore since we are giving the information to more than just the news media), is still somewhat daunting and intimidating.

The civilian sector had so much insight into social media that I decided to learn from them, modify their skills to work for law enforcement, and teach those skills to my colleagues. What I share with the various police departments and refer to in this chapter are some of my experiences and professional tips.

As a police officer, I am naturally gifted with a Type "A" personality, and no one is going to tell me how to do something. This is partly because I am frequently called upon by people to have all the answers. From giving marital advice during domestic disturbances, performing life-saving measures by doing CPR on a gunshot victim, to knowing the evacuation distance for a potential bomb, I'm always counted on to have the answers.

Where I was fortunate in my quest of learning social media, was the fact I was able to humble myself and learn from masters in the field. People like Jay Baer, whom I had the pleasure of listening to at an event, as well as reading his book, "Hug Your Haters." His tips and techniques for dealing with customer service issues which arise on social media, allowed me to evolve as a customer service guru, in a profession which is regularly beaten down.

Let this be a huge learning point for you; When you don't know how to respond to a hater on social media, ask how a law enforcement agency with a strong reputation would respond. You see, we don't have the luxury of banning people from our pages, nor can we delete people's posts (there are some exceptions), as our social media platforms technically belong to the public, and there are things like the First Amendment and Public Records Request Acts, which we have to honor. Because of this, we've essentially become masters of dealing with the haters on social media, while at the same time, showing our professionalism, empathy, and compassion in the type of responses we give.

Standing Out As A Person, Standing Out As A Department

Regardless if you are going to use social media as a person, or a department, you are required to do it right. Notice I wrote "required" as opposed to "you should." The reason why I wrote it that way is that I have seen too many people who think they know what they're doing on social media, only to screw it up, and then not realize the significance of their actions.

For some odd reason, when you try to guide or correct people on something they did wrong on social media, people become offended and defensive. I think it has to do with an ego thing - "since everyone is doing social media and getting it, I can too."

If you are one of these people, you need to lay down your sword and listen to those who have more experience than you in the subject matter. There's a reason they do what they do, and there is a reason you do what you do. Keep an open mind and learn from all of the experts in this book so that you too will do social media the right way.

Become a master of what you're doing, and where you're going to do it. If you are a new department or business, and you are going to start posting on Facebook, then you need to know Facebook inside and out, period. Now granted, the platform changes almost daily, but you should be in tune enough to know when something does change.

Once you know all you need to know about how the platform works, do yourself one substantial giant favor. Click on the settings tab and go into the "back side" of the platform and learn what every button does, and what every feature does when it is turned on and turned off. The scary thing is that creating a Facebook profile is as easy as providing your name, email address, date of birth, and gender. Once a profile is created, people go on and start "playing." No one takes the time to learn about safety and security settings, and alert functions until it's too late.

After you have mastered the platform you are going to use, take a look at where your industry is as a whole, regarding using the platform, and social media in general. Make sure you are doing it right and doing it well, both as an individual and as a business or department.

This means having a consistent tone and online characteristic. You can't respond to one person with, "Thank you for reaching out to me, and I look forward to engaging with you here on social media," and then respond to someone else with a simple "Thank you." You don't want to confuse people and need to keep in line with your developed posting guidelines or standards. There's nothing wrong with simply stating "thank you" but just make sure you're consistent.

Put Your Psychology Hat On

Once you have developed a substantial presence on social media, you'll need to take a step back and look at what others are doing on social media. I often laugh because any time a new feature comes out on social media, or a unique style of video or photo, marketers and the rest of the world jump on the bandwagon and beat the thing to death. For example, you might remember when marketers would write something like, "What this grandfather did next for this bikini model will shock you," in hopes of luring you to clicking on their link, video, or photo. After about the 100th post like that, no one clicked because they knew it was "click bait."

After you've observed and figured out what's going on, try to figure out how to be unique and stand out above everyone else. Maybe you should do the complete opposite of everyone else. Perhaps you wear a neon blue suit whenever you do a live video, or you have a particular way of opening up your videos. Whatever it may be, you need to find out what captivates people's attention, and more importantly, how you get them to interact with you.

Now deliver value to your community and do it on their terms.

Don't Be A Lawyer, Doctor, or Scientist

Let's face it - people in these professions get paid well because they can have specialized knowledge, write well, and understand the topics, issues, and documents of their profession. They also communicate well among their peers and colleagues, but many of them suck when it comes to interacting with their clients, patients, and the general public. Don't worry, most of my cop buddies suck too when it comes to being - human.

If you can't explain something in simple terms, or you don't have a creative or entertaining side to your possibility, then you need to acknowledge your limitations and hire someone who can help your business grow.

At the same time, if it's you or your brand that you're trying to grow on social media, and you don't have these skill sets, then you need to learn them. For some, that might mean taking a shot of Jack Daniel's Whiskey, and for others, it means taking acting lessons.

Think Outside The Box

I'm a police officer. That was my calling in life since I started as a young police explorer scout in 1986. But since becoming involved in social media, my next calling is somewhere out there helping someone, a brand, or new company, evolve and even erupt into something great.

When it comes to using social media, don't back yourself into a corner just because of who you are as a professional. Be aware that by keeping an open mind and trying new things, you just may find a new aspect of your profession that you can highlight using social media to become a rock star in your industry or profession.

———

With over 25 years' experience in law enforcement, Mike Bires is a leader in the law enforcement social media community. He is the lead team member for a law enforcement agency in Southern California, and co-owner of a training and resource company, https://LawEnforcement.Social. Mike has been influential to those outside of the law enforcement arena, as he shares his experiences involving all forms of negativity, both online and offline, and how it helps him and his profession to propel forward with one simple mission; Making people feel important and feel safe. You can reach out to Mike on social under the handle of @iSocialCop

CHAPTER 53

SEVEN LEGAL TIPS TO HELP YOU SAFELY DO BUSINESS ONLINE

BY MITCH JACKSON

There's no way I could have finished this book without sharing a few "legal tips" to help all the business owners, professionals, and entrepreneurs, stay safe and sound on the social media platforms. While this may be the final chapter in my book, it's also, in my opinion, one of the most important when it comes to business and law.

Before we go any further, please appreciate the fact that although I'm a pretty darn good California lawyer, I'm not your lawyer. As such, no legal advice is being given in this book or chapter. If you have any questions, please immediately reach out to a qualified lawyer in your state. OK, let's get started.

Do Business as a Corporation or Limited Liability Company (LLC)

The unfortunate question in today's business world isn't if you'll be sued, it's when. According to recent statistics, the average small business owner will be sued at least 3 times during his or her business lifetime. Because social media allows almost anyone to start and promote their business online, without any significant costs or experience, I think we'll see this number double over time. Knowing this, I encourage you to please be smart, plan ahead, and take steps to protect yourself and your business before something terrible happens.

Corporations and LLCs allow you to put a protective shield between your business, and personal life. If you correctly set up, run and manage your company, your personal assets will be protected if a claim or lawsuit is ever brought against your business.

What I've seen in the real world is that most people don't set up their corporations and LLCs correctly. Those who do often times drop the ball down the line when it comes to managing the entity. There are numerous initial and annual filing, registration, legal, tax and insurance requirements that all must be handled and completed correctly. The point of this chapter is to make you aware of these requirements. An experienced professional in your city and state can hold your hand and make sure you do everything right.

One more thing. In my opinion, you should not do business as a sole proprietor or general partnership. For the above reasons (and many more), there's just too much liability attached to doing so. Doing business as a sole proprietor is by far the biggest mistake I see people make when doing business online. Instead, form a corporation or LLC and do business as a legal business entity that offers protection to you and your family.

Protect and Respect Intellectual Property

Use Intellectual Property (IP) law (copyrights, trade names, trademarks...) to protect your products, services, and ideas. If you have something worth protecting, it is essential to take the necessary IP steps to protect your legal rights. I'd recommend that you contact an experienced lawyer in your state to discuss options and needs. The US Small Business Administration website offers several useful resources you may want to review. For trademark options and protection, contact Joey Vitale at IndieLaw.com For your patent needs, reach out to Karima Gulick at https://kgulick.com

Stay out of trouble by respecting the IP rights of other people and companies. Don't use someone else's pictures, videos, and music without their written permission. You may be breaking the law and exposing yourself to litigation and money damages.

There are plenty of resources on the Internet that allow you to use or purchase images, videos and songs for your online work. Either create your own or take advantage of these sites and you'll never have to worry about an intellectual property claim being filed against you.

Promote Your Products and Services Through Your Business

When communicating on social media, make sure your audience knows that you're doing so on behalf of your business.

By doing so, the protective shield I mentioned above will usually limit the claims against your business and stop them dead in their tracks. Your personal life, assets and bank accounts will not be exposed to your business liabilities.

For example, when you begin a live stream, let your audience know that your content is being presented and shared on behalf of your company and not you personally. You can do this by simply including something like the following in the first 30-60 seconds of your show- "Today's live video is being brought to you by the XYZ Company, a leader in the mobile app community."

What's important to remember is to share this fact towards the beginning of your broadcast so that it's clear that the information, products and services provided are by the XYZ Company. This is easy to do but rarely done. It's also a good idea to repeat this type of message every 5-10 minutes to give notice to people who join your presentation late. I know this sounds like a hassle but it's just the smart thing to do.

For the same reasons, your websites, blogs and other digital platforms and communications should clearly give notice that your company is a corporation or LLC. This includes all logos, emails and letters.

Use Contracts and Other Written Agreements

Almost everything you do online involves contract law. Be smart and communicate and confirm all deals, proposals and agreements in writing. No, a phone call, email or text is not good enough. Life would be a lot simpler if a digital wink is all that it takes to create a binding agreement but, it's not.

Before representing another person or company's product or service, read all contracts and agreements. Communicate any issues and confirm all agreements in writing.

Influencers need to follow all disclosure laws. If you're a brand or agency hiring an influencer, make sure you put all terms and conditions, including disclosure requirements, in writing.

Mediation and Arbitration Clauses

When individuals and small businesses are using contracts to support their online efforts, I recommend communicating clearly in writing, in large bold print, a mediation and arbitration provision. Have a place next to the paragraph for the other person to initial and date. Note that the laws in each state vary so check with local counsel about how to add these clauses correctly to your contracts in your state.

The fact of the matter is that having mediation and arbitration clauses in your agreements will increase the chances of you having the opportunity to resolve a dispute with another party without the need for litigation. Not only will you save a considerable amount of time and aggravation by avoiding litigation, you'll also save a great deal of money.

Attorney Fees Clause

A good attorney fees clause will do two things. First, it will help eliminate frivolous lawsuits because the winning party, subject to a court's approval, will be entitled to have her attorney fees paid by the other side. The end result is that people will think twice about suing you or your business.

Second, a properly drafted attorney fees clause may allow you to retain a good lawyer who you may not otherwise be able to afford. For example, if a client comes into my office with a good case but can't afford to pay my hourly rate, I may still take the case if there is an attorney fees clause. I know that if I win the case I will get paid by the other side and this is an added incentive for me to agree to get involved.

Venue Clause

A well written and communicated venue clause will determine where all legal disputes will be filed and resolved. Smart business owners have venue clauses in all their contracts and invoices.

For example, let's say you have venue clause that states all claims, disputes and litigation will take place in Orange County, California. A disgruntled New York based customer will need to travel to Orange County to resolve all disputes. If litigation becomes necessary, the New York customer will need to hire California legal counsel to handle his dispute or claim in Orange County.

A proper venue clause can be an effective deterrent to frivolous or minor claims. It can also be an excellent tool to help you keep your litigation expenses to a minimum.

Conclusion

I enjoy and embrace the Internet, social media, and live streaming platforms. At the same time, I also recommend using established offline legal tools to protect your online business marketing, branding, and sales.

Please review and discuss these tips with your business partner, advisor and lawyer and see how you can incorporate these approaches into your everyday online business efforts.

CONCLUSION

If you're part of my LegalMinds Mastermind and reading this book, then you know what's coming next.

It's a mantra that I'm sure everyone in my community is tired of hearing but, it's the key to success in business, social media and life.

Take action!

What you are holding in your hands is powerful information that can change your business and practice forever. But here's the deal, nothing is going to happen unless you take massive action and start executing.

Don't let this opportunity pass you by. Don't wait until tomorrow to get started.

Start taking action right now to create massive change.

While you're enjoying this journey, remember to make time for your health, family, and friends. And never stop making each day your masterpiece!

Mitch

TESTIMONIALS FROM OTHER BUSINESS OWNERS AND PROFESSIONALS WHO ARE USING SOCIAL MEDIA TO MARKET THEIR PRACTICES AND BUILD THEIR BRANDS

"Making social media an integral part of our marketing has transformed our small law firm's practice. In a very competitive market, we have been able to compete against the big firms. Smart marketing through the various social media platforms allows us to spread our digital footprint. The only regret we have is that we should have begun these efforts sooner!"

Bernard Nomberg, Esq. | https://www.nomberglaw.com

———

"Social media has greatly enriched my personal, professional, and financial life. I have met amazing people, like Mitch Jackson, Jim Hacking, John Fisher and many others, that have become wonderful friends, colleagues, and mentors. From an outreach standpoint, there is no greater tool than social media to reach thousands of potential clients (and friends) with a little, or no, budget. It truly is an awesome world we live in!"

Scott Welch, Esq. | https://welchlawllc.com

———

"No lawyer knows more about how to actually use social media to get business than Mitch Jackson. And he does it in a way that not only produces business, but maybe more importantly, produces new relationships. I've benefited from his wisdom, even though I've used only a small percentage of what he's shared.

A book by Mitch would be worth it, but this is more than that. The result of those new relationships is that Mitch knows the experts in every area. And they have been willing to share what they know with Mitch, and whoever is smart enough to buy his book.

You can go buy 10 or 15 books, or you can buy this one and get the best of those. If you are interested in using social media - whether to foster new relationships, enhance your status and brand, or drive new business - getting this book is a "no brainer."

Walter Reaves, Esq. | http://www.waco-criminal-attorney.com

———

"Mentor. When I think of Mitch Jackson, I think of what a wonderful teacher he is. Mitch has built an amazing community of forward-thinking lawyers who thrive on new tips, hacks and processes to improve their social media skills. Mitch has worked with the best of the best - Tony Robbins, Gary Vaynerchuk and Seth Godin, just to name a few. He generously shares the knowledge that he has gained, never counting the cost but always willing to jump in and assist other lawyers and social media practitioners. Now, with his new book - The Ultimate Guide to Social Media - Mitch shares all of his best stuff. For a very small investment, you can gain a wealth of knowledge from one of the best social media experts in the country."

Jim Hacking, Esq. | https://hackinglawpractice.com

———

"Social Media has allowed me to stand out from the crowd and show my clients who I am as a person and as a criminal defense attorney. Whether I am boxing in the gym, walking my dog BeBe, or inside the Courtroom trying a case, the use of video allows me to show my clients a sense of commitment, dedication, and hard work all by being authentic to what I love to do each and every day."

Allyson Kacmarski, Esq. | https://www.attorneyallyson.com

———

"There is no question that because we have leveraged social media into our marketing efforts that we can now stand toe to toe with larger firms. Social has been an amazing ride so far and we are looking forward to where it is headed in 2019. This book allows any small or medium size firm to compete in any market and make no apologies. It will help you shake up your market."

Daryl Dixon | https://www.daryltdixonlaw.com

———

"I started a podcast about appellate practice in Georgia—a very niche area. Not only did I become friends with some of the prominent appellate lawyers I was interviewing, but I also started getting recognized as an authority. I was at a conference, and a stranger told me she's listened to every episode! I've also been invited to guest on other podcasts and judge student oral argument competitions. The best part is how easy it was to start; I spend about 4 hours and $40 per month on the podcast. If it works for appellate law, it'll work for any subject."

Ryan Locke, Esq. | https://thelockefirm.com/

"It's no secret that Social Media has changed the way we communicate.

Communication is now faster, cheaper, and ten times more far reaching than twenty years ago. Everyday new digital applications and platforms are being developed to connect people faster. Without a focus or plan, I began marketing my legal practice on Social Media five years ago. I saw the potential to make a big profit, but I did not have a blueprint. Attorney Mitch Jackson has developed a marketing strategy that simplifies marketing through social media that is easy enough for the least tech savvy person in the world. Mitch's blueprint is based upon basic human principles, and he's used the tool of social media to connect you to the community you serve."

Johnnie Finch, Esq. | http://johnniefinchesq.com

———

"Lawyers need to embrace social media and use it creatively, in non-traditional ways, to engage with the world, capture people's attention, and build relationships and influence. No lawyer does this better than Mitch Jackson. His use of social media and his passion for it has truly inspired me. If you're a lawyer and wondering how to use social media effectively, I encourage you to take a look at what Mitch is doing and to read his book."

Joshua Goldstein, Esq. | https://immigrationlawyerslosangeles.com/

———

"Social media has expanded the Experts.com brand. We have built awareness of our service and drastically improved our network of attorneys and expert witnesses by engaging with individuals and companies on multiple different platforms. I recommend the use for all professionals. Just use it professionally."

Nick Rishwain, JD | Experts.com | Vice President of Client Relations & Development https://Experts.com

———

"Social media and social networking activity way back in 2008 has been a real boon in rocketing myself (an unknown author and legal futurist) and my businesses globally. I practically built my speaking and consultancy business (EntrepreneurLawyer) from scratch using social media, at no cost. News of The Naked Lawyer Ebook sensation rippled around the world via social media channels leading to worldwide lucrative speaking and consultancy engagements. As a result, I've been blessed to make new and close friends in business and life all around the globe, and continue to do so even more of late due to the interest in my latest venture, Robot Lawyer LISA. Social media is a wonderful environment in which to help others with direct introductions and sharing information of interest. I really love this awesome aspect of social sharing and caring."

Chrissie Lightfoot | CEO EntrepreneurLawyer Limited | CEO Robot Lawyer LISA
http://entrepreneurlawyer.co.uk/

———

"Social media inspires me to have a purpose for my firm, a Why, we do things. That what I get out of social media the need to have a purpose, mission and to find ways to help others."

Michael DelSignore, Esq. | https://www.delsignoredefense.com

———

"What we are seeing with the internet and social media today is truly a once in a generation type of event. Social media has allowed me to make connections with lawyers and referral sources that I consider good friends, but whom I've never actually met in person. Just 10 minutes ago, I was on an impromptu video conference with 5 other lawyers to discuss marketing strategies for our law firms. That would never have happened even 10 years ago, and certainly wouldn't have happened without the help of social media. Thank you, Mitch, for all your help and guidance in showing us how to use this incredibly powerful tool!"

Jim Hart, Esq. |https://jameshartlaw.com

———

"Social media enables me to connect with people all over the world who I otherwise never would have had the pleasure and ability to meet. It has become the centerpiece of my referral generating and marketing activities. It is a very big part of my life. Some of the most important relationships and friendships I have formed in the last few years have their roots in communities I am an active part of on social platforms. These communities mostly are educational. My life personally and professionally has been enriched as a result of these online activities."

Jennifer B. Gardner, Esq. | http://jgardnerassociates.com

———

"Social media (and Live streaming) is not about your business. It is about transparency, building bonds and establishing relationships. Add value without any expectation of return and everything else will take care of itself."

Don E. McClure, Esq. | https://attorneymcclure.com and
https://soytuabogado.com

"Social media has helped me break out of the traditional lawyer mold. It was very taboo when I first started practicing to show clients your personality. Now social media allows me to engage with clients and potential clients in a more friendly way and they can see that I'm really a pretty relaxed person when not working on their cases. It's fun to let the non-lawyer side out to play on social media."

Carol Williams, Esq. | https://clwimmigration.com

———

"Social Media has had a huge impact on my practice, simply because it gives me access to a large number of people while I'm sitting in one place. It has allowed me the opportunity to foster relationships with people (whether peers or future clients) that I likely would have never met due to proximity. Additionally, social media allows me to witness the entrepreneurial journeys of others, which serves as inspiration and provides a guide to things I want to add or improve regarding my practice and brand."

Shade' A. Dixon, Esq. | https://www.thdlegal.com

———

"As a weird mix of introvert and extrovert, social media has enabled me to communicate my message to my audience and community in ways I could have never imagined. It's not about how many likes I get, how many people I have on my list, or how much income I make. The feeling that I get when a complete stranger sends me a message to tell me that my last video, my last post, my last article, changed their life, is absolutely priceless. If you focus on producing great content and serving your community through social media, you will be richly rewarded. Look at social media as a way to let your light and creativity shine, to show your uniqueness to the world and make the impact you were born to make."

Leila Nosrat, Esq. | http://www.leilanosrat.com

———

"Just like you, your clients and prospects are very busy. When faced with an important decision and too many choices about who to work with, many will take the path that is the easiest and has the least amount of friction. With social media, you can help create that environment in advance by being visible, by sharing valuable content, and by positioning yourself as a leader in your practice area. Focus on being helpful, smart, and approachable, which is what your clients need, want, and deserve. It's time."

"*Social media has made an enormous impact on my business. I not only rely on it to stay on top of social and digital media in order to provide my clients with the best and most efficient integrated marketing advice about how they should be using it, but it allows me to be all over the world even when I'm not there. I have created and nurtured relationships with professionals all over the globe simply because I have a device at the end of my hand or on my desk that allows me to reach out and interact with whomever I want at any moment I want on whatever topic I want. I don't have to rely on anyone else to deliver my message for me and neither do you. These are extremely powerful tools that I recommend you use, too.*"

Nancy Myrland | http://www.myrlandmarketing.com

———

"*I have had the pleasure of knowing and interacting with Mitch Jackson for several years now. He's been a tremendous mentor to me, for all things relating to social media, and online marketing. Mitch has also surrounded himself with experts in all aspects of legal marketing and SEO, which means, if he doesn't know the answer, he knows someone who does. Many of those experts are part of Mitch's group, LegalMinds, and have contributed chapters to his great new book. Mitch himself is an absolute master of social media. From my extensive observations, and my own travels around social media circles, there is no lawyer who is more prominent online. Despite his worldwide recognition, amazingly, he still finds the time, and cares enough, to make himself available to newbies, and veterans alike. Therefore, if you are a lawyer who wants to take your online presence to the next level, you absolutely must connect with Mitch, join his LegalMinds Mastermind, and read his book. Don't think twice!*"

Tina Willis, Esq. | https://injuryattorneyflorida.com

HAVE MITCH JACKSON SPEAK
AT YOUR NEXT EVENT!

Mitch has spent most of his adult life practicing law, trying cases, and studying the art of communication. His interests in helping others and learning how to effectively communicate began at an early age while growing up at The Saddle and Surrey Guest Ranch in Tucson, Arizona.

At the ranch, his family entertained guests from around the world which included famous authors, politicians, athletes and a few celebrities like, Walt Disney and John Wayne. The family was also active in promoting tourism in Arizona and as a result, his mother was featured on the cover of Newsweek magazine and his father was a leader in the local community heading up Rotary, the Chamber of Commerce, and most of the major Travel Associations. In fact, he was also one of the cowboys in the old Winston cigarette ads.

Mitch grew up riding horses, hunting and fishing. Together with his friends, they would spend weekends hiking and backpacking throughout Arizona and exploring old mine shafts deep beneath Old Tombstone and the surrounding area.

In high school Mitch's interest gravitated to motocross, scuba diving in the Sea of Cortez, playing football, a little baseball, and competing as a ranked Arizona tennis player throughout Arizona and California. He also became an expert hang gliding pilot.

After graduating from the University of Arizona, Mitch took a management position at Caesars in Lake Tahoe, California. His summers were spent sailboarding on the lake and winters skiing in the mountains.

Mitch eventually attended law school and that's where he met Lisa Wilson, his partner and wife.

Over the years, Mitch has received numerous recognitions including the 2013 California Lawyer Attorneys of the Year (CLAY) Award for litigation. According to California Lawyer Magazine, this award recognizes attorneys who have changed the law, substantially influenced public policy or the profession, or achieved a remarkable victory for a client or for the public and have made a profound impact on the law.

In 2009, Mitch also was named one of Orange County's "Trial Lawyers of the Year" by the Orange County Trial Lawyers Association.

Both he and Lisa have also each received the prestigious AV rating by Martindale-Hubbell (highest ability and ethics rating available) and their firm is listed in the Bar Register of Preeminent Lawyers, an exclusive listing reserved for less than 5% of all distinguished law practices in the United States.

When he's not trying cases, Mitch enjoys sharing law, business, ethics, and social media marketing and branding tips with other professionals around the world via his LegalMinds Mastermind (legalminds.lawyer). Mitch is also a fourth generation Rotarian and both he and Lisa are past presidents of their Rotary Club. Mitch also served as an Assist District Governor and Rotary District Interact Chair.

Lisa and Mitch are the proud parents of two wonderful children. Alexandra is in her last year at the USC Gould School of Law and Garrett is in his first year at the USC Marshall School of Business.

SPEAKING

Mitch enjoys speaking and sharing, through storytelling, ideas and solutions relating to law, trial advocacy, social media, digital and technology. Most topics include a component designed to empower his audience to share their human side to help them disrupt, hack, and improve their companies, causes, and professional relationships.

His favorite topics include those designed to show entrepreneurs, business owners, and other professionals how to effectively build their brand, expand their sphere of influence from local to global, and create top-of-mind awareness on the social media and digital platforms.

Mitch is an early adopter of livestreaming (live video) and has spoken at the New York and San Francisco Periscope Summits and keynoted at Summit.Live in Los Angeles. He's also appeared on live video shows with Katie Couric, Anderson Cooper, Seth Godin, Peter Diamandis, Gary Vaynerchuk, and dozens of other well-known celebrities.

Over the past two years, Mitch has shared the stage in front of 2,000 people with David Meerman Scott at the Tony Robbins Business Mastery Event in Las Vegas (Mitch has been featured in David's last two best-selling books). Mitch also spoke at the Clio Cloud Conference in New Orleans to share his thoughts about using technology and specifically, VR, AR, MR, and AI, during litigation and in trial.

In his capacity as a legal expert witness, Mitch shared his advice as a contributing consulting expert to the California State Bar's "Effective Introduction of Evidence in California- Chapter 54 Electronic and Social Media Evidence." He also was honored to consult on, and be quoted in, "Shame Nation" written by Sue Scheff with the foreword by Monica Lewinsky.

Mitch enjoys crafting personalized presentations to compliment the theme and message of your event. Every presentation given my Mitch is customized to compliment your unique needs and goals. Once Mitch is introduced and takes the stage, you can sit down, relax and enjoy the show. Reach out with questions to 800-661-7044 | mitch@jacksonwilson.com | Streaming.Lawyer/speaking

LEGALMINDS MASTERMIND

Two years ago, Mitch created the LegalMinds Mastermind. Today's it's grown to a global community of amazing professionals embracing social media and digital to help consumers, market their practices, and build their brands.

LegalMinds is for lawyers, and other professionals, who believe that social media, digital and technology are changing the world. Each week the community focuses on sharing expert tips, approaches and techniques, via live video meetings, to tap into the power of the social media to build brands, create new relationships and generate more income.

Mitch invites you to read and watch the member written and video testimonials and learn more about his mastermind community by visiting LegalMinds.lawyer